CONTEMPORARY VENEZUELA

and Its Role in International Affairs

COUNCIL ON FOREIGN RELATIONS BOOKS

CONTEMPORARY VENEZUELA
and Its Role in
International Affairs

Edited by
ROBERT D. BOND

A Council on Foreign Relations Book
Published by
New York University Press · New York · 1977

Copyright © 1977 by Council on Foreign Relations Inc.
Library of Congress Catalog Card Number: 77-76055
ISBN: 0-8147-0991-5 cloth
       0-8147-0992-3 paper

Library of Congress Cataloging in Publication Data
Main entry under title:

Contemporary Venezuela and its role in international
    affairs.

    "A Council on Foreign Relations book."
    Includes bibliographical references and index.
    1. Venezuela—Relations (general) with foreign
countries—Addresses, essays, lectures.   2.   Venezuela—
Politics and government—1935-   —Addresses, essays,
lectures.   3.   Venezuela—Economic conditions—1918-
—Addresses, essays, lectures.   I.   Bond, Robert D.,
1946-
F2326.C66   327.87   77-76055
ISBN 0-8147-0991-5
ISBN 0-8147-0992-3 pbk.

Manufactured in the United States of America

Contents

[v]

CONTRIBUTORS

DANIEL H. LEVINE is Associate Professor of Political Science at the University of Michigan. He is the author of *Conflict and Political Change in Venezuela.*

PEDRO-PABLO KUCZYNSKI is President of Halco Mining. Formerly he was chief economist of the International Finance Corporation of the World Bank. In 1974-75 he served as an external adviser to the Central Bank of Venezuela. He is the author of *Peruvian Democracy Under Stress: An Account of the Belaúnde Administration, 1963-1968.*

FRANKLIN TUGWELL is Associate Professor of Government at Pomona College. His publications include *The Politics of Oil in Venezuela.*

KIM FUAD is News Editor for Venezuela for United Press International. He is an authority on Venezuelan petroleum, and is a frequent contributor to *Resumen* and *Business*

Venezuela. He is currently at work on a book on Juan Pablo Pérez Alfonso.

JOHN D. MARTZ is Professor of Political Science at the University of North Carolina and Editor of *Latin American Research Review.* Among his publications on Venezuela are *Political Participation and Mobilization: The Venezuelan Campaign of 1973* (with Enrique A. Baloyra) and *Acción Democrática: Evolution of a Modern Political Party in Venezuela.*

ROBERT D. BOND is a Research Associate at the Council on Foreign Relations and was formerly Visiting Assistant Professor of Political Science at Vanderbilt University. In 1972-73 he conducted field research in Venezuela on business interest groups and economic policy-making under a grant from The Ford Foundation.

Abbreviations

AD	Acción Democrática
Bs	bolivares; Bs. 4.3 = U.S. $1
CARICOM	Caribbean Community and Common Market
CIEC	Conference on International Economic Cooperation
COPEI	Comité de Organización Política Electoral Independiente (Christian Democrats)
CORDIPLAN	Oficina Central de Coordinación y Planificación
CVG	Corporación Venezolana de Guayana
FEA	Federal Energy Administration
FIV	Fondo de Inversiones de Venezuela
GDP	gross domestic product
GNP	gross national product
GSP	Generalized System of Preferences; authorized by U.S. 1974 Trade Act
ICE	Instituto de Comercio Exterior

IDB	Inter-American Development Bank
IEA	International Energy Administration
IMF	International Monetary Fund
LAFTA	Latin American Free Trade Association
MAS	Movimiento al Socialismo
mbd	million barrels per day
MEP	Movimiento Electoral del Pueblo
NIEO	New International Economic Order
OAPEC	Organization of Arab Petroleum Exporting Countries
OAS	Organization of American States
OPEC	Organization of Petroleum Exporting Countries
PETROVEN	Petróleos de Venezuela (the state oil company)
SELA	Sistema Económico Latinoamericano
UNCTAD	United Nations Conference on Trade and Development
URD	Unión Republicana Democrática

Introduction

This is the first book to survey systematically the role of contemporary Venezuela in international affairs. It examines Venezuela's foreign policy goals and how they interrelate with domestic political and economic development objectives. By analyzing the various factors which determine Venezuela's actions on the world scene, the book seeks an understanding of the country's present—and possible future—international role. There are, in addition, several general areas of knowledge to which the book's chapters contribute: the comparative analysis of the politics of development; the evolving pattern of Latin American interstate relations; Venezuela's role in world petroleum affairs; the problems of "North-South" relations between developed and developing countries; and the interests and policies of the United States.

The book is the result of a series of discussions held at the Council on Foreign Relations during 1975-76 on Venezuela and its foreign relations. These discussions were prompted by an awareness that Venezuela was assuming an increasingly important but little studied role in hemispheric and international affairs. Well before the Arab oil embargo of 1973-74 and the subsequent quadrupling of petroleum prices, Venezuela was emerging as a significant international actor, but this development had gone generally unrecognized. Only a few experts knew that Venezuela was the third largest exporter of petroleum in the world, that it was the major single-country source of United States oil imports, that it pioneered in founding and nurturing the Organization of Petroleum Exporting Countries (OPEC), or that it played a leading part in redefining the relationship of host countries to the international oil companies. But the "energy crisis" focused considerable international attention on Venezuela. Journalists, businessmen, analysts of foreign affairs, and government and international officials began asking questions about the foreign relations of this leading Western Hemisphere member of OPEC.

Six specialists on Venezuelan affairs were asked to prepare papers on various aspects of the nation and its foreign relations. The authors were selected for their expertise in their subjects, not for any committed positions. There was no attempt to impose a common framework for analyzing and evaluating Venezuela and its actions. Yet a number of common assumptions and themes emerged from our discussions. First, we are generally supportive of Venezuela's efforts to achieve social and economic development through a democratic political system, and we share an appreciation of how difficult a task it has been for the political leadership to forge a democracy in the past two decades. Clearly, a high social and economic cost has been paid to institutionalize Venezuelan democracy, and an immense amount remains to be done to incorporate the marginal sectors into the society. But Venezuela remains one of those rare examples—a developing country able to combine substantial socio-economic progress with widespread political participation *and* political stability. Second, we share a guarded optimism that Venezuela will be able to meet the formidable challenges it faces: the extension of social and economic democracy to the majority of the population; the achievement of economic growth that is less dependent on oil earnings; and the successful management of its newly nationalized petroleum industry. Third, we agree that Venezuela is playing an essentially constructive and responsible role in world affairs, and that both the substance and the style of its foreign policy may contribute to the formation of a more prosperous and peaceful world order. While we are at times sharply critical of Venezuela and its foreign policy actions, it is always within the context of trying to explain why and how its international activities relate to the nation's politics and to its pressing development needs.

Needless to say, our perspective on Venezuela is not universally shared. There is, from the left, a strong critique of Venezuela which often argues that the leaders have betrayed their own promises, institutionalized capitalism, conciliated the military and economic elites at too high a cost, contributed to the marginalization of the poor, repressed dissidents, and squandered oil wealth—all in subservience to the imperialist powers. The corresponding critique from the right charges the leadership with having sacrificed economic rationality to socialist ideology, discouraged much-needed foreign investment, incompetently managed petroleum affairs, pursued misconceived foreign policies, and so on. Neither perspective is represented in this volume, and ample evidence to refute both is implicit in the essays that follow. We were not trying to give equal space to a full range of contrasting views. From the outset, our intention was to produce a volume that critically analyzed Venezuela and its international role—not one that was in support of any preconceived positions.

Now let me add a few introductory words on each of the chapters. The book begins with three essays analyzing the linkage between domestic political and economic concerns and the conduct of Venezuelan foreign policy. In the first chapter Daniel Levine examines the strengths and weaknesses of the Venezuelan political system and argues that the Venezuelan democratic experience strongly influences the conduct of foreign affairs. Next, Pedro-Pablo Kuczynski contributes an assessment of the Venezuelan economy, paying special attention to Venezuela's prospects for achieving economic growth that is less dependent on oil earnings. In Chapter 3 Franklin Tugwell offers an exploratory inquiry into the prospects for Petróleos de Venezuela, the new state oil company. Chapters 4 through 7 deal more specifically with Venezuela's role in international affairs. Kim Fuad analyzes Venezuela's past, present, and probable future role in OPEC. John Martz discusses Venezuelan foreign policy toward Latin America, pointing out that this has been the most active yet least coherent area of Venezuelan diplomacy since 1974. Next, in his second contribution to the volume, Franklin Tugwell appraises the challenges Venezuela's new international role poses for the United States. The book concludes with my overall assessment of the origins, conduct, and probable future of Venezuelan foreign policy.

I wish to express my appreciation to James R. Greene for his skillful work as chairman of the Council's Venezuela survey discussion group, and to Milton Charlton for serving as rapporteur. The authors join me in sincerely thanking the following individuals for critically reading and commenting on earlier drafts: Maurice Bernbaum, Gene Bigler, Jorge Dominguez, Norman Gall, Jeffrey A. Hart, Ronald G. Hellman, James R. Kurth, Walter J. Levy, Joan Lipton, Abraham F. Lowenthal, and Thomas Sonandres. All of the authors also join me in expressing appreciation to Robert Valkenier for his assistance in editing the individual essays. Thanks are also due to Lorna Brennan and her staff for arranging the meetings. Susan Stoller merits special mention for her excellent assistance at all stages of this project.

My deep personal appreciation is owed to Abraham F. Lowenthal, Director of Studies at the Council on Foreign Relations while this book was in preparation and now head of the Latin American Program at the Woodrow Wilson International Center for Scholars. Without his active encouragement and counsel the book might never have appeared. Finally, I would also like to thank the Tinker Foundation for making possible this publication as well as other projects on Latin America and the Caribbean being carried out here at the Council on Foreign Relations.

Robert D. Bond

[ONE]

Venezuelan Politics: Past and Future

Daniel H. Levine

Since the mid-1960s, a wave of repressive measures and military coups has swept away many of Latin America's most promising and seemingly best-established democracies. The collapse of democratic politics in countries like Argentina, Brazil, Peru, Uruguay, and Chile has convinced many observers that the political future of Latin America lies with authoritarian regimes of one form or another. Such governments are no longer seen as temporary setbacks on the road to democracy, but rather as the logical result of the Latin American process of economic development and political change.[1] In this bleak landscape, Venezuela provides a vigorous exception. Having survived many challenges over the last two decades, Venezuelan democracy now stands out for its stability, strong leadership, and openness. On the surface at least, the prospects are bright.

Yet during the 1973 election campaign, Carlos Andrés

Pérez, now President of Venezuela, was widely quoted to the effect that the next few years would be the "last chance" for democracy in his country. Was this mere electoral rhetoric, or is there a deeper basis for concern about the future of the Venezuelan political system? How can the prospects for Venezuelan democracy be accurately weighed, distinguishing immediate concerns from long-term trends, putting strengths and weaknesses together in balanced perspective?

Assessing the future of any political system is always a tricky enterprise. Predictions which were plausible in the past may have been based on situations which no longer exist. In time, once-potent social forces lose their power while new elements exercise an influence hitherto unnoticed or only partially understood. De Jouvenal argues that a central function of politics is to make non-political forecasts possible: by providing a stable framework for social and economic life in general, the political order sets knowable limits to action, thus permitting both individuals and institutions to make reliable predictions in the business of daily life.[2] But social and political forecasting are mutually dependent; for, while political systems give order to daily life, they in turn rest on particular social foundations. As these change and evolve, political systems built in earlier times may find adaptation and response difficult. As we shall see, Venezuelan politics may be in just such a situation.

Over the last few decades, demographic, social, cultural, and economic change has been deep and broad-ranging in Venezuela. As a result, the parameters of national politics have shifted considerably since the days when the bases of the present political order were laid down. For this reason, simple extrapolation from the past will not necessarily yield reliable assessments of the future. To understand the prospects for Venezuelan democracy, knowledge of its past must be

[8]

tempered with and strengthened by attention to its response to present and foreseeable trends.

The need for this careful kind of assessment became quite clear in the early days of the new *Acción Democrática* (AD) government, which took power in 1974. The election which returned AD to power reversed a long-term trend to party fragmentation and dispersal. AD regained an absolute majority of popular votes (last enjoyed during the short-lived democratic experiment of 1945-48), and anticipated challenges from right and left failed to materialize.[3] In general, the political landscape was dramatically simplified. Many smaller groups were eliminated as the electorate polarized around AD and its social-christian rival, COPEI, which together took over 85 percent of the vote. In addition, once in office, AD pursued a number of vigorous initiatives. In its previous periods in power (1959-63 and 1964-69), the party had moved cautiously and pragmatically, moderating programs of social and economic reform in order to gain conservative support for a still shaky democracy. After 1974, enjoying a clear majority and finally free of the immediate domestic threats to stability which had plagued earlier AD governments, the administration of Carlos Andrés Pérez moved to complete the nationalization of petroleum, promulgated strict limits and controls on foreign investment, and implemented new measures to combat unemployment and urban poverty. Finally, buoyed by the surge in world oil prices, the new regime expanded its role in international affairs—as lender, spokesman for other Third World raw materials producers, and sponsor of new inter-American institutions bypassing the United States, such as SELA (the Latin American Economic System).

In this way, a regime which most domestic and foreign observers had assumed would be simply a carbon copy of earlier AD governments moved instead toward ambitious

[9]

domestic programs and a vigorous expansion of foreign policy. How capable are the authorities, the regime, and the political system as a whole of carrying these initiatives through to a successful conclusion? How will they stand up to the pressures and strains of changes now foreseeable? How, finally, will the evolution of domestic political forces and perceptions shape Venezuela's role in international affairs? Assessing the future on these dimensions requires attention to both survival and efficacy: the ability of the system to persist in its present form over the medium term (15-25 years), and the capacity of its leadership to achieve important national goals.

The analysis which follows is organized into three major sections. First, I examine the sources and fundamental patterns of Venezuelan democracy, with particular attention to the accommodations, compromises, and implicit "rules of the game" on which it has been built. With this analysis well in hand, potential sources of change and their political consequences are considered. Finally, a concluding section outlines available alternatives to democracy in Venezula, assesses the likelihood of their coming to power, and speculates on the potential consequences of their implementation.

Origins and Bases

It is ironic that the mid-1970s should find Venezuela as the surviving "showcase" democracy of South America.[4] Certainly the historical record is not one to encourage adherents of democracy.[5] Throughout the nineteenth century, Venezuela suffered through periods of intermittent civil war, punctuated by a seemingly endless succession of *caudillos*—so-called "strongmen" representing unstable and shifting alliances of local and regional leaders.[6] The nation was extremely poor,

[10]

and government, though authoritarian, was weak—unable to accomplish much in any field. The consolidation of national power began in this century, as the victory of *caudillos* from the Andean state of Táchira was closely followed by the discovery and exploitation of oil on a large scale, which provided the revenues for a strong central army and state machine. Indeed, Juan Vicente Gómez (who ruled 1908-35) and his successors built so strong and repressive a system that the first fity-eight years of this century saw only three years of anything which would be called popular democratic rule—the brief and abortive experiment of 1945-48, known in Venezuela as the *trienio*. Politics in the *trienio* was marked by widespread, bitter, and unrelenting conflict, culminating in military intervention and a decade of brutal repression. The experience of these years marked Venezuela's political leaders deeply. They became convinced that their own failure to control and channel political conflict had opened the door to military rule.[7] They learned, in addition, that political leadership involved more than adherence to ideology and program—compromise, conciliation, and negotiation became key political values.

The full effect of this learning experience became apparent after 1958. For with the overthrow of Marcos Pérez Jiménez on January 23, 1958, Venezuelan politics turned a new leaf, entering a period of democratic rule which continues today. The apparent vigor of contemporary Venezuelan democracy may make us forget how fragile a thing it once seemed: only a decade ago, the prospects for democratic survival seemed weak and tenuous at best. But democratic institutions did survive and prosper, overcoming economic problems and defeating both a succession of military coups and an extended attempt at guerrilla war by the left. Sheer survival against such concerted opposition reveals deep roots and a number of carefully nurtured strengths which deserve closer attention. How was this success possible? What does it tell us about present and future prospects?

To simplify drastically, Venezuelan democracy survived after 1958 in large measure because survival was the primary, immediate goal of Venezuela's leadership. Rather than press at once for radical reforms in business, agriculture, social welfare, education, and the like (as demanded by party activists), political leaders instead devoted great effort to conciliating old enemies, building coalitions in government, Congress, and private organizations, and establishing the legitimacy of the new political system.[8] Underlying this strategy was the belief that social and economic reform could have lasting impact only if put into effect by solid and durable institutions. Thus, the first goal of AD leaders was to stabilize new institutions by committing a broad range of elites and organizations to their survival. For these reasons, the reform of political procedures and the extension of guarantees of survival to previous political enemies became paramount.[9] This concerted emphasis on methods for incorporating opposition groups reflects the impact of the *trienio* experience on Venezuelan leaders as they faced the future in 1958. They saw clearly that, despite overwhelming popular support (at least as measured in votes),[10] democracy in the 1940s had fallen victim to intense civil conflict which led to calls for military intervention. To avoid a repetition of such extreme and bitter conflict, AD's leaders made coalitions, institution building, and stabilization their first priority.

The political arrangements built in the 1960s reflect these concerns in their extensive provision for compromise and caution. In concrete terms this meant limitation of reform programs as the price for conciliating coalition partners and potential enemies in society. Reform was not abandoned by

[12]

any means, but a characteristic *style* of action developed, avoiding major ideological disputes and therefore shelving proposals for fundamental reorganization of agriculture, business, or other major institutions such as education. As an alternative, "technical" solutions, involving the application of *more* resources instead of restructuring the situation, were emphasized. An emphasis on consultation, procedural guarantees, and "technical" solutions is visible across a broad range of issues.[11] Moreover, relative to the resources available, a great many problems, particularly in the area of human resources, were barely touched, leaving the present government with an enormous amount of ground to make up.[12]

In general, the picture I have drawn emphasizes broad patterns of compromise and conciliation. Lest this seem too idyllic, let me point out that any process of incorporation, whereby previously hostile elements are brought into new institutions and patterns of action, presupposes (and indeed may be contingent upon) a measure of exclusion—some are brought in, others are shut out. In Venezuela, the drawing together of center and right was stimulated and hastened along by the alienation of the far left. Perhaps more than any other single factor, the development of a leftist strategy of insurrection and guerrilla warfare helped consolidate democracy. Old enemies like the Church, the military, and business groups came to see AD and its regime as the only thing standing between them and total liquidation at the hands of a successful revolution on the Cuban model. AD's leaders, particularly President Rómulo Betancourt, exploited this situation to the hilt, extracting the maximum degree of support at home and abroad by portraying the democratic regime as the only effective counter to communist revolution.[13]

The pattern of accommodation and conflict resolution outlined above is relatively easy to reconstruct. But after all, it

[13]

was only a method, a method intended to reduce the intensisty of open partisan conflict, confining it within limited and controllable channels.[14] Why was the method successful? How were leaders able to impose it? Four factors were central to success: (1) powerful organizational structures and enduring popular loyalties; (2) autonomous and effective leadership; (3) favorable economic conditions; and (4) the peculiar configuration of the international scene.

Consider the question of party organization. The method of caution and compromise outlined above required AD leaders to make many policy concessions, often in contradiction to party doctrine and principles. The result was high intra-party tension and a series of damaging divisions (in 1960, 1962, and 1967) in which more radical elements split off to form independent political movements.[15] Despite these splits, top leaders were able to impose compromise and ride out the crises because of the great strength of party structures and the extremely powerful role they give to leadership in Venezuela. This tradition of organizational strength and leadership autonomy has its roots in the very origins of AD as a party. Historically, AD came on the national scene as spokesman for a broad coalition of the marginal and dispossessed of Venezuelan society—above all, lower classes from peripheral regions.[16] The foundation of AD coincided with accelerated social change (tied to the impact of oil on the economy) resulting in extensive social and geographical mobility and a general loosening of traditional ties throughout the society. Many individuals and groups of all types were on the move in Venezuela, and AD, appearing on the scene at the right moment, was able to unify and represent a heterogeneous coalition of these groups. Party ties became a central kind of social affiliation, knitting together and often overriding more limited group and sectoral loyalties. Thus, for example,

[14]

peasant, trade union, and student activists were simultaneously group leaders and party militants. As such, they could be called upon by party leaders to modify strategies, tactics, or goals in order to accommodate the long-range political interests of the party. In this way, party organization *per se* became strong and complex because it incorporated and reinforced other kinds of loyalties and affiliations. In addition to cutting across group ties, AD penetrated the society vertically as well, creating organizational ties from the national level through regions to blocks and precincts—in cities, towns, and countryside alike.

This set of party-based structures took root in the 1940s and, after surviving a decade of brutal military repression after the 1948 coup, became firmly established in the democratic period as the *major* channel of political action. To be effective in Venezuelan politics, groups and interests have been largely required to work through the matrix of party organization. This structural trait, added to the heterogeneous composition of Venezuelan parties, gave leadership a great deal of leverage *vis-à-vis* any single group. Moreover, in the case of AD, the combination of public office with party office gave leadership many key resources in its struggle to control intra-party dissent. Thus, in many ways the particularly powerful organization of Venezuela's political parties, and the degree to which they continued to channel popular support, strengthened the hand of leaders in their search for stability.

Most major political parties have followed AD's organizational model, combining a heterogeneous social base (with different classes, groups, and interests joining within each party) with a professional, hierarchically organized, and relatively autonomous leadership. While AD has dominated Venezuelan politics over the last thirty years, opposition parties have nevertheless grown steadily, holding power from

[15]

1969 to 1974. Thus, one must also indicate at least briefly the major characteristics of key opposition political parties.

Of these, the most important is clearly COPEI. The 1973 elections marked another step toward a two-party system in Venezuela, with AD and COPEI taking over 85 percent of the popular vote between them. Indeed, AD's surprising resurgence and return to majority status in 1973 may obscure a long term trend of potentially greater significance, *i.e.*, COPEI's steady growth in popular support. Since 1958, COPEI has consistently expanded its national support, moving from about 15 percent of the popular vote in 1958 to well over a third in 1973.

What sort of party is COPEI? COPEI is a Christian democratic party, marked by a deep commitment to the translation of Christian social doctrine into political principles and programs. The party is Christian in inspiration (unlike the secular and often anti-clerical AD), but not confessional in character—it is a political party, not an arm of the Church. Along with its ideological roots, the most profound influence shaping COPEI has undoubtedly been the figure of Rafael Caldera, founder of the party, dominant leader since its inception, and President of the Republic from 1969 to 1973. The combination of ideology and dominant leadership helps one understand COPEI's general political stance and its record in office under Caldera. While over the years AD has gradually moved away from insistence on ideology and toward a more pragmatic approach to politics and policy, COPEI by contrast has taken pride in its ideological consistency. More-over, Caldera's lengthy domination of the party hindered the emergence of figures of comparable stature; hence, the COPEI administration which took power in 1969 was largely untested, yet strongly committed to its own programs and philosophies. While much of the learning process described here for AD was the result of experience in power, COPEI's top officials lacked this chastening background.

Thus, despite its relatively weak position as a minority government (elected with only 29 percent of the popular vote), once in power COPEI made no official coalitions, paid remarkably little attention to the needs of normal political fence-mending, and (primarily because of inexperience) committed several potentially serious blunders, such as its initial attitude to OPEC described elsewhere in this volume by Fuad. My point here is not primarily to criticize COPEI, but rather to lay the basis for arguing that the party is probably now experiencing the same kind of learning process that AD went through some time before. With a term in office under its belt, and the accession of a new generation of leadership within the party, COPEI should emerge from the present period in opposition considerably strengthened and more mature.

The other opposition parties are considerably less important. In this heterogeneous collection of leftist parties, two are worth more than passing attention, the MEP and the MAS. The MEP (People's Electoral Movement) emerged from a major division within AD over the 1968 Presidential candidacy. Led by Luis B. Prieto and Jesús Angel Paz Galarraga, the MEP took a large proportion of AD's trade union and organizational strength on leaving the party in 1967. But in the 1968 elections, Prieto failed to win, and the party has been in sharp decline ever since.

The MAS (Movement Toward Socialism) continues to attract the fascinated attention of political observers, despite a disappointing showing at the polls in 1973. Why does it attract such attention? The importance of the MAS lies less in its electoral or trade union strength, than in what its very existence has to say about the evolution of the left in Venezuela. The MAS grew out of the expulsion from the

[17]

Communist Party of many members who protested the Russian invasion of Czechoslovakia. On leaving the Party, these leaders (including some of the most brilliant figures of the Venezuelan left) founded the MAS as the party to elaborate a fresh, nationalist, and independent socialist alternative for Venezuela. They reject both the reformism of AD and COPEI and the rigid Stalinist positions heretofore characteristic of Venezuelan Communism.[17] In addition to its ideologcal significance, the MAS is also noteworthy in that its very formation reflects abandonment of guerrilla war and insurrectionary strategies as unsuitable for Venezuelan society. Instead, emphasis is placed on mass organization, essentially within the bounds of the present political system.

In a general sense, political organization provides a framework for action, a set of structures which can be put to many uses. Any complete analysis must go beyond structures to take account of the unusual skill and toughness of the generation of political leaders which built the current system. All too often, we assume that political outcomes are the inevitable result of social and economic conditions—that crises arise and follow a logic of their own. But problems are rarely insoluble *per se;* rather, they become so because leaders define them in such a way as to create and sustain insoluble situations. But as I have noted, in Venezuela top political leaders and many others in social, cultural, and economic life devoted considerable effort after 1958 precisely to redefining political problems and group relations in order to make solutions possible. This prudent leadership, backed by organizational structures which concentrated power in its hands, was fundamental to the consolidation of democracy.

This said, it is nonetheless important to avoid confusing skill with serendipity. Political outcomes may be caused less by the actions of leaders than by a happy combination of circumstances. While I believe that effective leadership *did* make a great difference to the survival of democracy in Venezuela, it remains true that formulation and implementation of its characteristic style of action was greatly facilitated by the abundant income generated by the petroleum industry. As a general rule, it is easier to build coalitions when there are goods to distribute than when scarcity prevails. While the decision to seek compromise and stability as primary goals was independent of resource availability, oil income certainly made the whole process easier, if only by facilitating broader pay offs to competing groups.

Finally, international forces figured heavily in domestic political equations. A convenient way to assess their interaction is to consider the major domestic sources of opposition to democracy following the overthrow of Pérez Jiménez: the military and the left. The struggle against each profoundly shaped the political system and its domestic and foreign policies. In the first few years after 1958, many coups were attempted by officers hoping to re-establish military rule. All were defeated and *golpista* elements were gradually isolated and purged from the officer corps. Their attempts were often supported by foreign dictators such as Rafael Trujillo of the Dominican Republic, and by economic elites fearful of what they perceived as the "socialism" of AD. But these concerns were soon laid to rest by economic policies which favored and protected domestic industry, restrained labor demands, and in general carried through the cautious line sketched out above.

President Betancourt's intensive efforts to neutralize opposition on this flank, however, carried a price in growing leftist dissatisfaction, which soon took form in guerrilla war. After Castro's victory in Cuba, Venezuela became a major theater of guerrilla struggle in Latin America, and active conflict lasted well into the 1960s. But ironically, as we have seen, the left's

[19]

turn to insurrection was probably the decisive factor in consolidating Venezuelan democracy, as the threat of communist revolution drove center and right together behind the AD regime.

The twin threat from right and left provides a good example of the extent to which domestic politics can stimulate major foreign policy initiatives. After 1958, a central element of AD foreign policy was the "Betancourt Doctrine," which urged non-recognition of *de facto* regimes and their expulsion from the Organization of American States. The "Doctrine" is thoroughly explored elsewhere in this volume, particularly by Martz and Tugwell. In the present context, it is important only to note that it was simultaneously directed at dictatorships of the right (most notably Trujillo) and later at armed leftist movements and their apparent patron, Cuba. Looking outward through the lens of domestic politics, President Betancourt saw the survival of democracy in Venezuela as dependent on the isolation and defeat of dictatorships throughout the region. His adherence to a non-recognition policy led to broken relations with many nations, and to Venezuela's leading role in seeking sanctions against the Dominican Republic and Cuba. Betancourt's successor, Raúl Leoni, also adhered to a non-recognition policy, although he applied it more loosely. But with the taming of the military and the defeat and decline of guerrilla activity, the case for strict application of the Betancourt Doctrine seemed less persuasive. Thus, when COPEI came to power in 1969, President Caldera abandoned non-recognition in favor of a policy of "ideological pluralism."

In general, under Leoni and more notably with Caldera, foreign policy reflected a gradual waning of the threat from the left and a growing desire to play down Venezuela's identification with United States policy, as emphasized by Betancourt in his strong support for the Alliance for Progress.

[20]

President Caldera's preference for ideological pluralism was coupled with a desire to promote what he termed "international social justice" through increasing emphasis on the economic issues dividing North and South, instead of the political conflict between East and West. He believed that such economic issues (involving trade, commodity prices, and the like) were crucial to the future, and would displace the issues which had dominated the past.

Over time, then, it is possible to see a trend in the evolution of Venezuelan foreign policy, shifting as the main concerns of domestic politics evolved and changed. As open threats to democratic survival at home began to disappear, foreign policy gradually moved *away* from a primary political concern with the international defense of democracy and *toward* a broader concern for economic issues (with a concomitant increase in ideological tolerance).[18] Given this trend, it is perhaps worth speculating on the way in which a renewal of domestic instability (or a sharpened sense of isolation and fragility derived from the spread of authoritatian rule) might affect foreign policy. If the trend just described is accurate, one might expect such developments to generate a more aggressive political role abroad, with a lessened concern for maintaining Venezuela's newly minted role of international lender and champion of the Third World.

It is important to avoid confusing a decline in these new roles with a reduced concern for the defense of oil prices. First of all, it is by no means clear that a concern for oil price stability and a defense of commodity prices in general necessarily go together, or that Venezuela, though its concern for petroleum, is thereby committed to regional solidarity. In any case, if there is any single constant in the foreign policy of Venezuelan democracy, it is its concern with the stabilization of oil prices and the gradual increase of governmental revenues.[19] As Fuad and Tugwell point out elsewhere in this volume, Venezuela was one of the original sponsors of OPEC in 1960, and its concern for producer solidarity has been constant. Given the overwhelming importance of petroleum to Venezuela, it could hardly be otherwise.

In summary, a political system developed during the 1960s with several salient and enduring characteristics. Politics was marked above all by caution, prudence, and the broad conciliation of diverse interests (excluding the extreme left). The great strength of this system has been its ability to handle diversity, an ability in large measure contingent on the continued vitality of organizational structures, effective leadership, abundant resources, and a favorable configuration of international forces which pushed old enemies together in common defense. As we have seen, the style which Venezuelan political leaders developed for handling diversity emphasized conciliation and coalition building. This characteristic style of action grew out of a profound learning experience which taught political elites the value of pragmatic compromise as opposed to all-out insistence on ideology. The learning experience is visible in foreign policy as well. First, policy has changed and evolved flexibly over time. More fundamentally, the style of action characteristic of domestic politics in Venezuela, with its stress on building institutions *within which* differences can be resolved, spills over into foreign policy. Tugwell's essay on US-Venezuelan relations, elsewhere in this volume, shows very clearly the predominantly compromise-oriented and institution-building character of Venezuelan foreign policy.

The Venezuelan system seems quite coherent and successful, particularly when set against the failure of more aggressive reformist regimes elsewhere. But as noted at the outset, policies and orientations built to meet the challenges of one era may themselves rigidify and thus hinder adequate response to new and different situations. How strong and durable is the system just described: how adequate are its style of action and its program orientations to the kinds of problems likely to face future political leaders? Let me turn now to consider these questions.

Problems and Scenarios

I have argued here that much of the success of Venezuelan democracy is due to the continued strength and vitality of political party organization. Party organization is not only a vehicle for formulating policy or reconciling diverse interests. It also serves to channel and control popular participation. Thus Venezuela is one of the rare examples of an "under-developed" country which has been able to combine widespread popular participation with political stability—precisely through the mechanism of party organization.

But the Venezuelan party system acquired its basic form over thirty years ago, and in a sense continues to reflect the social alignments of a bygone age. The dominant political parties (AD and COPEI) are still firmly rooted in the rural areas and peripheral regions where they made their initial organizational successes many years ago.[20] Yet in these same years Venezuela has undergone massive demographic change, and is now highly mobile, young, and literate. In terms of urbanization alone, almost three-quarters of the population was classified as "urban" in the 1971 census—in 1936 urban population was less than 30 percent of the total. Urban areas also have grown much faster than the countryside, and larger

[23]

cities have grown fastest of all. This rapid urban growth reflects both natural increase and, more importantly, a massive migration out of the countryside.

The extremely rapid transition from rural to urban poses new and difficult challenges for Venezuelan governments and for the political organizations on which they rest. The sheer problem of providing adequate services at an ever-increasing pace is difficult, even for resource-rich Venezuela. Moreover, in political terms, these population movements reveal a shift from older, more stable, and politically organized settings into new environments in which attempts to build political organizations have enjoyed only sporadic success. The migrant populations concentrated in the *barrios* of many Venezuelan cities are little affected by party organizations. No major party has yet been able to organize lasting support among them. But *if* a distinctive feature of Venezuelan democracy has been its ability to combine mass participation with stability through party organization, and *if* political power continues to hinge on electoral resources and mechanisms, what impact will the emergence of a relatively unorganized mass of urban voters have on the system's long-term viability? [21]

A visible consequence of increasing urbanization and the organizational failure of major parties in the cities has been the extreme volatility of urban voting. In the four national elections held since 1958, the popular urban vote has swung widely across the political spectrum, returning in 1973 to AD after a long absence.[22] But it is unclear as yet if AD's victory is the leading edge of a new trend, or simply another swing of the pendulum. Taking the latter as a working hypothesis, consider what might happen to Venezuelan politics if elections continue to be marked by massive shifts in the urban electorate and an unabated decline in the political weight of stable and "safe" rural areas.

[24]

One possible scenario involves a severe weakening of party organizations as social and affective groupings, and a correspondingly increased emphasis on leadership personalities as a focus of political conflict and loyalty. To some extent, this was already visible in the 1973 election campaign, in which foreign and local media experts had a major impact on electoral strategy, emphasizing candidate personality and Madison-Avenue-style tactics to a remarkable degree. Of course, in any election campaign it is difficult to sort out the relative impact of issue, party affiliation, and candidate appeal. The personality of the candidate is always in evidence to some extent. But a long-term shift from organization-focused to leader-focused conflict would reflect and reinforce a decline of one of the unique strengths of Venezuela's leaders—their control over a massive net of organizational ties throughout the nation, from which they derive support and through which they control and direct action at many levels.

The weakening of party organization would also seriously affect the political elite's ability to represent and reconcile a broad range of interests. This capacity to live with diversity and reconcile opposing interests without institutional breakdown is one of the basic strengths of the current system. But if the organizational foundations of this ability wither away, how long can the system itself survive? How soon will it be before Venezuelan politics falls into the stereotyped Latin American mold of competing *caudillos*, each with a personal following, all eager for a share of the spoils and little else?

Perhaps not long at all. Yet social processes rarely have "inevitable" endings. By their conscious actions political leaders can redirect social trends, thus altering the likely distribution of outcomes.[23] Venezuelan politicians are well aware of their organizational failures in the cities, and have tried many strategies to penetrate the urban masses. But the problem is not only political; organizational campaigns and strategies alone may not suffice. For the ability to build enduring political organization is closely tied to a variety of factors in community life, most notably stable employment, access to services, education, and, in general, the existence of stable ties between the *barrio* and the larger society. If these conditions (particularly stable employment, which is central to the rest) are not improved, then party organization *per se* is unlikely to prosper. In Venezuela, party organization remains closely linked to a dense network of other, typically work-related groups such as unions or professional associations. But most migrants, lacking advanced skills and steady jobs, are marginal to these associations, and hence marginal to the national organizational system as a whole.[24]

Considered in this light, the dilemma of urban political organization reveals the extent to which survival and efficacy are intertwined for Venezuelan democracy. For the ability to maintain and expand the organizational base of the political system depends in large measure on expanding the general benefits and opportunities available to the urban poor. Here Venezuela's political elite begins to pay the price of caution in earlier times. The accommodation strategy of the 1960s led to the relative neglect of rural areas, thus stimulating further migration to the cities where, in turn, earlier failures to promote employment and union organization more vigorously produced a situation in which migrants lack stable jobs or associational ties. Although some of the policies of the new AD government are intended to expand jobs, services, and union organization, their impact is still unclear. Moreover, as Kuczynski points out elsewhere in this volume, despite these good intentions Venezuela's resources are unfortunately of the type that require *capital*- rather than labor-intensive development. While industrial employment has expanded substantially over the last decade, many migrants, lacking advanced training and skills, become part of what Lisa Peattie has aptly termed the "backwash sector"—those permanently left behind by economic and social progress.[25]

A problem immediately arises for Venezuelan policy-makers. The enormous increase in petroleum revenues in the early 1970s was, in all probability, a one-shot affair. Revenues now seem likely to remain steady in the foreseeable future, with few sudden jumps. But the surge in income was accompanied by the initiation of ambitious lending and investment programs overseas *and* major increases in demands for goods and services at home. If my analysis of urban support holds true, then the trade-off between external and internal resources commitments is likely to become sharper as time passes.

Meanwhile, previous political experience has produced a leadership group which is highly skilled in the arts of mobilization, compromise and maneuver, but less well-versed, perhaps, in the day-to-day business of implementing policy—delivering goods and services. It is generally acknowledged that although top leadership is of high quality in Venezuela, a serious problem exists at the middle and lower levels of the bureaucracy—precisely those charged with implementation and delivery. While the emphasis so far has been on the survival capacity of Venezuelan democracy, rather than on its ability to act effectively at home and abroad, empirically the two dimensions are difficult to distinguish. In the long run, the regime's ability to act effectively depends on the continued mobilization of popular support and broad inter-elite commitment to political institutions. But given the social changes outlined above, continued *political* capacities of this type may require a greater emphasis on policy implementation in the future.

The scenario just outlined paints a bleak future because of the failure of political organizations to incorporate new sources of popular support. Increasingly wild electoral fluctuations, added to the decline of organization in general, might rekindle a sense of political unease and instability in many sectors. This is, of course, just the kind of situation in which the military often intervenes to "restore order," or is called upon by civilian groups anxious to bolster their own claims to power with help from the barracks. Certainly there are ample precedents in Venezuelan history for such a scenario. There, as elsewhere, military intervention has followed extended periods of civil strife, violence, and discord. Indeed, as we have seen, a major motive for the caution and compromise which marked the 1960s was a desire to avoid such divisive situations, and thus remove a prime incentive for military intervention. But decline and fragmentation of the party system could substantially increase the prospects for military action.

Regrettably, it is easier to set the stage for possible military intervention than to be certain of the orientation of the officer corps were intervention to occur. There is little hard evidence concerning the social background and composition of the officer corps. Scattered data indicate, however, that in recent years the military education system has given increased emphasis to programs in the social sciences, technology, and management which go well beyond the traditional concerns of military academies.[26] On the whole, Venezuela's armed forces are relatively small, well-equipped, and highly financed. With the virtual disappearance of internal war, and the relative absence of major international threats, what are these forces doing? Although the military has had only a minimal role in the national planning process to date, the current direction of training does reflect an expanded interest in the planning, development, and administration of resource-rich and underdeveloped regions. In addition, the military has taken on a greater role in managing state enterprises ranging from aircraft and ship building to petrochemicals, shipping, and construction of various kinds. This emphasis on resource management provides a variety of fields to occupy some of the energies of the armed forces, while enabling them as well to build an effective national presence in areas bordering on Brazil, Guyana, and Colombia. With these preoccupations, and barring a dramatic escalation of domestic conflict, military intervention seems unlikely in the short term.

In the long run, of course, the experience derived from these new skills and roles may enhance the military's view of itself as the single institution most qualified to manage national affairs effectively. Certainly the recent experience of the military in Brazil and Peru forces one to consider this possibility carefully. It seems to me, however, that intervention on the grounds of the military's managerial skills would depend largely on prior breakdown in the economy and social order. Such developments depend on events in society as a whole, and not on the internal evolution of the military, which creates primarily a capacity and predisposition to respond. Should the economy falter gravely, or the social or political orders begin to unravel, then of course the military would stand ready to intervene.

Changes in the scope and content of political conflict could arise from other sources. One potential problem area which deserves attention is undoubtedly inflation. Venezuela has long been a high-priced economy, with labor, goods, and services all quite expensive by comparison with other Latin American nations. But prices, while high, were quite stable. Recently, however, Venezuela has experienced both "imported" inflation (tied to the increased cost of goods on the world market) and an additional inflation derived from governmental wage

[29]

and price policies. Although the inflation has been modest by regional standards (8.5 percent in 1974 and 15 percent in 1975), it is a new and unsettling experience for Venezuelans. Governmental fiscal policies have dampened inflation somewhat, but official price and wage policies have pushed it up. What are the likely political consequences of its continuation?

Extended bouts of high inflation are extremely corrosive of social loyalties. The decline of savings, the need to scramble for continuous readjustments, and the general uncertainty of the future which inflation brings, often lead to intensified political conflict. In a system such as Venezuela, which depends politically on the trade off between diverse interests in an expanding economy, a transition from abundance to a constant scramble for readjustment would doubtless lead to dramatic escalations in social tension. Venezuelan policy-makers and interest groups have become so accustomed to fiscal abundance that even a decline in the rate of annual budgetary increase is likely to generate considerable tension. Moreover, it is worth recalling that inflation typically squeezes the middle class sharply, undermining its aspirations and sense of security. Accelerated inflation was a major factor in middle-class alienation and sharpened conflict preceding recent military coups in Brazil and Chile, and the analogy to Venezuela is not difficult to make.

While the problem is clear enough, solutions to inflation are difficult in an open society, because normally some group must pay through limitations on income or consumption. In Brazil, for example, it has been argued that curbing inflation in the mid-1960s was accomplished largely at the expense of lower-level wage earners.[27] But in Venezuela a sharp drop in real income for lower classes would be politically suicidal, while the easing of import restrictions (to undercut the high prices of local goods by encouraging imports) runs into determined opposition from domestic business. So far, inflation has been kept within tolerable bounds through careful fiscal policies and caution in the use of new "petrodollar" incomes, but a continuation of such policies is central to avoiding the potentially damaging impact of high and sustained inflation.

Beyond questions of economic and fiscal policy, offical relations with the private business sector in general may be a source of growing political problems in the future. The central focus of attention is no longer on the issue of nationalization (now effectively settled for the major foreign-owned extractive industries), but rather on the role of the local private sector *vis-à-vis* the state in economic development. As the major channel for petroleum income, the Venezuelan state has long played a key role in the economy; and with recent nationalizations and the jump in official revenues, this role is sure to grow. So far, domestic private business has flourished under democratic rule, and its main complaints have concerned taxes, labor legislation, and the threat posed by integration into the Andean Pact where high-priced Venezuelan goods would be at a disadvantage. As Kuczynski and Tugwell point out in their essays in this volume, if the economy is to be reoriented with the goal of creating a dynamic, self-sustaining export capacity, problems are likely to arise with the private sector, which is protected, high-priced, and relatively inefficient. For the moment, emphasis has been placed on developing greater capacity in government-owned export industries. But as these expand, private industry will be under growing pressure to become more competitive, and tensions may grow over official tariff, export, wage, and labor policies. So far, however, business continues to expand, profits remain high, and the private sector continues to play the democratic game in which it has done so well.

Ultimately then, the future of Venezuelan democracy rests

[31]

on two related conditions: first, the extension of social and economic democracy to new sectors of the population; and second, the continuation of favorable economic conditions. The former will consolidate popular support and make organization easier while enriching the future of the nation by stimulating the development of Venezuela's human resources, thus eliminating the tragedy and waste of malnutrition, poor health, inadequate housing, and insufficient education. The latter condition depends in large measure on the price and supply of petroleum and the quality of economic management. Although petroleum income is likely to stabilize (and even perhaps decline slightly) in the near future, the general situation is good. The data Kuczynski presents in his essay on the economy give reason for optimism here. The extension of benefits is more problematic, and hinges on the capabilities and resolve of Venezuela's political and administrative elite. Both conditions are necessary, but not sufficient in themselves, for one can only judge the "survivability" of a regime in relation to the alternatives available. In closing, then, I would like to examine briefly several possible alternatives to Venezuelan democracy, consider their potential consequences, and set them against the enduring strengths of the current system.

FACING THE FUTURE: ALTERNATIVES AND CONSEQUENCES

Facing the challenges of the future, Venezuela's political institutions can count on several enduring strengths, most notably great wealth and effective leadership. The wealth has been present in increasing measure for over fifty years, and all indications are that it will continue relatively unabated in the medium term. Politically, the most remarkable aspect of contemporary Venezuela is the successful transfer of leadership between political groups and generations. By first exchanging power between political parties (in 1969 and again in 1974), and then handing leadership over to a new generation in each group (in 1974 and after), Venezuela appears to have solved a puzzle which has proven nearly impossible for many other nations—how to make institutions endure beyond their founders. This very success, added to the growing weight and capacity of the state, surely bodes well for the survival capacity of the institutions themselves, and for their potential flexibility in the face of new and as yet unforeseen problems.

Before launching into a detailed discussion of possible alternatives to democracy in Venezuela, it may be well to devote some thought to just what continuation of the present system means. If AD should retain power in the next administration, it is reasonable to expect an extension of present trends, with one notable *caveat*. As the available surplus from petroleum income declines, *any* administration will have to retrench in some policy areas. AD is a party basically oriented to domestic politics—foreign policy arouses relatively little enthusiasm in the party. For AD then, retrenchment (should it be necessary) seems most likely to center in foreign policy areas peripheral to the nation's central interest in petroleum. Thus, for example, a gradual withdrawal from experiments in regional solidarity may be in order.

If AD is more of the same, what of COPEI, the major opposition party? Throughout this essay, I have implicitly grouped AD and COPEI together as the basic parties of the democratic system, on the assumption that more unites than divides them. Although in general I would maintain that position, some differences may be noted here. First, COPEI as a party is more concerned with foreign policy than AD is, and thus is perhaps more likely to maintain initiatives in this area, retrenching elsewhere if necessary. Second, as we have seen, some observers argue that COPEI in power under President Caldera was rigid and ideological in style. Here I would argue that the learning process described above for AD will probably reduce the gap between COPEI's greater tendency toward a consistent philosophical position and AD's more pragmatic stance. It is important to emphasize, however, that such differences in style are matters of degree—neither party fits neatly in a category of "ideological" or "pragmatic," and in any case constraints on any democratic group in power (*e.g.*, the need to maintain popular support, safeguard oil income, and expand domestic industry) are so great that the available room for maneuver is quite limited.

The alternatives to the present system and its leadership are quite different now from those of the 1960s. At that time, three major possibilities dominated the scene: first, military dictatorships of a straightforward repressive variety; second, democracy of the AD-populist brand; and third, leftist revolution more or less on the Cuban model. Both domestically and internationally this set of alternatives has all but disappeared. First of all, leftist insurrection has been effectively defeated at home, while in Latin America as a whole, the attractiveness of Cuba as a model for change is much reduced. At the same time, electoral democracy, while prospering in Venezuela, has gone into eclipse throughout the region, and little scholarly attention is paid to its prospects and possibilities. The election of Salvador Allende in Chile made this "path" momentarily fashionable once again, but military intervention there as well has made democracy seem "old-hat" to liberals and conservatives alike. Finally, the nature of military rule has itself changed. The traditional stereotype of the *caudillo*, out for plunder and little else, has been largely replaced by institutionalized, permanent, and ideological military regimes.

[34]

As I noted at the outset, Latin America is now marked by a notable trend to authoritarian regimes of various sorts. Brazil, Peru, and Chile are leading cases. Though these countries all are quite different from one another, in each of them military rule is pervasive and seemingly permanent. Despite Brazil's reputation for favoring a more free-wheeling role for foreign enterprise (in contrast to Peru's highly publicized experimentation with "radical" social and economic schemes), available evidence casts considerable doubt on the substance of this difference. In both nations the state is heavily involved in the economy; and recently, economic problems, rising unrest, and a change in top leadership in Peru have led to abandonment of the regime's more radical programs, and a sharp turn to the right. The major difference between the cases lies perhaps in the greater repression associated with the Brazilian experience, and here Chile lines up clearly with Brazil as an anti-leftist alternative.

How likely are any of these alternatives for Venezuela? What difference would they make to national life if implemented? Consider first the prospects of the left, surely the weakest pretender to alternative status. Leftist parties have never demonstrated mass appeal in Venezuela, and attempts to impose revolution by force have been decisively defeated. Moreover, international support for such adventures has disappeared. Thus, despite the fact that the left continues to fascinate foreign scholars, I believe it can be effectively dismissed as an alternative in Venezuela. Ironically, the best hope for the left probably lies with the military. If democracy were overthrown (for example, in one of the scenarios sketched above), the left would stand a chance of assuming leadership underground—a better chance in any case than in open political struggle. Conversely, an attempt might be made (following the Peruvian example) to penetrate the military,

[35]

gaining allies and converts in the officer corps. But these are awfully tenuous threads on which to build a political strategy. If the left is dismissed as a viable alternative, one or another form of military rule remains. Which is more likely if military rule comes at all in the foreseeable future? Venezuela's own situation and traditions suggest an experience more on the lines of contemporary Brazil or Chile than the Peru of the "revolutionary" phase. There is no reliable evidence of ideological tendencies within the Venezuelan military predisposing it to Peruvian-style institutions and policies. In any case, it is important to realize that such solutions are more meaningful in societies such as Peru, where there is much untapped organizational material to work with. But Venezuela, like Chile in 1973, is *already* highly organized and politicized. Hence, the problem facing military rulers would be less one of incorporating excluded sectors of the population than of excluding and repressing the already organized. Much effort would undoubtedly be devoted to terror and repression.

Leftist rule would clearly bring far-reaching changes to Venezuela, particularly in the organization of political and economic life, but the possibility is so remote that detailed projection is not warranted. Would a shift from democracy to military rule make a notable difference to domestic or foreign policy? Posed in this way, the question directs attention primarily to economic programs. But I would like to note, first, that in terms of social, cultural, and political life, authoritarian rule would make an enormous difference. For all its faults, Venezuela today is an open and free-wheeling society, where civil liberties are respected and genuine attempts are being made to expand popular institutions and programs. A return to military rule would perforce destroy this flourishing and vigorous life—probably in a sea of blood. For the more complex, politicized, and mobilized a society becomes, the more extensive and thorough-going is the repression necessary for authoritatian rule to survive. The overthrow of democracy would thus be a human tragedy of vast proportions.

In terms of economic policy, it is difficult at this juncture to see how a move to military rule would have much impact. Unlike Chile, ideological debate over socialism vs. free enterprise has not been central to Venezuelan political life. Thus, even military rulers would be unlikely to denationalize the iron ore or petroleum industries, although a looser attitude toward joint ventures and foreign investment in general might accompany military rule. It is also difficult to see how a turn to military rule would alter the role of the state in the economy. This role is already great and, unlike Peru, it is not a case of transforming a weak state into an agent of change. Instead, the major economic impact of military rule at home would probably lie in the reduction of redistributive programs and closer, less conflictful, relations with the private sector, most notably through the repression of organized labor and the revision of job security legislation.

In foreign policy, military rule would probably herald more notable changes. Any shred of the Betancourt Doctrine would of course disappear. In terms of economic policy, given the overwhelming importance of petroleum to national welfare and govermental revenues, the constraints on Venezuela are so great that little substantive change is likely to ensue. However, if as I have suggested, military intervention should take a more "rightist" rather than "leftist" orientation (using these terms with full awareness of their misleading and ambiguous character), then the rhetoric and activities involved in playing the role of Third World champion would probably be substantially cut back, and involvement in schemes for regional integration substantially set aside. In addition, external initia-

[37]

tives might be abandoned (or at least slowed down), given military preoccupation with internal problems and the need for extensive repression.

A more indirect, but quite significant consequence of military rule for Venezuelan foreign policy arises in the area of style of action discussed above. In both domestic and foreign affairs, I have noted a strong relation between style and substance—a style oriented to compromise and coalition-building and a substantive concern for moderation in policy terms. Both style and substance are rooted in political experience at home. But a military regime would surely be less devoted to building institutions for compromise at home, and in foreign policy as well this "compromisory" orientation would doubtless suffer. One example, suggested by Fuad (in this volume) is the probable demise of what has been a non-ideological, mediating role for Venezuela within OPEC. Other attempts at institution-building, on a regional and area-wide basis (e.g., initiatives in the Caribbean, or SELA) would also suffer.

From the present vantage point, however, these possibilities are remote, and Venezuelan democracy, at least for the foreseeable future, seems strong and viable. This vitality springs from a mixture of the system's own strengths and its leaders' ability to take advantage of favorable economic conditions and international trends. Of course, nothing is permanent in politics, and little can be taken for granted. The major problems facing Venezuelan democracy have changed notably over the years, and can indeed be traced to the very successes of the past—successes producing patterns of action and expectation which may no longer be adequate to changed conditions. Since taking power, the administration of Carlos Andrés Pérez has faced up to this dilemma, gradually loosening many of the definitions, rules, and implicit parameters set up to guide Venezuelan politics through the turbulent 1960s. Here lies the meaning of seeing the coming years as a "last chance" for democracy—a "last chance" to readjust its structures, procedures, and policies to changed conditions. Seen in this light, President Pérez is less a "radical" and innovator than, like his political mentor Rómulo Betancourt, a man who tries to move and change with the times, adapting to altered circumstances, rarely caught by surprise. The same learning process visible in so many areas of the system as a whole is clearly reflected in the experience of individual leaders like President Pérez. Indeed, this flexibility and willingness of Venezuelan leaders to design and build new bases on which to meet future challenges is perhaps the best guarantee of democracy's survival in the years to come.

NOTES

1. For an articulate and convincing exposition of this school of thought, see G. O'Donnell, *Modernization and Bureaucratic Authoritarianism: Studies in South American Politics* (Berkeley, California: Institute of International Studies, 1973).

2. B. De Jouvenal, *The Art of Conjecture* (New York: Basic Books, 1967) p. 240.

3. The challenge from the right was thought by many to lie in the continued strength of ex-dictator Marcos Pérez Jiménez, who had drawn a considerable vote in 1968. His support, however, proved extremely volatile, and all but disappeared in the 1973 vote. The hopes of the left centered on the Movement Towards Socialism (MAS), a new party based primarily on a 1970 division of the Communist Party. But the MAS, too, did much more poorly than

expected, pulling only 5 percent of the Presidential vote despite an intensive and much-ballyhooed campaign.

4. The only other country in South America that even comes close to fitting the label "democracy" is Colombia, and that nation's persistent economic problems, unrest, and rigid social structure make it an unlikely candidate for "showcase" status.

5. The historical analysis presented here draws heavily on my book, *Conflict and Political Change in Venezuela* (Princeton: Princeton University Press, 1973). Given this general debt, no further reference will be made to the book, except to indicate the location of more extended discussions of particular points raised below.

6. For an excellent account of regionalism, caudillism, and civil war in nineteenth century Venezuela, see R. L. Gilmore, *Caudillism and Militarism in Venezuela 1810-1910* (Athens, Ohio: Ohio University Press, 1964). The transition to a new system at the beginning of this century receives a very good discussion in R. J. Velásquez, *La Caída del Liberalismo Amarillo* (Caracas, 1973).

7. In his address to Congress, on taking office in 1959, Rómulo Betancourt put the lesson of the past in these words: "Underground, in prison, in exile, or living in precarious liberty at home, we understood that it was through the breach opened in the front of civility and culture that the conspiracy of November 24, 1948—of unmistakable regressiveness and supported by some with ingenuous good faith—was able to pass—a conspiracy which overthrew the legitimate government of Rómulo Gallegos." R. Betancourt, *Tres Años de Gobierno Democrático* (Caracas: Imprenta Nacional, 1962), I, p. 13. Rómulo Gallegos was elected President for AD in 1947. For an extended discussion of *trienio* politics, see Levine, *op. cit.*, especially chapter 3.

8. Coalition government was the rule in the first ten years of

[40]

democracy under the Presidencies of Rómulo Betancourt (1959-64) and Raúl Leoni (1964-69). Although the composition of coalitions changed, the orientation to coalition rule remained strong among AD leaders. Coalitions at the level of government were mirrored in Congress and other institutions. For example, in trade unions and professional associations, a system of proportional representation was instituted after 1958, insuring that all major groups would be represented. In this way, the development of parallel and mutually exclusive organizations in the same field was avoided.

9. For more extended discussion of this point, see Levine, *op. cit.*, or J. D. Powell, *Political Mobilization of the Venezuelan Peasant* (Cambridge: Harvard University Press, 1971). Bonilla provides interesting data on the extent to which Venezuelan political leaders are free of paranoid and extreme views of opposition. Cf. F. Bonilla, *The Politics of Change in Venezuela: Volume II, The Failure of Elites* (Cambridge: The MIT Press, 1970), p. 328.

10. In the various elections held from 1945 to 1948, AD consistently took almost three-quarters of the popular vote.

11. Dinkelspiel sees this as a general orientation of Venezuelan public administration. See John R. Dinkelspiel, "Administrative Style," in L. Rodwin et al., *Planning Urban Growth and Regional Development: The Experience of the Guayana Program of Venezuela* (Cambridge: The MIT Press, 1969), pp. 301-315. Specific examples are legion.

12. Cf. V. E. Childers, *Human Resources Development: Venezuela* (Bloomington: International Development Research Center, Indiana University, 1974).

13. On Betancourt's relations with the military, see E. Lieuwen, *Generals vs. Presidents: Neomilitarism in Latin America* (New York: Frederick A. Praeger, 1964), pp. 86-91; R. Alexander, *The*

[41]

Venezuelan Democratic Revolution (New Brunswick: Rutgers University Press, 1964), pp. 105-117; and P. Taylor, *The Venezuelan Golpe de Estado of 1958: The Fall of Marcos Pérez Jiménez* (Washington: Institute for the Comparative Study of Political Systems, 1968), pp. 68-71.

14. It is important to remember that conflict was *not* eliminated, but instead regularized and built into the regular procedure of politics. The institutionalization of conflict was expressed in the limitation of legitimate resources and methods of action to those explicitly political vehicles, like elections or the Congress, which were controlled by the political parties. The importance of concentrating conflict in a limited number of resources and methods of action is discussed for Venezuela in Levine, *op. cit.,* especially chapters 3, 8, and 9. For a general statement of this perspective, see S. Huntington, *Political Order in Changing Societies* (New Haven: Yale University Press, 1968), especially chapter 4.

15. The 1960 division produced the MIR (Movement of the Revolutionary Left) which soon became allied with the Communist Party in the promotion of guerrilla warfare. In 1967 the party divided over the choice of a presidential candidate, with more socialist elements leaving to follow Luis Beltrán Prieto in the formation of MEP (the People's Electoral Movement). The 1962 split was of less long-term importance.

16. On the social basis of affiliation to AD, see the recent ecological analysis of voting data presented in D. J. Myers, "Urban Voting, Structural Cleavages, and Party System Evolution: The Case of Venezuela," *Comparative Politics,* 8:1, (October, 1975), pp. 119-151.

17. For an analysis of the positions of the MAS, see my "Urbanization, Migrants, and Politics in Venezuela," *Journal of Interamerican Studies and World Affairs,* 17:3 (August, 1975), pp. 358-72.

[42]

18. For example, by the end of his term in office, President Caldera had moved close to re-establishing relations with Cuba, a step finally taken by the new AD government.

19. A detailed analysis of the evolution of Venezuelan policy toward petroleum is provided in F. Tugwell, *The Politics of Oil in Venezuela* (Stanford: Stanford University Press, 1975).

20. See David Myers, *loc. cit.*, for detailed ecological data which support this argument.

21. I have explored this question at some length, in the context of recent studies of urbanization in Venezuela. See my "Urbanization, Migrants, and Politics in Venezuela," *loc. cit.*

22. For a full analysis of urban voting patterns in Venezuela, see Myers, *op. cit.*, and J. Martz and P. B. Harkins, "Urban Electoral Behavior in Latin America: the Case of Metropolitan Caracas, 1958-1968," *Comparative Politics*, 5:4 (July, 1973), pp. 523-550. The day to day process of political organization among the urban poor is discussed well in T. Ray, *The Politics of the Barios of Venezuela* (Berkeley: University of California Press, 1969), and L. Peattie, *The View From the Barrio* (Ann Arbor: University of Michigan Press, 1972).

23. The autonomous role of leadership in reshaping social and political alternatives has received increased attention in recent years. A good general discussion is provided in A. Lijphart, "Consociational Democracy," *World Politics*, 21:2 (January, 1969), pp. 207-223. For further development of this perspective, with case studies from European and Latin American experience, see J. Linz and A. Stepan, eds., *The Breakdown of Democratic Regimes* (Baltimore: The John Hopkins University Press, 1978).

24. The roots and consequences of urban marginality remain the

subject of some controversy. Peattie, *op. cit.*, offers an excellent discussion, emphasizing the fact that marginality is not a matter of *personal* disorganization or even necessarily of community apathy. *Barrio* dwellers form a variety of personal ties and local associates. The problem lies, instead, with linkages from the *barrio* to the larger society, which are difficult to build and sustain.

25. Peattie, *op. cit.*, especially chapter 11.

26. The Venezuelan trend noted here follows similar developments in Brazil, Peru, and other countries. The evolution of the Superior War College in Brazil is examined in great detail in A. Stepan, *The Military in Politics: Changing Patterns in Brazil* (Princeton: Princeton University Press, 1971). Stepan compares Brazilian developments with those in Peru in his article, "The New Professionalism of Internal Warfare and Military Role Expansion," in A. Stepan, ed., *Authoritarian Brazil* (New Haven: Yale University Press, 1973), pp. 47-68. An excellent overall review of developments in the military throughout Latin America is A. Lowenthal, "Armies and Politics in Latin America," *World Politics*, 27:1 (October, 1974), pp. 107-30.

27. On economic policy in Brazil, see T. Skidmore, "Politics and Economic Policy Making in Authoritarian Brazil, 1937-1971," in Stepan, ed., *Authoritarian Brazil*, pp. 3-46, and A. Fishlow, "Some Reflections on Post-1964 Brazilian Economic Policy," in *ibid.*, pp. 69-118.

[T W O]

The Economic Development of Venezuela—A Summary View As of 1975-1976

Pedro-Pablo Kuczynski*

INTRODUCTION AND SUMMARY

This essay attempts to interpret recent events in the economy of Venezuela and to relate them to the international context. The rise in oil prices which began in 1973 has focused international attention on the member countries of the Organization of Petroleum Exporting Countries (OPEC), in whose founding in 1960 Venezuela and Saudi Arabia played the leading roles. The questions being asked about Venezuela fall into two broad categories: Economically, can Venezuela

* The views in this paper are the personal ones of the author and are in no way attributable to institutions with which he is or was associated. Basic statistical data are presented at the end of this essay.

[45]

invest its new wealth productively, in order to generate economic expansion less dependent on oil and to distribute the benefits of growth among its people more equitably than in the past? Politically, how will the new prosperity affect Venezuela's relations with other Latin American countries and with the United States?

This essay looks at the economic aspects of these questions from the admittedly special vantage point of 1975-76. Barely three years have passed since Venezuela began to receive the large additional income from oil, a rather short period to enable an outside observer [1] to say anything meaningful about the future. After a historical introduction, the paper then comments on the economic and financial impact of the higher oil revenues in the period 1973-75, including Venezuela's new role as an international lender. The analysis of the future focuses on the Fifth Plan and its relations with the issues of employment and income distribution, and industrialization.

This account takes a perhaps somewhat optimistic view of Venezuela's past economic performance and prospects. While it is true that the economy is marked by a high degree of dualism, which is reflected in greater inequalities and in a lower level of social development than might otherwise be expected at the average income level attained by Venezuela, there have been strong achievements in the past, and there are tangible assets which augur well for the future.

Economic management during the recent period of adjustment to the much higher oil revenues which began in 1973 has been relatively restrained, considering the size of the temptation. By creating the Venezuelan Investment Fund, essentially a forced savings scheme in the public sector, the government was able to conserve a substantial part of the additional income. Although public outlays still rose rapidly, the general tone of fiscal policy was to avoid excesses. Venezuela did not make large-scale military outlays, which occurred in other countries with similar increases in revenue; it channelled a relatively high proportion of its revenues in 1974-75 into untied contributions to international financial agencies and into assistance to some of the smaller Latin American and Caribbean countries; a large part of the increase in domestic outlays was devoted to investment; import growth did accelerate substantially but still at a slower rate than in the majority of OPEC countries; finally, while inflation made an appearance for the first time in many years, it did so in a much less virulent form than in most of the rest of the world.

Further back, in the early 1960s for example, Venezuela faced a period of fiscal and balance of payments stringency. The nation was able to adjust then, admittedly at a time of lesser expectations than today. There were difficulties of a social character, but in the process of adjustment the government was able to implement a strong agricultural policy and the beginnings of a more aggressive industrial development. In the 1960s, a period of secular decline in international oil prices, Venezuela was able to achieve some diversification and social progress while maintaining a moderate rate of economic expansion.

Thus in the past, at least since 1958, Venezuelan economic management has shown that it could maintain steadiness in good and bad times. The experience of the past may be needed again in the future, since Venezuela might be entering into a period of relatively slow growth or even stagnation in real terms of its oil revenues. Even when new sources of production are developed in the 1980s, they are likely to be costly. Fiscal revenues from the Orinoco "tar belt," for example, are likely to be much less per unit of output than in the case of existing wells. Moreover, as other oil countries are tempted to increase oil output in order to finance ambitious development efforts, the price unity of OPEC may be more difficult to maintain. Finally, there is the challenge of making the recently nationalized Venezuelan oil industry work.

Moreover, the other tasks of Venezuelan development are not easy. The program of industrial diversification through state enterprises, which is to be sharply accelerated under the 1976-80 public investment program, will not yield foreign exchange resources in any size comparable to those from oil, and at far greater capital costs per dollar of output. Downstream investments may not be forthcoming; the employment generated will be small.

Venezuela should examine closely the range of viable development choices before the nation. The most viable alternatives probably lie between the one extreme of a purely dual oil economy with employment largely provided by the public sector (a choice which was rejected many years ago) and the other extreme of a largely industrial economy (which is probably unattainable with the relatively high wage rates already prevailing at the present relatively early stage of industrial development). Implicitly perhaps, the choice seems to be tilted towards an economy where services and urbanization will have a growing role—financial services, education, construction—with heavy, resource-based industry hopefully providing some export diversification away from oil. Opportunities also may exist for a technologically modern agriculture, if the conditions can be created for productive technological transfer.

The expectations of the Venezuelan public and the development of the oil sector will perhaps be the major variables in determining future economic viability. Venezuela can finance a reasonably rapid growth—in the six to eight percent annual range—if it gradually replenishes its oil resources through the development of new fields and if the delicate interplay of social aspirations and financial realities is handled with the skill shown in the last 15 or 20 years. In addition, very high priority needs to be given to education and to the improvement of productivity, both in the public and private sectors. From the vantage point of 1976, Venezuela has sufficient financial resources to meet these needs: high international reserves, virtually no foreign debt, and a large reservoir of an appreciating natural resource. Past experience suggests that these assets can be employed usefully.

STRUCTURE OF THE ECONOMY AND HISTORICAL BACKGROUND.

Similarly to other oil-exporting countries, the Venezuelan economy has a high degree of dualism. The oil and gas industry (including refining), which provides only about 37,000 jobs directly, in 1975 generated 77% of the central government's current revenue, 96% of merchandise export earnings, and 29% of gross domestic product (GDP).[2] At the other extreme, agriculture which employs about 680,000 persons or approximately 19% of the labor force generated only about 5% of GNP. As in other dualistic economies, Venezuela exhibits a pattern of personal income distribution that is more characteristic of countries with a lower per capita income level than Venezuela's per capita income of about US $2,000 (in 1974), the highest in Latin America. A more modern pattern of distribution might have been expected. According to the available estimates,[3] the lowest 20% of income groups receive only 3% of total income, compared to an average of about 4% for Latin America. Except for the rapid growth of the salaried urban "middle" class, which has led to a less uneven income distribution at the top than in other major Latin American countries, the scant available data

[49]

suggest that income distribution did not improve materially in the last 15 or 20 years. Distribution is not only lopsided as between income groups, but also between urban and rural areas. For example, incomes in Caracas are on average close to four times those in rural areas. Even without manufacturing, there is a wide range between the wages of blue-collar workers in petroleum (Bs2,500 per month in 1972) and more traditional activities (for example, Bs700 per month in a representative shoe factory in 1972).

The pattern of development of Venezuela has nevertheless until now been quite different from that of some of the countries of more recent oil prosperity, which have only had the oil resource. Even though oil has been the major source of foreign-exchange earnings for half a century, Venezuela has over the years developed a diversified domestic economy, with substantial agricultural and manufacturing sectors. Human resources development has moved ahead at a rapid pace, especially in the last two decades. Venezuela's development is thus at a far more advanced stage than most, if not all the other major developing oil-exporting countries. While the financial impact of the higher oil revenues since 1973 has been no less in Venezuela than in other major oil-exporting countries, the institutional and managerial capacity of Venezuela to adjust productively to the change is no doubt higher than in most of the other members of OPEC.

A brief look at past development patterns may be useful. Before oil production developed on a significant scale in the mid-1920s the economy of Venezuela was largely rural and relied for its dynamism, much as many developing countries do today, on exports of a few agricultural commodities. As oil income rose, the government, the main direct beneficiary, began to recycle it into public investment and especially into government employment in the Caracas metropolitan area.

Migration into large urban areas accelerated. By now, only 22% of the population live in rural areas. Over the years, successive governments, especially since the overthrow of the Pérez Jiménez regime in 1958, have made a special effort both to keep up agricultural development and rural incomes and to decentralize industry away from the Caracas area. As a result of special price incentives and other promotional policies, during the 1960s agricultural output in Venezuela rose at a faster rate than in any other major Latin American country, enabling the country for a time to reduce its heavy relative dependence on imported foodstuffs. Under the impetus of Juan Pablo Pérez Alfonso, who was Minister of Development and Minister of Mines of the Betancourt administration (and had been Minister of Mines earlier in the 1945-48 Acción Democrática administration), the Corporación Venezolana de Guayana (CVG) was created in 1960, and fairly rapidly a government-controlled group of basic industries was established in the Guayana region, which is rich in hydroelectric resources and minerals. Although the central government did not have an unusually large direct weight in the GDP up to 1973, the fact that the government has been virtually the only primary recycler of oil wealth within the economy has given it a key role in planning new areas of priority for development.

The evolution of the economy over the last 30 years has not always been smooth.[4] Income expanded rapidly up to 1957, spurred in part by a tripling of crude oil production. However, in 1958 the incoming administration inherited a fiscal crisis. The stabilization program introduced at the time coincided with the beginnings of a long-term glut in the world oil market. Oil prices dropped steadily over the next seven years from an average realized price for crude and products of $2.50 per barrel in 1958 to about $1.90 in 1965, a level at which they stagnated for the rest of the decade. As import prices rose

[51]

steadily, the terms of trade for Venezuela deteriorated by 54% in the period 1958-70. The growth of manufacturing output, which had initially taken advantage of the relatively easier stages of import substitution behind high protective barriers, slowed down: value added in manufacturing fell from an average annual rate of growth in the 1950s of 9.7%, the highest in Latin America, to a still respectable 6.9% in the 1960s.[5] Partly in order to offset the slower rate of growth, the government assumed an active role in the development of basic sectors, particularly agriculture and the new industries in the Guayana region. The other basic reason for these new directions was of course the desire to "sow the oil," in the phrase coined by Arturo Uslar Pietri in 1936, into high priority diversification of the economy. The new policies were quite successful in some areas. For example, the annual average growth of 5.4% in agricultural output during the 1960s was the highest of any major Latin American economy. Nevertheless, the decade of the 1960s was a period of only modest economic expansion for Venezuela. While in the 1950s GDP had increased at an actual average rate of 7.6%, the annual average increase fell to 4.5% in the 1960s. With the rapid expansion of population, per capita income in the 1960s rose by only 1.3% annually, compared to a Latin American average of 2.4%.

Since about 90% of petroleum output is exported, and imports in 1974 accounted for about 36% of non-petroleum GDP, Venezuela has an obvious interest in developments in the international economy. In the last few years, these trends have been particularly important. The rapid increase in imports in 1974-75 (slightly more than a doubling from 1973 to 1975) has been the most important safety valve against domestic inflation. On the other hand, the unit price of the imports themselves went up by about 30 to 40% over the same

[52]

two-year period, contributing substantially to domestic inflation in 1974 and 1975. On the side of exports, the sharp recession in the industrial countries and the resulting decline in demand for energy led major OPEC producers in 1975 to face a reduction in demand for their oil, resulting in cutbacks in production ranging from a slight decline in the case of Iran, to a fall of close to 40% in Libya, and about 30% in Venezuela. Even so, in 1974 Venezuela supplied about 25% of US oil imports, a proportion which is significant but declined rapidly to about 13% in the first half of 1976, as the United States has relied increasingly on supplies from the Middle East.

As in the past, oil revenues and the way they are used continue to be the keys to the economic future of Venezuela. Whether the new oil wealth, which is due entirely to a higher economic rent for a limited natural resource, can lead Venezuela to develop its economic potential depends on many variables, but two are probably of overriding importance: managerial ability, especially to organize efficiently the new public investment ventures; and the distribution of the benefits of the new wealth through employment, income and social services. But before looking into the future, it is worth looking at what happened in the period 1973-75, during the initial and sudden impact of the rise in oil revenues.

The Impact of Higher Oil Revenues, 1973-75

Although the largest increase in international oil prices came at the end of 1973, there was already a substantial upward trend in the course of that year.[6] The important measure of this increase is the average revenue per barrel exported collected by the Central Government, which rose from $1.65 in 1972 to $2.29 in 1973, $8.75 in 1974 and $9.43

in 1975. The impact upon central government finances is
summarized in Table 1.

TABLE 1

Summary of Central Government Finances, 1972-76
(billions of Bolivares at current prices)

	1972	1973	1974	Prelim. 1975	Estimate 1976
Current Revenues	12.5	16.4	42.8	41.0	37.0
Current Expenditures	10.4	11.5	16.5	20 5	22.0
A. Current Account Surplus	2.1	4.9	26.3	20.5	15.0
Transfers to Special Funds [1]	—	—	14.1	9.0 [3]	3.5 [3]
Other Capital Expenditures [2]	3.6	4.8	11.4	12.0	14.0
B. Total Capital Expenditures	3.6	4.8	25.5	21.0	17.5
C. Surplus or Deficit (−) (A—B)	−1.5	0.1	0.8	−0.5	−2.5

1. The Venezuelan Investment Fund and the Funds for Agricultural Credit,
Industrial Credit, Medium- and Small-Scale Industry and Export Promotion, all of
them established in 1974.
2. Excludes funded debt amortization. The concept of capital expenditures shown here
is wider than capital formation as shown in the national accounts, which is the
important concept from the point of view of economic growth. Capital expenditures
shown here include large financial transfers to autonomous agencies.
3. Bs1 million in 1975 and Bs1.5 million in 1976 represent the Government
contribution to the share capital of PETROVEN. The revenue of PETROVEN,
beginning in 1976 and equivalent to 10% of the net operating income of the various oil
companies, is not shown since PETROVEN is an autonomous enterprise.

Source: Banco Central de Venezuela, *Informe Económico, 1974, 1975,* but with various
adjustments in the definition of current and capital expenditures; 1976: estimates by
the author. The definition of the Central Government is that used in the *Informe.*

Several statistical facts stand out. The first and most
important is the trend in current fiscal revenues, rising by
160% from 1973 to 1974, and then declining as oil output fell,
initially slowly in 1975 and more rapidly in 1976. The

increase in revenues in 1974 was accompanied by a large increase in current expenditures of about 44% in that year, although the absolute amount of the increase was modest in relation to the growth in revenues. The additional current expenditure went primarily for two items: higher wage rates (both public and private sector wage rates went up by about 18% in 1974), and larger transfers to various agencies, especially to the agricultural marketing agency (which received Bs1.8 billion in 1974 in order to finance higher farm prices and larger subsidies for imported foodstuffs). Another major feature was the very large increase in expenditures included in the capital account, not counting the Venezuelan Investment Fund, which itself received Bs13 billion in 1974, Bs8.1 billion in 1975, and a smaller sum at the end of 1976. Most of the allocations to the Fund in fact did not enter the domestic spending stream and went in part into foreign loans and assistance and in large measure into domestic savings whose counterpart was an increase in the international reserves of the country.

What has been the record of the government as recycler of the additional income in 1974-75? In general terms, the public sector has done well in channelling resources into high-priority investment areas and has avoided a consumption binge. It is too early to judge whether the additional expenditures have had a significant redistributive effect. Although the rise in current outlays was large, at a rate which could certainly not be sustained for more than a couple of years, it was not unreasonable in relation to expenditure possibilities. A greater emphasis was correctly placed on public investment rather than on public consumption. The creation of the Investment Fund made a significant contribution to attenuating inflationary pressures, by withholding from domestic spending half the Bs27 billion in additional revenues

[55]

obtained in 1974. Finally, great restraint was exercised in new expenditures for defense equipment. Outlays for defense went up from Bs1.4 billion in 1973 to Bs2.0 billion in 1974, and Bs2.5 billion in 1975, with much of the increase for salaries and little for orders of new equipment. In 1975, defense absorbed 6.2% of central government expenditures (net of the Investment Fund) and about 2.0% of GDP. These are rather modest magnitudes in comparison with those in some of the other major oil-exporting countries.

Despite the moderation of fiscal policy under rather extraordinary circumstances, the suddenness of higher expenditures has created very high expectations for the future. Certainly, the pace of expenditure growth, both for consumption and investment, could not be sustained for very long even under optimistic assumptions about oil revenues. For example, Bs4 billion of central government funds was directly spent in 1974 on food and agriculture, subsidizing food imports, expanding special low-interest credit to increase farm output, especially of cattle, and increasing by 30% on average the support prices for farm products. This rate of commitments can probably not be maintained in the future. The same is true of the increases in capital spending in 1974 and 1975. Eighty percent of the increase in public investment represented transfers to autonomous agencies and state enterprises such as those in steel (SIDOR), petrochemicals (IVP), aluminum (ALCASA) and electricity generation (EDELCA). While these entities have large well-defined investment programs, some of the other agencies do not, with the result that central government transfers to them led to an accumulation of agency deposits in the commercial banks in the course of 1974.

The government has been preoccupied with transferring some of the additional resources for productive investment in the private sector. Two efforts in this direction have been the

[56]

Agricultural Credit Fund and the Industrial Credit Fund. Assistance for agriculture is obviously of high priority. Agricultural output grew relatively slowly in 1970-74, at an annual average rate of 3.7%, and imports of foodstuffs rose rapidly over the same period from $140 million to $350 million in current prices, and to about $440 million in 1975, plus the value of 300,000 to 400,000 head of cattle annually imported clandestinely from Colombia. Unfortunately, the form of government assistance to agriculture places excessive emphasis on subsidized loans, the risks of which are well known. Similar risks exist in the case of the Industrial Credit Fund, although perhaps to a lesser degree as the terms are somewhat less subsidized.

The Venezuelan Investment Fund was established in May 1974, for two basic purposes. Initially, the main function was to be to sterilize a part of the additional oil revenue and thus enable the country to accumulate and conserve foreign-exchange reserves for future use. At the same time, the Fund was to have a second but rather different function: namely, to act as a development bank for the large diversification projects in the public sector. These diverse objectives have not always been understood. There was initially some critical comment of the Fund and a fairly serious turnover in its relatively small staff. In fact, however, the record of the Fund in both of its major areas of activity has been a creditable one. About 75% of the approximately $5 billion in assets which it had at the end of 1975 was in the form of short-term international reserves invested through the Central Bank. A very small proportion was in high-grade marketable international bonds, mostly with five-year maturities. The emphasis placed on liquidity is understandable in view of the fairly rapid pace at which the government expects the Fund to disburse its commitments for domestic projects. As of the end of 1975, the Fund has lent

[57]

and partially disbursed $480 million for the SIDOR steel expansion project, $70 million for the ALCASA aluminum project, and $200 million for the expansion of the Venezuelan Shipping Company.[7] The remainder of the assets consist of Venezuelan financial assistance and commitments to international organizations and to Central America.

While the Fund has a certain degree of financial freedom, it is in fact an executor of the government's plans and wishes. It would be unrealistic to expect the Fund to become a commercial vehicle or a foreign assistance agency, a fact which has not always been taken into account by the many bankers and officials from abroad who—largely unsuccessfully—knocked at the doors of the Fund in 1974-75. Their ardor may be dimmed in the future since the Fund received only a small budgetary allocation at the end of 1976, because no significant balance-of-payments or fiscal surplus was expected for the year. However, even if the Fund were to pass from the scene in the next few years, the role which it played in the transition period of 1974-75 was of genuine importance for domestic financial management. By sterilizing a large part of the additional revenue, it moderated the adjustment of the economy to the sharp and sudden rise in income.

A significant proportion of the additional income in 1974 was saved not only through the Investment Fund but also in the form of liquid private sector savings (for example, through time and savings deposits and mortgage bonds, the outstanding amounts of which rose from Bs14.3 billion at the end of 1973 to Bs24.9 billion two years later, or an annual increase in real terms of 21%). Gross savings as a percentage of GDP rose from 25% in 1973 to 35% in 1974, and fell to somewhat below 30% in 1975.

On the external side, the adjustment of 1974-75 was also reasonably successful, reflecting the higher propensity to save.

It is true that imports rose rapidly in 1974 and 1975, but based on official data, the growth (48% in 1974 [8] and 41% in 1975) was somewhat more modest than the average for OPEC countries as a whole (67% in 1974 and about 60% in 1975). In real terms, and adjusting for the higher price of imports, the growth in imports in 1974 amounted to about 20% against an increase in real GDP of 4.5%.[9] In terms of decisions about imports, which take place at current prices, the propensity to import a given percentage of the GDP in fact fell from 18.8% in 1973 to 16.8% in 1974. Although the import data are still preliminary, the impression that Venezuela was on an "import binge" in 1974-75 is somewhat misleading, since in fact a smaller proportion of the additional income was imported than in the past.

Still, Venezuela, similarly to the other major OPEC countries, has turned out to have a much greater "absorptive capacity" for imports than was expected by some observers at the beginning of 1974. In a sense, the economic behavior of these countries has been no different from that of an individual consumer who, as a result of a large recent increase in income, will move to a higher absolute level of consumption together with a higher absolute and relative level of saving.[10] The question is of course the actual size of that additional saving. In the case of Venezuela, the marginal shift toward saving was particularly important, at least in the initial stages of the upward income adjustment.

The growth in imports, moderate as it was in relation to the OPEC average, was a safety valve against inflation in the sense that it provided an outlet for the additional domestic demand. Although imports did provide a release for pent-up domestic demand, they also spread through the economy the "imported inflation" of prices from Venezuela's major suppliers, especially the United States (which accounted for 46% of

[59]

imports in 1974).[11] While government fiscal policies as a whole tended to moderate total domestic demand, government price policies, which attempted to improve the distribution of income, tended to be inflationary. The rise in crop support prices in April 1974 amounted to about 30%. At the same time, the government decreed an average 18% increase in the wage rates for workers in the lower income brackets, which was the major factor in the rise of about 20% in the overall national wage index for the year. While Venezuelan inflation has been modest by the standards of major Latin American economies and even of industrialized countries, the average cost-of-living rise of 8.6% in 1974 and of 10.3% in 1975 has been unusual in an economy characterized in the past by its price stability. The acceleration of inflation in 1975 was due to a variety of factors: the delayed effect of the 16.5% rise in wholesale prices in 1974, a somewhat more expansionary fiscal policy and also the reactivation of private fixed investment which, together with the high level of public investment, created shortages of various products, cement in particular. The acceleration of inflation occurred despite the attempt of the authorities to introduce a total price freeze in the spring of 1974, which was modified in September 1974 by a system of controls over the prices of essential goods.

As in the past, oil output and prices were the key variables in determining export earnings and fiscal revenues. When international petroleum prices were raised by 125% at the end of 1973, Venezuela was still at a high plateau of petroleum production. Output in 1973 averaged 3.37 million barrels a day compared to a peak of 3.71 million in 1970, and an average of about 3.46 million in the decade 1963-73. In the meantime, domestic consumption, stimulated by very low retail prices, went up from 157,000 barrels per day in 1963 to

253,000 in 1973, an average annual growth rate of 4.9%. In 1974, output began to drop.

The average daily extraction rate was 2.98 million barrels in 1974, and fell to the vicinity of 2.4 million barrels in 1975, with daily output in the region of 2.2 million barrels in the last few months of the year. The one-third cutback in production was steadier and more continuous than in other OPEC countries, and was the result of a variety of causes: the reduced demand by industrialized countries (an 8% drop from the beginning of 1973 to mid-1975), deliberate conservation by the Venezuelan government, and two mild winters on the US east coast (which still absorbs almost 50% of Venezuelan exports of crude and products). There may have been other factors, such as the increased competitiveness of Middle East sources as a result of depressed freight rates, especially on super-tankers. There appears to be no evidence that the impending nationalization of the oil companies played a role.

The result of the drop in output upon the balance of payments and the Central Government budget is obviously significant. In 1974, tax and royalty revenue from hydrocarbons was the equivalent of $8.7 billion (out of total budget revenues of $10.2 billion) while realized export earnings were $10.4 billion. For 1975, these totals fell to about $7.4 billion (including royalties) and about $8.5 billion respectively. The outcome for 1976 at the time of writing is still somewhat uncertain. In very general terms, assuming an output of 2.3 million barrels per day and international petroleum prices on average 5% higher for the year as a whole, fiscal and foreign exchange income would be slightly higher than in 1975.

The acceleration of inflation in 1974-75 was the one noticeable but apparently temporary weakness in the adjustment of the Venezuelan economy to its new higher level of

[61]

income. In other areas of economic management, the adjustment was by and large quite successful. The question of course is what will happen in the longer-run future. Before looking in that direction, we will review briefly Venezuela's new role as an international lender.

VENEZUELA AS AN INTERNATIONAL LENDER

While the role Venezuela played as an international lender in 1974-75 is unlikely to continue on the same scale for very long, the rapidity of Venezuela's response and the areas to which it channelled its lending certainly reflected favorably upon the degree of international responsibility of the country. As John Martz shows in another essay in this book, international lending was also an important component of foreign policy.

The Pérez administration has been very aware of the negative impact of the higher oil prices on oil-importing developing countries, especially on the smaller countries of Central America and the Caribbean.[12] While wishing to help, the government has also tried to avoid the inevitable problems of direct bilateral aid to sovereign countries. As a result of these considerations, a two-pronged approach to international assistance was evolved by the government during 1974-75: the bulk of the international financial collaboration of Venezuela was to be with international agencies (mainly the IMF, the World Bank and the Inter-American Development Bank), but direct assistance on the part of Venezuela was channelled to the smaller neighboring countries, including Guyana and the various Central American countries, where Venezuela felt that it could make an effective contribution.

The sums made available by Venezuela were large in

relative terms, particularly in 1974. In that year, Venezuela committed SDR 450 million (the equivalent at the time of US$540 million) through the Banco Central to the IMF Oil Facility, of which $303 million had been disbursed by year-end. The Investment Fund committed and disbursed a $500 million loan to the World Bank and Venezuelan commercial banks took up a Bs100 million note issue, also from the World Bank.[13] Disbursements of public sector lending abroad in 1974, made up largely of the loans to the IMF and the World Bank, totalled about $850 million, or 14% of the current account surplus.[14] The pace diminished somewhat in 1975, as the balance-of-payments surplus became smaller. The major commitments included another contribution to the IMF Oil Facility (SDR 200 million) and a commitment over a five-year period to establish a $500 million trust fund within the Inter-American Development Bank. In addition, various commitments totalling up to $150 million were entered into (although in some cases not signed) in 1974-75 with three regional development finance institutions: the Caribbean Development Bank (of which Venezuela is a member), the Andean Development Corporation, and the Central American Bank of Economic Integration. Altogether, including the financing of oil sales to various Latin American countries—particularly to the six countries of Central America (with Panama), Jamaica and Peru—disbursements in 1975 were probably on the order of $400 million, or about 26% of the current account surplus. In addition, there was a short-term loan to finance coffee stocks of Central American countries but it did not lead to significant disbursements because the price of coffee below which the scheme would have entered into operation was in fact overtaken when international coffee prices began to recover in mid-1975.

The oil-refining agreement with the Central American

[63]

countries and Panama is of long-run importance, since it places Venezuela in the bilateral aid business, at least for the period 1975-80. During that period, the Venezuelan Investment Fund will lend to the central bank of each of the six countries an annual sum equivalent to the difference between the actual realized export prices of Venezuelan crude (i.e., the price the importing country would have paid) and US$6 per barrel, based on the volume of imports of Venezuelan oil by Central America in 1974. The import subsidy would thus cover about half of Central American oil imports, which total about $300 million annually, excluding the re-export trade of Panama. The import subsidy will decline each year, as the base price of $6 per barrel is raised annually by 16.6% until the subsidy disappears at the beginning of 1981. The sums thus lent, which are expected to reach a gross total of about $500 million, can be paid back in six years or, alternatively, the money can be used for approved development projects (such as those assisted by international financial agencies), in which case the maturity is extended to 25 years.

The international financing effort by Venezuela has been an important one. In comparison with some other major surplus countries within OPEC, the current account surplus of Venezuela is relatively smaller in per capita terms, its domestic needs are large, and its petroleum reserves are relatively low. Judged against these parameters, Venezuela's disbursements of official international finance in 1974-75 were substantial in relation to the OPEC effort as a whole, accounting for about 15% of the total gross OPEC flow during those two years.[15] On the other hand, the major part of this flow of resources, both in the case of Venezuela and of other OPEC countries, has not been on "soft" terms.

The pace of official international lending by Venezuela is likely to slacken, probably quite rapidly, as the current account surpluses diminish in the next few years. Nevertheless, a related question which remains thus far unanswered is whether the new prosperity can contribute to the rise of Caracas as an international financial center, with a substantial international capital market. A real financial center has to be based on a substantial corporate clientele nearby, plus appropriate hospitable conditions such as currency convertibility, a minimum of red tape, realistic interest rates, and a tax system which is favorable by international standards. Venezuela meets some of these conditions, but it is too soon to judge its potential for expansion into an international financial center.[16]

ISSUES AND PROSPECTS

After considerable discussion both within and outside the government, the Fifth Plan was officially announced in mid-1976. Covering the period 1976-80, the Plan has some ambitious physical and financial targets. It will raise obvious issues about the path of Venezuela's economic development.

The Plan does not aim to provide a comprehensive strategy for developing the economy. Rather, it is a list of major public expenditure targets with various investment projects attached. The degree of preparation varies, from relatively advanced projects in heavy industry, which is likely to be the major absorber of funds, to more general aims in the area of social and human needs. The major issue concerning the Plan is probably not so much the volume of resources needed to finance its expenditures, which are likely to slip somewhat, as the development strategy which it implicitly represents. The strategy is clearly one of diversifying the economy from oil into heavy industry. While the general aim is commendable and the shift is likely to be gradual, the strategy has wide-ranging implications for employment prospects, the distribution of income, and the availability of resources for investment itself.

To what extent is it feasible and desirable to pursue diversification away from oil? A point could be reached when the expenditure on new industrial investments was so large that, even after substantial external borrowing, oil output would have to be stepped up in order to prevent a large fiscal and balance-of-payments gap from arising. A rise in oil output beyond external demand would certainly run counter to the requirements for OPEC oil-pricing policies. Indeed, one or two major OPEC countries appeared to be running into such a problem in 1976. For Venezuela, therefore, it will be important to hold current and capital expenditures within limits which can be financed without sudden major increases in oil production, given a reasonable amount of external borrowing. Unless some sort of equilibrium can be kept between the various conflicting claims of running such a policy, diversification might run into the problem of oil prices which decline in real terms. This kind of "fine tuning" has to be practiced by all major oil-exporting countries, since otherwise the cartel will not be able to defend a united price front.

The range of choices open to Venezuela in devising a development strategy is rather narrow. Because of relatively high wage rates, industrialization combined with high factory employment (the strategy successfully followed by some East Asian countries) is not really feasible. Nor is complete dependence on oil. The emphasis on resource-based industries is no doubt right, as long as it is followed by other complementary policies. The strategy which is implicitly being pursued is a combination of resource-based activities (oil and heavy industry) with an urban services economy. In order to increase the chances for success of such a strategy, however, policies probably have to become somewhat more explicit than they are at present on a range of issues such as social services, training and education, manufacturing for the domestic market, and small- and medium-scale private enterprise.

FINANCING RESOURCES AND THE 1976-80 PLAN

For the next four or five years, when no major new sources of oil supply can be expected to enter into production, oil output and prices and the demand for imports will be the key variables. If we suppose that oil export prices will keep up with world inflation, there would still be a deterioration in the current account balance of payments, since the expected rate of growth of the economy will require imports to increase faster than the income from oil and the interest earned on foreign assets. In the past five years, the elasticity of imports on the non-petroleum sectors in relation to GDP rose from 1.3 in 1970 (in other words, for every percentage point increase in GDP, imports rose by 1.3%) to 1.6% in 1973, and almost to 2 in 1974. Even at a more normal level in the range of 1.2 or 1.3, Venezuela's imports (as in most developing countries) will go up faster than the national product and quite possibly faster also than current foreign exchange earnings, of which oil exports and interest income are the major components. The tendency is likely to be accentuated by the high import content of major planned public investments. Unless the above assumption about oil prices is drastically wrong, therefore, the current account surplus in the balance of payments is likely to become insignificant and may even turn into a deficit in the next two years or so.

At a given international price for oil, the key variable in the outlook for the balance of payments and indeed for the whole economy is the extraction rate of oil. The issue that will continuously face economic policymakers is to design the right blend of oil output with external borrowing. To what extent should Venezuela step up oil production (thus depleting a scarce resource or, in a sense, "borrowing" against future production) or borrow financial resources abroad? There are clear constraints on both courses of action. To expand oil output in existing fields is not easy or necessarily economical, as wells which would have to be re-opened are marginal.

Borrowing abroad has its negative aspects also. It is true that, as a net international lender with a solid financial basis, Venezuela was able in the fall of 1976 to obtain a seven-year $1 billion loan at the lowest interest premium of any major international Eurocurrency loan syndicated since mid-1974. The highly liquid position of a number of major international banks, whose lending in their own domestic economies (especially the United States) was stagnant, combined with the high international reserves of Venezuela, contributed to the success of the loan. This success occurred despite the fact that the loan was essentially used to refinance short-term external debts of various autonomous agencies which, having been held on a short fiscal leash in relation to their ambitious spending plans, circumvented established procedures by borrowing at terms of less than one year.[17] Another loan of $1.2 billion was completed early in 1977.

Thus there are signs which might lead to concern both within and outside Venezuela, both on the issue of short-term management of public finances outside the central government and on the longer term outlook for the balance of payments. This type of forecast of the balance of payments may well be greeted as pessimistic, particularly by those who, as a result of the recent bonanza, have grown accustomed to the idea that

Venezuela should be a net lender and not a borrower. In fact, there are good reasons why Venezuela has again become a net borrower of moderate sums in the international capital markets. Venezuela is in the full swing of expanding and diversifying its economy; even at a per capita income level of $2,000, it is unlikely to be able to generate all the savings necessary for the task. It therefore needs to borrow in order to sustain a reasonable rate of economic expansion. Another factor is that Venezuela is in an excellent position to borrow. Until mid-1976, it had had no net external debt. In fact, the official obligations of foreigners to Venezuela at that time substantially exceed the funded external public debt; the income from those obligations also exceeded the very low debt service, which was equivalent to less than 1% of export earnings. The question in borrowing policy will therefore be not so much whether to borrow but what to borrow for and how much, in view of export earnings prospects and debt-servicing capability.

At least for the next few years, it is thus unlikely that there will be a significant external resource constraint, as long as government spending does not increase beyond reasonable bounds, and a careful balance is maintained between the rate of oil extraction and external indebtedness.

A related question concerns the availability of domestic resources in light of the fairly ambitious public investment plan. The initial publicized discussions of the draft Fifth Plan prepared by CORDIPLAN, the planning agency, mentioned a target of around Bs130 to 140 billion (in 1975 prices) of public investment in the period 1976-80. This original target was based on the requests of the various spending agencies. Approximately one-third of the total was to be for large state-owned manufacturing projects, about 20% for electric power and transportation (including construction of an east-west

[69]

railway from the Guayana industrial area to the main markets in the central region and the west), and another 20% for the petroleum sector. Only about 5% of the original requests were for education, health and social welfare. The proposed plan was thus heavily weighted toward very large capital-intensive schemes. The main objection to the preliminary figures, however, was their size in relation to the country's financial and executing capability. A lively public debate ensued, in which it was clear that the Finance Ministry favored a substantially smaller target. In the end, in mid-1976, a final public investment program was announced for a total of Bs94 billion (in 1975 prices) for the period 1976-80.

The new target of Bs94 billion is still high and will require a very substantial fiscal and administrative effort if it is to be attained. It includes Bs21 billion of petroleum investment, an amount which is considered sufficient to maintain existing production but not to make a start in major new developments, such as the heavy oils on the north bank of the Orinoco river. For such a start to be made, at least another Bs15 to 20 billion would have to be added. In practice, there is likely to be some slippage in various sectors, so that the total plan target can realistically be considered to be about Bs80 to 85 billion.

If a modest sum of Bs15 to 20 billion is included to start new petroleum developments, the plan—in reality a public investment program—can for practical purposes be considered to be about Bs100 billion. The plan would thus work out on average to an annual target of Bs20 billion. This is about three times actual public investment expenditures of about Bs6.5 billion in 1974, equivalent to 5.1% of GDP. The new target would be equivalent to about 10% to 11% of GDP, assuming an 8% average annual growth rate of GDP in constant prices during the period 1976-80. If it is assumed for the sake of argument that one quarter of the total could be financed from abroad

[70]

(with net borrowing of about US $1.2 billion per year), the remainder would have to come out of net domestic savings. Assuming that domestic savings return to a normal level of about 25% of GDP, about a third would then be channeled to the public sector.

Such an effort, while large, would not be as big as it appears at first sight, for two reasons. First, at least Bs12 billion of the public investment effort will be covered by transfers of the oil companies to PETROVEN, making possible investment which would have previously been carried out by the private sector. Second, there are Bs20 billion available in financial resources from the Investment Fund, which represent past savings.

These types of illustrative calculations should not be taken too seriously, since there are major assumptions which could turn out to be wrong. For example, it is assumed that the physical and administrative capacity exists to actually build and productively spend the amounts envisaged. The macroeconomic assumptions about oil revenues, GDP growth, domestic savings, and prices and the level of public investment itself could, and probably will, turn out differently. Still, the point which emerges is that a public investment program of the general order of magnitude which is being tentatively planned assumes a fairly substantial evolution of the Venezuelan economy toward a much larger and more effective role for the public sector. Whether and how this can happen and what the effects will be is partly a matter of opinion. But a few things are clear to the government and to outside observers. On the revenue side, the efficiency of state enterprises has to be improved considerably if they are to generate sufficient savings. The private sector, including agriculture, will be called upon to pay more taxes (at present non-petroleum central government current revenues as a percentage of non-petroleum GDP are only 8%). In fact, the government in November 1976 presented to Congress a significant tax reform, with higher taxation of upper income groups. On the expenditure side, waste and excessively capital-intensive outlays will have to be controlled more effectively than in the past.

There is general agreement within Venezuela that a major element in the outlook for the economy will be the degree of success of the public sector in managing and developing the nationalized petroleum companies. The technical, managerial and financial resources required are large. This applies not only to keeping up the present rate of output of about 2.2 to 2.3 million barrels per day, but also to investment in order to develop new areas. Venezuela's proven recoverable reserves are relatively low compared to those of some other major OPEC producers. If an attempt is made to develop new sources of supply, the expenditures and technical complexities will be substantial. For example, a 150,000 barrels per day pilot plant to begin the research and development phase of the Orinoco tar sands is estimated to cost by itself Bs7 billion at today's prices. A major effort is being made by the Government to staff the new petroleum enterprises with the best people, including foreigners when no Venezuelans are available.

DIVERSIFICATION AND INDUSTRIAL POLICY

The largest part of public investment will be earmarked for industry, especially electricity, steel, aluminum, and petrochemicals. If all plans go ahead—an unlikely prospect—Corporación Venezolana de Guayana (CVG) and its subsidiaries in steel, aluminum and electricity alone would spend

Bs50 billion at today's prices in the next eight to ten years. Since these are also the best equipped agencies, this portion of planned investment is more likely to go ahead than the others. All these industrial plans have several points in common. They are highly capital-intensive and create little direct employment; some of them will require substantial downstream private sector investments if they are to be successful (this is particularly the case in chemicals and mechanical industries); and in terms of generating exports, very large investments will be required before a substantial diversification takes place beyond petroleum exports. For example, the large steel and aluminum projects mentioned below will generate exports and substitute imports worth about $1 billion annually at 1974 prices, after an investment of about $4 billion, compared to realized foreign exchange earnings from petroleum of $10.4 billion in that year.

In general terms, however, the emphasis on industrialization reflects the legitimate desire to overcome the fact that the manufacturing sector is substantially less developed than could be expected for a country at Venezuela's income level.[18] The emphasis of the public sector industrial plan is on resource-based capital-intensive heavy industry for export. Thus, SIDOR is expanding its present production capacity of 1.2 million tons of steel to 4.5 million tons by 1978. The program, which will enable Venezuela to produce domestically about 700,000 tons of products which are imported annually and to export about 2.5 million tons per year, has a total cost of about Bs14 billion. The exports will replace the unprocessed mineral ore exports of Ferrominera Venezolana, which took over when the U.S. Steel and Bethlehem Steel subsidiaries were nationalized in 1974. Although Venezuela's known resources of bauxite are of poor quality, a major expansion plan of the aluminum industry for export is underway, using imported raw material and cheap electric power from the Guri hydro-electric works. ALCASA (a joint venture of Reynolds Aluminum and CVG) is expanding from a capacity of 54,000 tons to 125,000 tons by 1978. A much larger project, at a total cost of about Bs2 billion in an 80/20 joint venture of CVG with Japanese interests, is under study; it would produce and export 280,000 tons of aluminum annually by 1980 or 1981. The possibility of a joint venture between Jamaica, Mexico and Venezuela to establish another alumina plant in Jamaica (which would sell to Venezuela) has also been discussed at the political level. The plans in petrochemicals are equally large, although perhaps less well defined because of the weaknesses in the Instituto Venezolano de Petroquimica (IVP), the state agency with a monopoly for the production of basic chemicals.

The successful development of industry requires several ingredients besides efficient planning of state-owned industry. One incentive is to make the bulk of private industry less dependent on protection from imports. A related issue is the relationship of Venezuelan industry to competition from Andean Group suppliers. Another requirement, especially for the major primary state-owned industries, concerns arrangements for downstream investments.

The question of downstream investments is particularly important at a time when Venezuelan industry is facing rapid adjustments. Foreign direct investment has been particularly important to private industry (according to the Central Bank *Informe,* there was $1.1 billion of foreign private investment outstanding in industry in 1974, with the largest amounts in the automotive industry and in chemicals). But foreign investment is likely to be more hesitant than in the past as a result of the national ownership requirements under Decision 24 of the Andean Group and possibly also to a lesser extent because of the policy of nationalizing basic resources. The entry of Venezuela into the Andean Group at the beginning of 1973 will gradually expose Venezuelan industry to greater competition, a healthy development. On the other hand, some adjustments are likely to be difficult. There are highly protected industries in which Venezuela is unlikely to be able to improve efficiency to a competitive level because of the heavy labor component at high wage rates. Textiles, clothing, small appliances and furniture are among these industries. Under the Andean Group arrangements, Venezuela can maintain duties on a list of products until 1985.

The task of making industry more efficient is a major one. The government took a first step in this direction in 1973 when it abolished the system of quotas and import licenses. The system gave infinite protection to some industries, and therefore required offsetting price controls. The new ad valorem tariff of 1973 is a clear improvement, although the average nomimal tarrif level of 75% is still high by international standards, and the lower level of protection has to some extent been offset by generous duty exemptions on imported raw materials. Nominal rates of import duties are obviously an inadequate measure of protection. A more useful one is to compare domestic with international prices. A 1971 survey by CORDIPLAN [19] showed that at the time the gross value of the industrial production (excluding petroleum refining) of Venezuela was Bs20 billion: the same output valued at world prices would have been of the order of Bs11 billion. Even though actual protection has no doubt fallen since 1971, because world prices have risen faster than prices in Venezuela, the rough-and-ready comparison is a good indicator of the level of protection for industry as a whole. Protection was particularly high for food processing, beverages and textiles and also for paper, glass and automobiles.

In general, the average nominal tariff is especially high for consumer goods (128%) and is more modest for intermediate and capital goods (48% and 34%, respectively), which are the products requiring special encouragement if downstream private investments are to take place with the new steel and petrochemical complexes. As a result of protection, profits in the domestic market have been relatively high (in 1971, for example, according to industrial survey data, pre-tax profits were of the order of 30% of fixed assets in modern industry) and capacity utilization has been low while effective taxation of the profits has been modest. In September 1973, the government established an export incentive scheme through tax rebates. So far there has been only a very modest growth of manufactured exports other than petroleum products and those of CVG subsidiaries. The reason is not hard to find. With present levels of protection, it would probably take an exchange rate substantially more depreciated than the going rate of Bs4.30 per US dollar, depending on the branch of private industry, in order to make sales abroad even marginally attractive financially in comparison with domestic sales.

With its present level of income, the Venezuelan economy can for the time being live with a relatively inefficient industrial sector. However, as the new government-owned export-oriented industries are developed, the need to improve the efficiency of the rest of the industrial system will increase. A few significant steps have already been taken but others are possible, especially in reducing tariff protection, and are probably easier to take in the present period of bonanza than they would be in less comfortable times.

Human Resources

An issue which is often emphasized in discussions about Venezuela's future is the need to improve and expand the managerial talent of the country. This is a rather complex question. The principal fact which stands out is the shortage of middle-level management and skills.

In general, as in the case of industrialization, the question about managerial resources is not so much the absolute level of training and skills available, but the level in relation to the high income per capita. The Venezuelan education system has in fact made rapid strides in the last 20 years, at least numerically. The enrollment ratio in primary education, a rather rough measure of educational coverage in the basic grades, rose from 52% in 1950 to about 77% in 1970, compared to a Latin American average of about 72%. Venezuela was ahead of some countries (for example, Brazil at 72% and Colombia at 62%) but behind others (Mexico at 82% and Panama at 84%) which have a lower per capita income level. In terms of the effectiveness of the primary school system in keeping pupils through the six-year cycle, Venezuela has done rather better than most other Latin American countries. Progress in secondary education has also been rapid, at a somewhat faster pace than the Latin American average. The enrollment ratio in 1970 was about 34%, comparable to that of Brazil, considerably higher than Mexico's (21%) or Colombia's (23%), but lower than that of Panama or of Trinidad and Tobago.

Despite rapid educational progress, there are still some areas of concern. The average literacy rate for those 15 years and older remains relatively low at 70% in 1970, comparable with Brazil but lower than the Latin American average of 73% and below countries such as Mexico and Colombia.[20] However, literacy rates for young people are much higher than those of older people. At the other end of the educational spectrum, higher education is turning out too many lawyers and social scientists, and not enough engineers, scientists and business

[77]

managers.[21] In the middle levels of technical education, vocational school enrollment is particularly low.

The Pérez administration is very much aware of these problems and has made education and training a major item of public investment. A scholarship program to send university students for full-time study abroad began on a crash basis in 1974. About 10,000 students are already abroad, a large number which reflects the importance given by the government to the program. The idea of opening the doors and windows of Venezuela to university training abroad is undoubtedly a good one, even if there is the normal degree of wastage.[22] However, training at the top has to be matched by much greater efforts at the middle level (occupations such as mechanics, plumbers, nurses), which is usually the Achilles' heel of organizations in developing countries. This is a very difficult task, not only because higher incomes create high expectations of reaching the university and professional levels, but particularly because educators do not agree among themselves on the best way to provide this type of training. Costly mistakes are therefore quite possible.

THE EMPLOYMENT ISSUE

The question of generating sufficient employment opportunities is closely linked to the distribution of income, since what is at stake is the creation of remunerative employment. In Venezuela, as in many other developing economies, the problem is not so much open unemployment, which is moderate, but the existence of a large pool of semi-employed people who survive on very low incomes. Out of a total population of 11.7 million at the end of 1974, there was a total labor force of 3.5 million, made up of 2.7 million men and

856,000 women. With economic development, the participation rate of women in the labor force has increased, especially in the cities, and reached a national total of 25% in 1974 (38% in Caracas), compared to 20% in 1961.

The statistical evidence on employment produced by the 1961 census and the household surveys conducted in 1971 and 1974 (by the *Dirección General de Estadística*) brings out several tentative conclusions, although these should be tempered by a healthy skepticism of the data. Open unemployment declined substantially from 13.3% in 1961 to 6.2% in 1971, although some of the decline may be due to understatement of the employment in small-scale manufacturing in the 1961 census; open unemployment appears to have stayed at about 6% from 1971 to 1974 while employment increased at a relatively high annual rate of 4.3%; the highest and most persistent rates of unemployment are among the young, especially the 15 to 24 age group, which averaged 12.2% unemployment in the second half of 1974. Factory employment has, surprisingly, been a major absorber of employment. In 1974, industrial factory employment occupied 338,000 workers (out of 591,000 employed in manufacturing as a whole) compared to 295,000 in 1971 and 150,000 in 1961. Factory employment has thus grown at an annual average rate in the last 13 years of 6.5%, a very rapid rate which is not far behind the rate of expansion of manufacturing output.

However, as one looks beyond these broad statistics, a significant degree of underemployment and poverty emerges. In the Caracas metropolitan area, for example, which had in 1974 an average income per household per month of about Bs1,200, 53,000 households (comprising about 200,000 people) had family incomes of less than Bs500 per month (equivalent at the current exchange rate to U.S.$116); the average monthly income for this group was only Bs160 (or

[79]

U.S.$37). Another 40,000 families (with about 230,000 persons) had incomes between Bs500 and Bs1,000 per month, and an average of about Bs800. Most of these people are in unorganized service activities in what social scientists now call the "informal sector." Outside of agriculture, 40% of workers are either self-employed or work in establishments with less than five workers. Within Venezuela as a whole, in 1974 approximately 30% of the self-employed had incomes of less than Bs100 per month, a level which obviously reflected their lack of steady employment. In the case of employees, the ratio of those below Bs100 per month in income was 16%, made up in a substantial proportion of domestic servants.

The government has correctly made a major issue of the poverty and underemployment question. However, in the short run, no instant successful "war on poverty" can be expected. Early in 1975, the government decreed that all enterprises with 10 or more employees had to increase their employment by 5% above the May 1975 level. In anticipation of the measure, businesses stopped hiring personnel ahead of the May base period, so that the effect of the measure was probably insignificant in comparison with what would have happened without it.

In reality, an effective employment strategy in Venezuela will be difficult to devise because the resources which the country has (such as oil, iron ore, and hydroelectric power) can be developed technologically only with highly capital-intensive methods. Under the Fifth Plan, more than two-thirds of public investment would go to these sectors (including petroleum), hardly a recipe for job creation. At the same time, if these resource-based basic industries can provide cheap inputs to the rest of the industrial sector, an auspicious beginning will have been made. To complement the effort, gradual changes in existing well-known price distortions

[80]

which encourage excessively capital-intensive forms of production will need to be carried out.[23]

CONCLUSIONS

The foregoing bird's eye view of the Venezuelan economy has been of necessity rather partial and perhaps also optimistic. There is no doubt that there are major areas of vulnerability for the future. The main one is clearly that the Venezuelan economy will continue to depend on oil as its mainstay for a long time to come. The major industrial development being carried out by state enterprises will not generate exports on a scale remotely comparable to petroleum. Even ten years from now, non-oil exports would not amount to more than about one-fifth of total merchandise exports, and that would already be a major achievement. Nor can the new investments be expected to lead to a radical downward shift of the import coefficient in an expanding economy. With oil the main variable in the economy, Venezuela is very vulnerable, as are other major oil exporters, to possible weakness in oil prices. This could be brought about if major oil-exporting countries as a group had to step up oil output in order to meet overambitious development goals. The danger of such a development is obvious not only in financial terms, but also in relation to the very high expectations of social and economic improvement which have been generated in most of these countries since 1973.

On the other hand, a sharp drop in oil prices is very unlikely. The cartel did make it possible to raise prices to the levels reached since 1973, but a major if not the major part of the increase (after almost twenty years of a secular decline in oil prices in real terms) was due to the world boom of 1972-73 combined with the increasing dependence of industrialized and developing countries alike on imported energy. So far, the latter phenomenon has not really changed and, in the case of the United States, is intensifying. Plans to change the trend are highly dependent on oil prices roughly in the present range or even higher.

Another major concern is whether Venezuela has the administrative capability, understood in the broadest sense, to succeed in its development plan. That is a hard question to answer. On balance, despite obvious weaknesses, the performance of the last two or three years suggests that it can succeed. Venezuela was able to save, through the Investment Fund, a sizable share of the additional revenue from oil. It has so far resisted the temptation of getting into large armaments expenditures. There has been waste, no doubt. However, in a democracy with a vocal press, there have been many checks upon profligacy, as has been shown repeatedly by Congress and especially by the Controller General.

The development goals for the next five years are quite ambitious, and will probably have to be cut back somewhat, but they are not unreasonably out of line with the financial and managerial resources of the country. The economic keys will be how well Venezuela can manage its oil industry, which requires very large investments, and how effectively the management of a growing public sector can be meshed with the private sector of the economy.

What are the international implications of this assessment? Clearly, the euphoria of 1974 is gradually giving way to a more realistic assessment of the economic future, where development at home is the overriding priority. A major flow of Venezuelan resources to its neighbors in Latin America and in the Caribbean is quite unlikely in the next few years. The fact that Venezuela in the fall of 1976 again became an international borrower will no doubt bring strong internal pressures to bear against further commitments abroad which are not of a strictly commercial nature. Venezuela will continue to be vocal internationally. The Sistema Económico Latinoamericano (SELA), whose major sponsor Venezuela has been, will no doubt stay, but the heady days of big initiatives bankrolled by Venezuela are over. There is plenty to do at home.

NOTES

1. The author served during the year 1974-75 as an external adviser to the Banco Central de Venezuela. The opinions in this essay are entirely the author's and in no way reflect those of the Banco Central de Venezuela.

2. The corresponding data for 1974, a year of sharp changes, were 85.1% of central government current revenue, 96.5% of merchandise export earnings, and 37.0% of GDP. This last figure is based on GDP in current prices, which exaggerate the increase in output in 1974 because of oil prices. On a constant price basis, the contribution of the hydrocarbons sector in 1974 was of the order of 14%, and that of agriculture about 7%.

3. As usual with such estimates for developing countries great care should be exercised in the interpretation of the data, which in the case of Venezuela are derived mainly from official sample surveys conducted in 1962 plus additional data for 1971, and are thus by now largely out of date. For an analysis of the 1962 data, see United Nations Economic Commission for Latin America, *Income Distribution in Latin America* (New York: UN publication sales number E.71 11. G.2, 1971); pages 52-61.

BASIC ECONOMIC DATA

Population	:	12.1 million (1975)
Growth Rate p.a.	:	3.4% (1961–75)
Per capita income	:	US$2,016 [1] (1975)
GNP	:	US$25.2 billion [1] (1975)
GDP	:	US$29.0 billion [1] (1975)

Sector composition of GDP (%)	In current prices 1970	In current prices 1974	In 1968 prices 1974	Growth rates in constant 1968 prices 1970–74
	100.0	100.0	100.0	4.2%
Agriculture	7.0	4.6	6.8	3.7%
Petroleum, gas & mining	19.0	38.4	14.3	–3.4%
Petroleum refining	3.8	10.5	2.3	–6.5%
Other manufacturing	12.2	8.8	14.0	7.4%
Construction	3.9	3.3	4.3	10.2%
Other (services)	54.1	34.4	57.3	6.5%

Geographic composition of foreign trade (1975)	Imports f.o.b.	Exports f.o.b.
Total value ($ billion)	5.5	11.1
Geographic distribution (%)	100.0	100.0

	1970	1974
United States	47.6	55.0 (est.) [2]
Canada	3.3	12.8
EEC	25.8	9.2
Andean Group	2.2	1.6
Other	21.1	21.4

	1970	1974
Labor force (thousands)	3,100	3,506
Unemployed	6.2%	6.3%
Employed in agriculture	22.5%	19.4%
petroleum, gas & mining (incl. refining)	1.5%	1.5%
manufacturing	16.2%	16.9%
construction	5.5%	6.3%
other	48.1%	49.6%

Balance of Payments Summary (US$ millions)

	1973	1974	1975	Projection [3] 1976
Exports f.o.b. (valued at petroleum reference prices)	5,645	15,197	11,117	11,000
Imports f.o.b.	−2,626	−3,876	−5,462	−6,400
Services incl. unrequited transfers	−2,122	−5,462	−4,123	−3,500
Current account balance	897	5,859	1,532	1,100

Capital to official sector (net)	102	−202	−2	⎤
Private sector capital (net)	46	−649	444	⎦ −1,400
Capital account	148	−851	442	
Errors and omissions	−321	−982	459	
Total (i.e. change in Central Bank reserves)	724	4,022	2,433	−300
Net international reserves of Central Bank at year-end (US$ millions)	2,401	6,423	8,856	8,500

1. US$ equivalents are computed at the market exchange rate (US$1 = Bs4.285) and do not attempt to adjust for relative purchasing power.
2. The estimate arises because of re-exports of Venezuelan oil refined in the (Netherlands) Antilles.
3. Projection by the author.

Source: Banco Central de Venezuela, *Informe Económico 1974, 1975,* and Dirección General de Estadística, various publications.

4. An invaluable source of analytical information up to the late 1950s is the published report by the World Bank, *The Economic Development of Venezuela* (Baltimore: John Hopkins University Press, 1961).

5. A comprehensive general statistical source for the 1950s and 1960s is *Latin America's Development and the Alliance for Progress* (Washington D.C., Organization of American States, 1973).

6. The figures used here are averages, since there is a wide range of export prices. In addition, export prices reflect differences in shipping distances and costs. The estimated market price of Saudi Arabian Light, a fairly representative crude, f.o.b. Ras Tanura (Saudi Arabia) has evolved as follows: $1.30 per barrel January 1970 (a price $0.63 below that of January 1955 in current dollars), gradually rising to $2.20 in January 1973, then to $2.70 in June 1973, $3.65 on October 16, 1973, and $8.18 on January 1, 1974.

7. A part of this is assigned to COVINCA, the agency in charge of developing a shipbuilding industry for Venezuela. It is not clear whether this very large project will go ahead on the scale originally planned, however. Although Venezuela has steel, it does not yet have the required engineering expertise and the costs are likely to be high initially.

8. This analysis is based on the preliminary data from the Banco Central de Venezuela (f.o.b. basis) as shown in the *Informe Económico 1974*. To the extent that the figures can be considered reasonably firm, they would show that earlier estimates of 65% growth in imports were too high.

9. In real terms, GDP increased only by 4.5% because of a 12% drop in petroleum output, which was more than offset by an increase of 7.4% in the GDP of the sectors other than petroleum. The problem of measuring an increase in real income to Venezuelans on the basis of an increase in income from foreigners (as a result of

[87]

higher oil prices) despite a decline in the output of oil, can be resolved by looking at real GDP adjusted for changes in the terms of trade. On this basis, with export earnings valued at current prices but adjusted for the terms-of-trade effect (i.e., adjusted downward to reflect the negative effect upon their purchasing power of the higher unit prices of imports), the increase in real GDP in 1974 was on the order of 12%. There are thus three possible measures of the growth of GDP in 1974: 4.5% in constant prices, 12% if the GDP is adjusted for the gain in the terms of trade, and 66% in current prices. The second measure is probably the best indicator of the real gain in welfare of the nation.

10. For a review of the literature on the behavior of individuals as regards consumption, see for example Ruth P. Mack, "Economics of Consumption," in *A Survey of Contemporary Economics,* Volume 11, Bernard F. Haley, editor, published for the American Economic Association by Richard D. Irwin, Inc., Homewood, Illinois, 1952. While governments presumably behave differently from individuals, the literature on consumer behavior provides one interesting background aspect to the economic behavior of some of the OPEC countries after the oil price increases at the end of 1973.

11. In 1974, Venezuela was the largest importer of US merchandise ($1.768 billion) among OPEC countries, just above Iran ($1.734 billion).

12. For an analysis of the effect of the higher oil prices on Latin American countries, see "The Impact of the Higher Oil Prices on the LDC's: The Case of Latin America," by the author, in Ronald G. Hellman and H. Jon Rosenbaum, editors, *Latin America: The Search for a New International Role* (New York: Sage Publications, Halsted Press, John Wiley & Sons, 1975).

13. The terms of the loan to the World Bank were 15 years at 8% annual interest; the note issue bought by the commercial banks was for 13 years at 7.5%.

14. Conventionally, net foreign assistance disbursements have been measured by the OECD countries as a percentage of GNP. On this basis, the percentage in the case of Venezuela in 1974 was 3.3%.

15. For a discussion of OPEC assistance, see Maurice J. Williams, "The Aid Programs of the OPEC Countries," in *Foreign Affairs*, Vol. 54, No. 2 (January 1976) pp. 308-324.

16. In 1975, the Bank of America moved the operating headquarters for its Latin American operations from San Francisco to Caracas. For a survey of some of the issues in the future of Caracas as a financial center, see *The Banker* (London), May 1976 issue.

17. In 1974, the government mandated the prepayment by a number of public agencies and state enterprises of various medium-term floating rate Eurocurrency loans totalling about $600 million. Shortly afterwards, however, these agencies turned around and began borrowing abroad again at short maturities which did not require Congressional approval.

18. Manufacturing, construction and petroleum refining accounted for 22.8% of GDP in 1973, and manufacturing alone for 11.4%. These proportions compare with an "expected" one of about 32% for industry and construction in a primary production-oriented economy of Venezuela's size and at its income level. The "expected" level is derived from *Patterns of Development 1950-70* by Hollis B. Chenery and Moises Syrquin, World Bank publication, Oxford University Press, 1975. The relevant values for Venezuela as of 1965 are shown on pages 99 and 206. I am grateful to Judith Dittmar for the adjustment to 1973 and to Dale Weigel for a discussion of the concepts involved.

19. CORDIPLAN, *Tercera Encuesta Industrial*, 1973, which contains 1971 data. A more recent survey of 1974 data has not yet been published.

[89]

20. For statistics on education in Latin America, see pp. 358-377 of *Latin America's Development and the Alliance for Progress, op. cit.,* OAS, 1973. The author has used this source, with adjustments for more recent estimates. Again, as in other areas of social statistics, care is needed in using these figures, many of which are estimates.

21. See, for example, the country data shown in F. H. Harbison and C. A. Myers, *Education, Manpower and Economic Growth* (New York: McGraw-Hill, 1964). A comparison between Venezuela and countries such as Korea or Taiwan is particularly striking (p. 47).

22. The program has also been criticized as introducting an alien mentality into the country, and accustoming managerial elites to use imported techniques. However, the success of sending 10,000 students abroad no doubt depends largely on whether the quality of the education they receive and their absorptive capacity justify the expense.

23. Among the problems to be gradually overcome are the differential between high protection for consumer goods and much lower protection for capital goods imports; a petroleum-based exchange rate which excessively encourages imports and discourages exports of non-petroleum products; and labor-benefits legislation which discourages hiring (such as a virtual prohibition against firings introduced into the new Labor Law of 1975).

[THREE]

Venezuela's Oil Nationalization: The Politics of Aftermath

Franklin Tugwell

As we free our oil industry from foreign hands, we make ourselves more dependent on it. If we are not capable of establishing a sound economic base by means of our own natural resources, we will have betrayed the profound meaning of this historic act.

Carlos Andrés Pérez

With this candid admission, the President of Venezuela expressed the mixture of pride and anxiety felt by many of his countrymen on the eve of the nationalization of the petroleum industry. The subsequent transfer of ownership and control went smoothly, receiving little worldwide publicity. The nationalized foreign companies did not like the compensation terms offered, but all the important companies accepted them, and there was little interruption of the production process itself. Nevertheless, it was a landmark event in many ways. At the time of takeover, the Venezuelan oil industry represented the largest single locus of American direct investment in Latin America. Its earnings have provided the basis of Venezuelan economic growth and prosperity for decades. And the industry remains the most important source of imported crude and oil products for the United States, in 1975 accounting for more than 17% of all petroleum imports and nearly 26% of those originating in non-Arab countries.

This essay is an inquiry into the prospects for Venezuela's nationalization venture, focusing primarily upon the political and organizational challenges the country is likely to face in making the new public enterprise a success.[1] The method employed is to draw from other cases of nationalization, (especially those which have taken place in relatively competitive polities and which have involved large and vital segments of the national economy) a cluster of "symptoms" and low-level generalizations to use as guidelines in analyzing Venezuela's case. Although it is impossible yet to do more than suggest tentative conclusions, the subject is important enough to warrant the effort.

ENTERPRISE IN THE PUBLIC INTEREST:
PROBLEMS OF ANALYSIS AND ASSESSMENT

A comparative review of the "aftermath" of nationalization is made difficult by the neglect of the public enterprise generally by economists and political scientists. There is a surprising lack, especially, of cross-national, theoretical analyses, those most important for prediction.[2] There are, however, a number of useful case studies, several of large-scale mineral-extractive industries that have been nationalized, which reveal enough similarities to suggest, if not a tight theoretical model of the political economy of the public enterprise, at least a cluster of characteristic problem-areas that might be useful in considering the future of Venezuela's oil industry.[3]

Perhaps the most striking conclusion to be drawn from these case studies is that there has been almost universal disappointment with the performance of public enterprises in the aftermath of nationalization. In the words of a student of the British experience, nobody, "—not the employess, not the managers, not the public, not the government—is satisfied with the way the nationalized industries have functioned during the last quarter century." [4] A second conclusion is that the same kinds of problems crop up with surprising frequency in different cases. These problems are worth reviewing, since they amount to a commonly accepted "indictment" of nationalization as a policy instrument, and they in turn point to some of the underlying reasons why public enterprise so often seems to run into trouble.

a) Politicization. One of the most frequent complaints is that nationalized industries suffer from improper and destructive political intervention in their affairs. This covers a wide range of difficulties. In Chile, for example, the state copper industry became embroiled in a debilitating struggle for control between different political parties, with the Communists being the worst offenders. In Great Britain public sector executives blame many of their problems on ministerial intervention, price controls, or the need to provide services which are unprofitable but politically necessary. Closely related to politicization, in the sense that they involve politically motivated intrusion into managerial decisions, are such things as payroll padding, favoritism in hiring—victorious parties always need jobs to hand out—and just plain corruption. Large public enterprises can easily become political "feeding troughs," especially in developing nations where controls may be less refined and the need may seem greater.

b) Labor Problems. Surprisingly, most nationalized industries also run into problems with labor, usually beginning soon after takeover, as the result of new and exorbitant wage demands, strikes, and a general breakdown in industrial discipline. Examples include Mexico (oil), Chile (copper), Peru (minerals), Venezuela (iron ore), and Great Britain (various). This is often due partly to the growth of union militancy in the years before nationalization, partly to the expectations generated by nationalist rhetoric, and partly to the restructuring of worker-management relations that occurs with government takeover. Nationalization often replaces the more pliable triangular bargaining system with a stark confrontation between workers and the state, in which labor no longer accepts the explanation that operations at a loss, due to "unreasonable" wage demands, will cost them their jobs. The public treasury, from their perspective, becomes bottomless. One of the most poignant illustrations of this is also found in Chile, where labor problems became so destructive that Fidel Castro, on his state visit, took time publicly to scold the copper workers for their behavior.

c) The Loss of Competent Technical and Managerial Personnel. Many industries in the developing nations, foreign control notwithstanding, have enough competent local personnel who have reached managerial and supervisory positions by the time of takeover so that they can continue to operate without extensive foreign help. However, many of these people often leave for other positions (at home or abroad) after nationalization, propelled by turmoil and strife and by a sense

[94]

that the standards of excellence to which they have become accustomed no longer obtain.

d) Decline in Efficiency and Productivity. These problems all leave their mark in the utilization of resources. Decreases in efficiency often lead to accounting losses and growing reliance upon the public budget for, first, investment capital, and then later, even for operating expenses.

This is a formidable list. Together these symptoms depict the familiar caricature of the nationalized "sick giant." Clearly, too, they are interrelated. Politicization, corruption, labor difficulties, featherbedding, the flight of qualified people, productivity decline, requests for subsidies—all seem to come together, as a package.

But not all nationalized industries fit this stereotype—though, to be sure, those that do have received the most attention. Is it possible, therefore to probe more deeply for the causes of these difficulties? What are the key variables that help determine whether a nationalization venture will be judged a success or a failure?

Perhaps the most important of these is the inherited condition of the industry itself—physical, administrative, and political. Too frequently the public sector is the legatee of an industry that is in serious trouble already, often on all these levels. Indeed, in an increasing number of countries it has become standard practice for the state to succor, by incorporation or subsidy or other means, large private companies or whole industries that are bankrupt or nearly so. There is no clearer warning of troubles after takeover; taxpayers and opposition politicians typically have short memories and are, perhaps rightly, especially demanding when it comes to the record of public enterprises. In the case of concessions-based mineral-extractive operations, the industry at takeover is often

CONTEMPORARY VENEZUELA

suffering from a lack of reinvestment, the result of foreign
reluctance to sink new capital into a venture that has become
increasingly risky.

In practice there seem to be only a few ways in which
public management as such can improve upon private control,
usually by restructuring the industry (e.g., to seek administrative or scale efficiencies) or by imposing new, publicly
approved goals upon decision-makers. It is, therefore, extremely important that any inherited problems and limitations
be recognized clearly at the time of nationalization and that the
new management be granted, in advance, the resources and
political support it will need to start off on a better footing.

Closely related to this is the broader question of the
standards to be used in assessing the performance of the
nationalized industry, in measuring productivity and placing a
value upon the product. Normally an industry is taken over
because its behavior under private management and within the
market framework is undesirable for some reason, and a
central goal of public ownership is to force social or political
"externalities" (e.g., dependence) or neglected roles or functions (e.g., provision of welfare through employment) into
managerial calculations. Thus it is of utmost importance that
new and clear-cut standards be developed—tailored, actually,
to the industry—publicized and applied in assessing the
industry's performance.[5] Because of the difficulty of doing
this, there is a tendency to rely upon the old standards, which
are readily available and widely understood. The result is easy
to anticipate: the public enterprise will be judged by private-
enterprise criteria, and its achievements will be poorly measured. What should be considered legitimate costs of accom-
plishing objectives will appear to be losses—and there will be
such costs because trade-offs are inevitable. This will lead to
widespread disillusionment and misunderstanding of what the

society has chosen. A second possibility is that management will seek instead to conform to purely private standards, recognizing that these are the operative ones. But, as one analyst has stated it: "Public enterprises, told to concern themselves with their profit and loss accounts, will also neglect public benefit. It has, I hope, been amply demonstrated that, to the extent that competition is absent, this neglect will often 'pay'." [6] In either case, the purpose of the nationalization is likely to be partially negated.

Along with a clear and realistic performance standard, it is also important for a nationalized industry to have political relationships that will facilitate the pursuit of efficiency according to the criteria by which it will be judged. This process of "boundary maintenance" is critical, for it will determine the extent and form of external intervention in decision-making. And appropriate organizational autonomy does not arise automatically from constituent statutes. Rather, it must be won through hard bargaining and carefully cultivated thereafter. Indeed, the more successful public enterprises seem to be those able to consolidate from the outset a system of working accommodations at the several points of interface with the polity—with the executive branch, Congress, parties, and organized labor. In this, the role of the President or chief executive often seems to be critical, especially in the early stages, but the nature and character of the political system sets the basic ground rules. It should be stressed that this is not just a matter of obtaining guarantees of autonomy from politics; the public enterprise is a political creature, and political intervention is both inevitable and proper. After all, it is to facilitate the imposition of politically determined objectives that most enterprises are nationalized in the first place. Rather, the issue is whether that intervention can be modulated and controlled. If it cannot, the industry may become a "feeding trough," an employer of last resort of political faithfuls, a battleground for the struggle of politicized unions.

Finally and especially critical in the case of mineral-extractive operations, there is the problem of maintaining the necessary international ties. Such enterprises often have a difficult time marketing their product because nationalization has severed or weakened administrative links to the integrated multinational corporations that controlled or coordinated this activity before. They are thus vulnerable to market fluctuations as well as reprisals by former concessionaires. Even if they escape reprisals, they risk ending up as "marginal suppliers," or suppliers of last resort, and are therefore highly insecure with respect to the stability of their sales.[7] Thus it is also important for them to consolidate working arrangements with those international decision-makers upon whom they must continue to depend, at least until alternative marketing arrangements can be secured.

To this point we have identified a list of problems common to nationalized industries and have noted several variables which seem important in determining whether these problems will crop up. Drawing upon the latter, it is useful to recast our analysis in the form of recommendations to the nationalizing government and to the management of the new public enterprise: (a) be sure to reorganize and compensate for inherited deficiences, and grant the new management, in advance, the resources and support it will need to revitalize the industry; (b) develop clear-cut standards that are tailor-made for the public enterprise and distinguish them from the standards applied to private enterprises; (c) seek out working political accommodations with key political sectors; and (d) carefully secure necessary marketing arrangements at the international level. These are first and foremost political tasks and therefore will be strongly influenced by the nature of the political system and by the political context of the nationalization itself. Using these as guidelines, what conclusions can be drawn about the Venezuelan case?

BACKGROUND: LEGACY OF MODERATE DECLINE

As is so often the case, the petroleum industry in Venezuela was nationalized after a long period of conflict and bargaining with foreign concessionaires, and the industry did suffer as a consequence. Venezuelan determination to domesticate the industry, to obtain greater national control over key industry decisions, and to win a larger share of company profits, mounted in the 1930s as the industry came to dominate the economy and as the government became more and more dependent on the revenues generated by oil exports. In the 1940s and then again after 1958, democratic governments committed themselves to the goal of replacing the concessions system with an arrangement that would assure greater national participation in decisions and earnings. Outright nationalization, no matter how desirable, seemed out of reach; few leaders were willing to disrupt the economy and jeopardize the fragile hold of democratic institutions. The funds for compensation were unavailable, and expropriation without it would bring severe reprisals in an international market dominated by large oil companies and guarded by their home governments.

Instead, Venezuelan leaders followed a policy of assertive experimentation, searching for, and trying out, alternative policy instruments that they felt would be helpful in achieving their objectives. These included such things as surveillance of company marketing decisions, tax increases (sometimes retroactive), back tax claims, reference prices (for tax purposes) and even special penalties for failure to meet production quotas.

At the international level, Venezuela took the lead in organizing the producing countries in a protective counter-cartel. OPEC, founded in 1960, was the product of collaboration between Betancourt's Minister of Mines and Hydrocarbons, Juan Pablo Pérez Alfonzo, and Saudi Arabia's Sheikh Abdullah Tariki. And as Kim Fuad's essay stresses, Venezuela continued to play a key role in that organization. The private oil companies, as might be expected, resisted the government at nearly every step. Their principal bargaining card was new investments, needed to add to proven reserves, bring in new technology, and generally maintain the health of the industry. In return for these investments they demanded a better "climate of investment." They also brought pressure to bear upon the government by building an alliance with the domestic private sector of Venezuela.

Throughout the 1960s the companies undertook little exploration and drilling for reserves, and these gradually declined from a high of more than 17 billion barrels to less than 14 billion in 1971. And they proved unwilling to make large investments in new refining technology. The government recognized the seriousness of these trends and took some measures to compensate. In 1966-67 it bargained successfully for a large desulfurization facility, and as part of the Hydrocarbons Reversion Law of 1971 it required the companies to contribute to a government fund to guarantee that their installations would be turned over to the state in good condition when the concessions ran out. But the decline in proven reserves could not be remedied without granting new incentives and new concessions, and this the government was not willing to do.

President Caldera, facing a decline in government income from oil—production peaked in 1970 and gradually fell off thereafter—cast about for ways to reassure the companies and bring reserves and production back up, but the AD-controlled Congress blocked his efforts. By the end of his administration, Caldera had concluded that state takeover was the only way to break the deadlock.

Then came the Great Oil Crisis, that cluster of events that included the revitalization of OPEC, the Arab-Israeli War, the blockade by the Organization of Arab Petroleum Exporting Countries (OAPEC) and, most important of all, the quadrupling of oil prices. At long last Venezuela found itself with enough funds, and in a strong enough position in the world petroleum market, to nationalize. On January 1, 1976, the industry became Venezuelan property, its management the responsibility of a new state holding company, Petróleos de Venezuela (PETROVEN). To celebrate the event, President Pérez traveled to the state of Zulia and raised the flag on the derrick of the well which, after it began production in 1914, is credited with opening the way for the subsequent development of the petroleum industry in the country.

Because of the legacy of nearly a decade and a half of sluggish growth and then decline, the government must now move quickly to revitalize the industry. It will need to make substantial investments in the next few years to discover new regular oil and to develop the heavy oil deposits in the Orinoco tar belt. In establishing PETROVEN the government granted it 10% of net income (before taxes, after royalty) on exported oil for its capital needs. Although this will suffice to keep production going, it will not be sufficient to pay for extensive exploration of new areas in the development of the Orinoco. For these funds PETROVEN will have to turn to the government. Depending on the other demands for capital and the sums involved (currently estimated at another $10-12 billion), this may cause problems.[8]

In most other respects, the nationalized industry seems to be in relatively good shape. For the time being, the government has kept largely intact the administrative structure of the larger companies, renaming them "operating units," and morale among the managerial personnel seems high. While much equipment is fairly old, this does not seem likely to cause major immediate problems. Most important, there has been adequate public recognition of the problems the industry has encountered, and there is a general awareness that large investments must be forthcoming.

Assessment: PETROVEN's Mandate

What do the Venezuelans expect from their industry, and how are they going to judge its performance? In particular, what do they expect it to provide them that the concessions system did not? On this score too, the government seems to have adopted a very realistic position. To be sure, as might be expected, Venezuelans are enjoying considerable nationalist gratification at winning out in a conflict with powerful foreign companies. Even here, however, the President has gone out of his way to stress that, if anything, the country is more, not less, dependent upon oil. The goal of decreasing the country's reliance upon foreign companies, and upon the U.S. market, remains; but the government has downplayed this in recognition of the fact that the other objectives are more important. More concretely, the government expects the oil industry to produce a steady flow of income, equal to, or slightly greater, per barrel than that produced by the private companies, and to provide the basis for a further growth of proven reserves (and the eventual utilization of heavy oil from the Orinoco region). Costs per barrel are almost sure to go up as the company catches up on needed investment and as production comes increasingly from older wells, but these problems seem to have been recognized and accepted.[9]

One problem, which is currently manageable but which is likely to prove troublesome in the future, is that gasoline and other refined products are sold within Venezuela at prices set well below levels in other countries.[10] According to one estimate, this represents an indirect annual subsidy of several hundred million dollars to the Venezuelan consumers, and domestic consumption, now just over 200,000 barrels per day, is expected to increase at about 8% per year while overall production rates remain level. Forced subsidy through price controls has been the bane of state industries elsewhere (e.g., Mexico); its extent is often obscured by accounting procedures, and it is often misjudged or missed entirely in public assessments of industry performance. A subsidy of this kind should be arranged so that its cost is clear and visible, and will not damage the image or standing of the state enterprise.

Another problem, which has already stirred controversy, stems from the failure of the government to seek changes in the tax accounting procedures. PETROVEN operating units are subject to the same tax laws that the private companies were, and as a result will almost surely end up their first year in the red. This is partly because of very high Tax Reference Values adopted in October, 1975—Exxon's Creole Oil Corporation has stated that these resulted in a government take of fully 98% of profits—and partly because of the 10% investment contribution plus the cost of the "technology agreements" (averaging some 19¢/barrel, after taxes, or 36¢/barrel subject to a 47% Venezuelan corporate tax rate) made with former concessionaires. The 10% investment contribution is especially confusing. Under private ownership this would be called profit remittance and treated as a dividend, but for the operating units it is treated as an expense, thus inflating their costs of operation and generating "paper" losses. Actually, adjusting for investment payments, income to the government per barrel is currently some 15¢/barrel higher than before nationalization (9¢ of this is due to higher realizations). But the confusion remains, and opposition leaders have already taken advantage of it. Late in March COPEI Deputy Abdon Vivas Terán called a special press conference to criticize the "losses," which he estimated would amount to some Bs. 920 million ($215 million) in 1976.[11] It is thus very important for the government to adopt a tax accounting system which is tailored to the nationalized industry and which, especially, legitimizes essential investment expenses. Failure to do so will leave the industry unnecessarily vulnerable.

POLITICAL CONTEXT AND ROLE

In the months prior to nationalization, Venezuela's President repeatedly affirmed his determination to guarantee the autonomy of PETROVEN and its operating units. As he put it in one interview: "What is essential is to grant PETROVEN the power to manage the industry without guild, political, or bureaucratic intervention, no matter how well intentioned these interventions might be." [12] To underscore this, he chose as President of PETROVEN General Rafael Alfonzo Ravard, head of the ambitious Guayana regional development corporation and a man with a long-standing reputation for strong, efficient and apolitical administration.

For a number of reasons, however, it will be very difficult to depoliticize the administration of the oil industry. Indeed of all of the problems PETROVEN is likely to face in the future, this is surely going to be the most serious. Oil and politics have been deeply intermixed in Venezuela for decades, and have become more so in the years since 1969. As the essay by Kuczynski points out, the government is currently mounting an audacious development program designed to build an economic infrastructure independent of oil; in this effort, petroleum revenues will be of the utmost importance. But the government is working very close to the margin; should this program falter, or should international prices weaken, the pressure upon PETROVEN will be enormous.

President Pérez has warned of difficult times ahead:

From 1976-1980 the petroleum industry will have an annual production of 2.2 million barrels per day. This volume of estimated production is reasonable, taking into account the weak situation of our proven reserves, especially reserves of light crudes. Nevertheless, freezing the level of production while consumption in the domestic market keeps growing at the rate of 8-10% will result in an inevitable reduction of fiscal income derived from oil, a reduction which *cannot be compensated* during this period by support from other sectors. This means that from the Bs. 25 billion that the state will receive from the oil sector during 1976, we will end up receiving some Bs. 22 million in 1980, that is *less money*, in both absolute and relative terms.[13]

In view of the past addiction of the state and the overall economy to a constantly growing fiscal bonus from oil, as well as the ambitious developmental scheme proposed by the government, there is a strong possibility that the industry will be asked to produce more oil, and sooner, than it would like, and this request may be urgent in nature.[14]

On a different level, petroleum policy is already a point of conflict between the government and its opposition. The Christian Democratic Party, COPEI, has attacked the government repeatedly for its handling of the nationalization process. Just before he left office, former President Caldera (COPEI) urged Carlos Andrés Pérez to nationalize immediately, and on subsequent occasions COPEI leaders have adopted much more nationalistic, even xenophobic, positions on oil, as have other opposition parties. After failing in its attempt to build a broad national consensus on the nationalization procedure, the governing AD party, Accion Democrática, was forced in the end to pass the nationalization law, as well as the terms of compensation, over the opposition of all other parties (except a minor group of supporters of former dictator Marcos Pérez Jiménez).[15] COPEI, in a widely criticized gesture, even prohibited its members, including Caldera, from attending the nationalization ceremonies on New Year's Day, 1976.

To be more specific, COPEI opposes the provision in the law (Article Five) permitting the government to enter into partnership agreements with private entities—this, despite the stipulation that these agreements shall be for a limited duration, that the state shall maintain a controlling share, and that prior authorization from both chambers of Congress meeting in joint session must be obtained. And it has steadfastly maintained that any development of the Orinoco deposits, where such agreements may be utilized to bring new technology to bear, should be entirely Venezuelan. COPEI has also made it clear that it will use any weaknesses in PETROVEN, which it has come to identify as an AD entity, as a weapon against the government. Recall that it was a Christian Democratic congressman who ferreted out the probable accounting losses of PETROVEN and tried to use them as a means of criticizing the payments to the former concessionaires agreed to by the government. It is clear that COPEI has chosen oil policy as a principal target in its overall endeavor to stake out a position to the left of AD on issues of national economic policy.

There is no question, therefore, that PETROVEN will remain an issue in future struggles between the parties. The legislature will be asked shortly to reconsider the Hydrocarbons Law, in order to accommodate the nationalized industry in its provisions, and legislative action will be required in any decisions to bring foreign companies in as partners (although Carlos Andrés Pérez has stated that he does not plan such agreements during his term of office).

AD is currently solidly in control of public policy, holding the presidency and a legislative majority. But should the party system fragment, as it has before, or should COPEI continue its steady growth, despite its more radical orientation on issues of economic policy, and take control of the government in the next election determined to reorient oil policy, the petroleum industry might find itself caught in political cross-pressures similar to those which have severely damaged nationalized copper in Chile.

Bureaucratic Control: Focus on Planning

The smooth operation of the Venezuelan petroleum industry since nationalization has surprised many people. This smoothness has been due in considerable part to the care taken by government planners to avoid destroying an efficient administrative system by hasty and ill-considered intervention. As one key member of the nationalization team, currently on the Board of PETROVEN, has put it: "The best news that the Venezuelan public could expect to have one year from now would be that operations have continued with as little change as possible." [16]

Within the government and PETROVEN, however, there remain unresolved issues of bureaucratic control which may be the source of future problems. There is, for example, a quiet but significant struggle going on between the PETROVEN management and the Ministry of Mines and Hydrocarbons over the extent and nature of ministerial supervision of the industry. PETROVEN is a state holding company with a board of directors and a president, all appointed by the President of the Republic. Beneath PETROVEN, actually owned by it, are fourteen "operating companies," which are the direct successors to the old concessionaires. The management of these has been maintained intact as far as possible to assure continuity. The largest foreign company, for example, upon takeover changed its name from Creole Oil Corporation to Lagoven, and a Venezuelan administrator, already a vice-president, became president. A number of functional coordinators have been created by PETROVEN to help it maintain working ties with and between the operating companies in such areas as production, finance, and technical development. The legal instruments make clear that there is a line of command from the President, to the Ministry, to PETROVEN, to the operating units; but these are unclear, as usual, about the scope and nature of the division of roles and authority. This is especially true with respect to the all-important planning function.[17]

PETROVEN administrators hope to retain much of the planning authority in their own hands, limiting the Ministry of Mines to setting the Tax Reference Values, stipulating overall production requirements, and reviewing and evaluating the conduct of the industry. They would like the Ministry to leave technical details and specific decisions to PETROVEN and the operating companies. However, the current Minister, Valentín Hernández Acosta, is clearly unhappy with this organizational model and does not, apparently, intend to abide by it. His comments in a recent interview make this clear:

We have to be as careful with Petróleos de Venezuela (PETROVEN) with respect to the technical matters and the development of the industry as we have been with the concessionary companies ... The experience that we have had is that the Ministry had more troubles, in making them respect the Law of Hydrocarbons, with the CVP [the former state enterprise] than with the concessionary companies ... With respect to technical matters, the Technical Office [of the Ministry] will continue working with as much, or perhaps more zeal than before ... the Ministry will have, with the Ministry of Finance, the responsibility for guarding the tax reference values of oil insofar as they affect the government of Venezuela. ... we cannot let Petróleos de Venezuela treat the subject from the purely commercial point of view, without taking into account national policy on prices as well as the commitments Venezuela has accepted in international organizations like OPEC.[18]

Another source of conflict is over the exploration and development of the Orinoco region. There is a group within the Ministry that wants this job very badly, but PETROVEN is very likely to demand primary responsibility in this activity.

To a degree, Ministry attitudes may reflect the ingrained adversarial outlook cultivated over so many years in relationships with concessionaires. Then too, the Ministry would actually have little left to do should PETROVEN take such a large role in planning and administering the industry.

Meanwhile, within the industry itself there are issues of bureaucratic control and functional role that are also unresolved. Some administrators feel strongly that planning and control must be centralized in the PETROVEN headquarters—the image is that of a large multinational, with branches—and others are in favor of a much more decentralized pattern of administration. Here old company loyalties and rivalries left over from the concessionary system may well be at work. At this point it seems likely that the centralizers will prevail, although the outcome of the jockying between PETROVEN and the Ministry of Mines may have an important effect.

Finally, there is the issue of what to do with the Venezuelan petrochemical industry, a state enterprise which is infamous for its poor performance over several decades. Many feel that this, also, should come under the administrative control of PETROVEN (as has the old CVP), but others, including the President, worry that the corruption and inefficiency will be catching.

Given the size and complexity of the Venezuelan oil industry, it is not surprising that these bureaucratic-administrative difficulties have arisen. Nevertheless, how and when they are resolved is of central importance to the future of PETROVEN. Among other things, this will influence the nature and extent of political control of industry decisions.

LABOR RELATIONS

As nationalizations go, Venezuela appears to have an important advantage as far as labor is concerned. A new contract is currently under negotiation between the oil-workers' union, FEDEPETROL, and the operating companies, and though there is some discontent among the rank and file over the government's unwillingness to grant special pay hikes in the wake of the takeover, few observers expect serious labor problems in the near future. In contrast to the strike-torn iron ore industry, there is a long tradition of labor support for the government's oil policies, and the labor force in oil, which is much older and more conservative, is concerned primarily with job security and the continuation of benefits under public ownership. In these matters, the government has made careful plans to assure a continuation of existing rights and privileges, including pension benefits, job stability, and collective bargaining arrangements.

MARKETING

In planning the nationalization, Venezuelan policy-makers realized that marketing would be a problem. In order to achieve greater independence, a principal objective of the takeover, the government has committed itself to restructuring and diversifying the country's markets. The object here is to circumvent, where possible, reliance on the private oil companies by making direct sales arrangements with governments, state enterprises, and public utilities.[19] Another goal is to reduce gradually Venezuela's dependence on the specialized markets in the United States to which the oil companies had oriented the industry. As I point out elsewhere in this volume, although Venezuela has for decades been the most secure offshore supplier to the United States, this fact has received no recognition by the American government. In the design of import controls and regulations, the United States has instead repeatedly categorized Venezuela with the most insecure sources of imported oil.[20] The latest example of this is the application to Venezuela of the "anti-OPEC" clause in the Trade Act of 1974.

In the short run, however, the option of restructuring market relationships simply was not available. There was not enough time, and Venezuelans were inexperienced in this phase of the business. Also, Venezuela's marketing is a much more complicated task than is the case in most oil-exporting countries, since nearly half of its oil goes abroad in refined form.

As a consequence, Venezuela found itself caught in an awkward predicament as the time for nationalization drew near. In order to ensure the smooth transfer of the industry and to avoid hurting established customers, the government sought to continue its existing marketing patterns. With the takeover, however, the bargaining relationship between the state and the foreign oil companies changed dramatically. As concessionaires, they were subject to extensive government control; as "off-shore" buyers, with future contractual arrangements with Venezuela still incomplete, they were freer to bargain hard for a more profitable arrangement. This new vulnerability touched many of the pre-takeover arrangements, such as the Article Five decision in the summer of 1975 and the compensation arrangements.

It also influenced the content of the "technical assistance agreements" in which the government agreed to pay the former concessionaires a fee, averaging about 19¢/barrel after taxes, for help in the next two years in operating the industry. Although these payments are in line with the per-barrel figures negotiated elsewhere, it seems clear that the amount to be paid is much greater than the services to be rendered— Venezuela will apparently continue to pay the expenses and salaries of the several hundred experts retained in this manner—and therefore ought to be viewed as a hidden subsidy, a payment for goodwill and the maintenance of an existing working relationship with the companies.[21]

The really critical dispute in government-company bargaining, however, was over prices. World demand for oil was depressed. Total underutilization of OPEC productive capacity stood at over 10 million barrels per day, and Venezuela's own production, in the month before nationalization, had dropped to 1.7 million barrels per day, down from an average more than twice this figure in 1970. In preparation for takeover, a group of Venezuelan experts worked out a price list they felt was in line with OPEC standards, and offered to sell 2 million barrels a day to the companies. The companies responded with offers to buy, but at prices that ranged from 20¢ to $1.00 per barrel below those asked by the government.

There followed a period of tense negotiations. As Fuad notes, no country has been a firmer supporter of the sanctity of OPEC price standards than Venezuela, and the government decided to stand firm by its proposals. The risk was substantial, since the budget for the following year was dependent upon a full 2.2 million barrels per day in export sales. Just sixty hours before the nationalization ceremony on New Year's Day, the government announced that agreement had been signed for just under 1.5 million barrels per day at the prices fixed by the government—too little, but as much as the companies would buy at the prices demanded.[22]

Then, in the latest example of what has come to be known as Venezuela's own special "petroleum luck," the market for oil in its principal markets began to improve in the first weeks after takeover. A cold spell drove up demand for heavy fuel oil on the U.S. East Coast, and partial recovery from recession strengthened demand generally. After two years of decline, the prospects for Venezuelan sales began to improve dramatically. Production, which had dropped in January 1976 to a low of 1.7 million barrels per day, by early summer was holding firm at 2.4 million barrels, exactly on target.

Venezuela's moderation in taking nearly two years to complete the nationalization was clearly sensible. If Carlos Andrés Pérez had taken the advice of former President Caldera or of members of his own party urging "immediate" nationalization, the country might have been forced to accept significant price cuts to move its oil. And this in turn might have damaged OPEC strength and determination. As it is, many in Venezuela feel that their firmness was an important contribution to OPEC solidarity at what may have been a low point in the world oil market.

To summarize, Venezuela was lucky in its first marketing venture; its determination to stand firm paid off. But it is still very vulnerable, both in terms of prices and in terms of the security of its sales agreements, and faces the danger of becoming a "marginal" supplier in the future unless it can pin down its market on a more secure, long-term basis. Those in charge of PETROVEN would like to do this in direct agreements with refineries, utilities, and state companies, but these buyers are currently asking substantial price reductions in return, something Venezuela is unwilling to grant.

Conclusion

Judging from the first year of operation, Venezuela's oil nationalization seems to be going well, at least in comparison to other nationalizations of a similar kind. Despite considerable pressure to move quickly, the government carried out the takeover in a relatively careful and prudent manner. Oil is flowing to markets at the planned rate; the refineries are in operation. The transfer of administrative control has been accomplished with few disruptions. Labor conflicts have not materialized, and do not seem likely in the near future to cripple the industry as they have elsewhere. And there has been no large-scale defection of administrative and supervisory personnel.

There do remain some urgent administrative/political adjustments which are likely to affect the future welfare of the industry in important ways. Accounting and assessment standards to be applied to the industry need to be clarified, if possible by means of adjusting the basic hydrocarbons tax legislation and by separating out the precise dimensions of the subsidy to domestic consumers stemming from price controls. The authority and role of the Ministry of Mines and Hydrocarbons needs to be clarified and delimited. And the all-important planning and coordination function needs to be "seated" within the overall PETROVEN/operating company framework. Here centralization in the hands of the PE-TROVEN staff directly under its president Alfonzo Ravard would probably be the best solution from the industry's perspective, but it remains to be seen if the role of the Ministry of Mines, until takeover, a powerful, competent, and ambitious bureaucracy, can be limited in this way, and if the operating units can be trained to treat PETROVEN as their legitimate "parent" company. Much depends on the willingness of Carlos Andrés Pérez to step in and take a strong stand on these matters.

The long-term prospect presents difficulties that may be more intractable. Despite the pledge of the government to assure autonomy to the oil industry, petroleum is almost certainly too closely intertwined with the Venezuelan economy and state for the industry to remain secure for long from disruptive political intervention. Venezuela is a vibrant, rough-

[115]

and-tumble democracy, and it is unrealistic to expect contenders for power to grant a special status to the oil industry, leaving it out of their struggles. Carlos Andrés Pérez and the AD party are firmly in control now, but the opposition has already demonstrated its willingness to use oil as a political weapon—indeed it has repeatedly denounced the character of the nationalization itself, placing a clear-cut "AD" label on the new public enterprise. Should the party system fragment, as seems possible, or should a party come to power intent upon imposing a more "radical" policy in oil, the industry will surely suffer. The technical assistance agreements, for example, are an obvious point of vulnerability. On the surface they appear an unnecessary subsidy to the international oil companies, an easy target for nationalist rhetoric. They may be essential, however, in securing an amicable and continuing market relationship. Thus they probably should be maintained, at least until independent marketing arrangements can be established.

Oil income remains the key to Venezuela's effort to mount, in the next half-decade, a long-delayed program of investment and economic restructuring designed to begin to free the country from its monocultural development trap. It would be a mistake to underestimate the extent of public and private addiction to petroleum-generated wealth. If current plans obtain, the years ahead will see the fiscal stimulus from oil leveling off and then gradually declining. These will be difficult years politically, if the response to similar periods in the past can be any guide. By the early 1980s the economy will either begin to grow on its own, and begin to generate a significant nontraditional export capability, or will almost surely sink gradually into stagnation. The temptation to avoid the difficult but necessary reordering of national economic relationships and instead turn back and extract more income from oil, more than seems prudent given current estimates of reserves and production capacity, will be very strong.

NOTES

1. I have examined the events leading up to the nationalization, in general terms, in my book, *The Politics of Oil in Venezuela* (Stanford, Calif.: Stanford University Press, 1975). For an excellent account of the political maneuvering surrounding the passage of the Nationalization Law, see the essay by John Martz, "Public Policy and the Politics of Consensus: Nationalizing Venezuelan Petroleum" delivered to the October 24, 1975 meeting of the Pacific Coast Council of Latin American Studies, Fresno, California.

2. On this point, see Alec Nove, *Efficiency Criteria for Nationalised Industries* (London: George Allen and Unwin, Ltd., 1973).

3. See, among others: Theodore H. Moran, *Multinational Corporations and the Politics of Dependence: Copper in Chile* (Princeton, N.J: Princeton University Press, 1974); Norman Gall, "Copper Is the Wage of Chile," *AUFS Reports*, Vol. XIX, No. 3 (Aug., 1972); Jack Richard Powell, *The Mexican Petroleum Industry, 1938-1950* (New York: Russell and Russell, 1972); Robert Ball, "The Lessons from British Nationalized Industries," *Fortune* (Dec., 1975); E. Eldon Barry, *Nationalization in British Politics: The Historical Background* (Stanford, Calif.: Stanford University Press, 1965); M.G. Webb, *The Economics of the Nationalized Industries* (London: Nelson, 1973). Also of interest in this context are M.L. Williams, "The Extent and Significance of the Nationalization of Foreign-owned Assets in Developing Countries, 1956-1972," *Oxford Economic Papers*, 27 (July, 1975), and Judith Tendler, *Electric Power in Brazil: Entrepreneurship in the Public Sector* (Cambridge: Harvard University Press, 1968).

4. Robert Ball, previously cited.

5. On this point, see P.W. Reed, *The Economics of Public Enterprise* (London: The Butterworth Group, 1973), Chs. 8-9.

6. Nove, previously cited, p. 138.

7. Moran, previously cited, p. 215, as cited by Gall.

8. Assuming the government gives this job to PETROVEN, as the latter would like. This has not yet been decided.

9. *The Organic Law Reserving to the State the Industry and Commerce of Hydrocarbons* states, in article 3: "The management of the foreign commerce of hydrocarbons shall have the following basic objectives:

"To attain the highest possible economic yield from exportation, in accordance with the requirements of national development; to secure and maintain stable, diversified and adequate foreign markets; to support and promote the development of new exports of Venezuelan products; to ensure, on suitable terms, the supply of materials, equipment and other elements of production as well as the basic commodities the country may require."

10. Gasoline is cheaper in Venezuela than in any country except Saudi Arabia.

11. *El Universal,* March 29, 1976.

12. *Resumen,* Vol. X, No. 125 (March 28, 1976), p. 20.

13. *Resumen,* previously cited, p. 20.

14. Indeed it appears as if this may have already begun: the industry seems to have exceeded planned output and early indications are that it may do so in 1977 as well.

[118]

15. See the essay by John Martz, previously cited.

16. *Financial Times* (London), "Survey of Venezuela," Nov. 17, 1975, article by Alirio A. Parra.

17. See Articles 6-7 of the *Organic Law Reserving to the State the Industry and Commerce of Hydrocarbons.*

18. *Resumen,* previously cited, p. 20.

19. See Article 4, *Organic Law Reserving to the State the Industry and Commerce of Hydrocarbons,* previously cited.

20. For more on U.S. policy toward Venezuela, see *The Politics of Oil in Venezuela,* previously cited.

21. Average per barrel profits for the 1966-74 period were only 41.3¢.

22. The government, at the time of takeover, planned to try to market the remaining 500,000 barrels a day in direct contracts, but it seems probable that, barring a change in market conditions, it would have been forced to grant price discounts to do so.

[FOUR]

Venezuela's Role in OPEC: Past, Present and Future

Kim Fuad

INTRODUCTION

When Ahmed Zaki Yamani was the target of a scathing attack by Iraq during the Bali conference of Oil Ministers of the Organization of Petroleum Exporting Countries in mid-1976, the Saudi Arabian oil minister typically got up and walked out. Not unexpectedly, his Kuwaiti colleague, Abdul Mutalib Al-Kazemi, joined him in a show of solidarity.

Then, surprisingly, Valentín Hernández of Venezuela stood up and also left the hall.

With three key OPEC ministers absent, Conference President Mohammed Sadli of Indonesia called a recess. Outside the conference room, the Iraqi delegation, taken aback by Venezuela's unanticipated support of Yamani, apologized. The conference then continued when a mollified Saudi resumed his seat.

[120]

At the meeting's conclusion, neither Venezuela—nor any of the OPEC nations pressing for an increase in oil prices—could persuade Saudi Arabia to modify its outright rejection of any price hikes. Hernández, however, indulged in a bit of opportune horse-trading by using his personal backing of Yamani, and acceptance of Saudi Arabia's intransigence on a price increase, as a bargaining lever to win concessions from the organization's largest single producer on the thorny issue of price differentials.[1] Later, Hernández would confess that his sudden departure from the conference room was a calculated gamble. He had sensed that OPEC unity, severely strained over the price issue, was in danger of splintering. Thus, he sought to force a recess in order to allow the hot tempers of his Arab colleagues to cool. His horse-trading success was the product of intricate OPEC give-and-take bargaining experience.[2]

This episode reveals one aspect of the complex and subtle role Venezuela plays in OPEC today. It is no longer in a leadership position, breaking political and technical ground and setting examples which it urges other OPEC partners to follow; instead, it now fulfills a discrete but influential role as a moderating force in the organization. Venezuela's current input is a far cry from that of Venezuelan oil minister Juan Pablo Pérez Alfonzo's, who virtually twisted the arms of his apprehensive Middle East associates in April 1959 to commit them to taking the first step toward founding OPEC, a move that would eventually surpass even Dr. Pérez's expectations.

It is the aim of this chapter to analyze Venezuela's changing role in OPEC, from the organization's early origins, through the difficult years of consolidation in the 1960s, the surge to power in the 1970s, and now the challenges of the future.

Overshadowed by the Persian Gulf in terms of production and reserves, Venezuela's continuing influence in OPEC and the world oil trade today results from its long experience and hard-won sophistication in oil matters. The early intense development of Venezuela's petroleum resources gave it both a political and technical headstart over the other OPEC members. Consequently, today the South Americans are respected as OPEC's statesmen.

Despite its many unique characteristics as an oil-exporting country, Venezuela grasped more than 30 years ago the need for producer unity. It thus played a major role in the creation of OPEC, guided the organization during the difficult formative years, and served as an important factor of cohesion.

Venezuela's continuing influence in OPEC rests upon four pillars of strength: (1) its historical and traditional role in the organization; (2) the need for a moderator in OPEC, a role for which Venezuela is ideally suited; (3) Venezuela's willingness to use oil as a negotiating instrument; and (4) the technical contributions Venezuela has made and will continue to make in the organization.

A Brief History of OPEC

Even seen as the inevitable consequence of global economic evolution, the 60-year process that transformed Venezuela from a Latin American backwater into a major oil power, with a pivotal role in OPEC, is remarkable.

Commercial oil production in Venezuela, which began in 1917 and antedated the majority of its OPEC partners by from 20 to 40 years, was the result of the search for new sources to satisfy booming demand following World War I. The fortuitous combination of prolific fields and the complacent dictatorship of Juan Vicente Gómez encouraged foreign oil companies to convert Venezuela into the world's largest net exporter of oil.

The virtually uncontrolled early exploitation of mineral resources by foreign companies was an experience that all other OPEC countries had in common with Venezuela. However, by the time that this process began to accelerate in the Middle East, Venezuela had been producing on a major scale for over 30 years. In the 1940s, Caracas began to take political steps that, when emulated by other oil-exporting states, resulted in new and radical—for the time—policies; these were to become the framework for a modified balance of power in world oil circles.

In the 1940s Venezuela, guided by Rómulo Betancourt and Pérez Alfonzo, permanently altered the government-industry relations that had prevailed under the 27 years of Gómez dictatorship and successor regimes. The demand for an equal division of profits between the government and foreign oil companies had led to the establishment of the famed 50-50 split under the administration of General Isaías Medina. However, Betancourt and Pérez Alfonzo had claimed that the Medina administration failed to achieve this goal; and when they came to power in the military-civilian coup of 1945, the Junta decreed a special once-only levy of $27 million which gave the state 50 percent of profits generated by the oil companies. In 1949, the 50-50 principle was consolidated by an additional measure that provided for a 50 percent tax on any sum by which a company's net profits for any year exceeded the government's total revenue from that company's activities in Venezuela. This formula, quickly adopted by the Middle East, was Venezuela's initial major impact on the policies of other oil-exporting countries.

It was also in the 1940s that Pérez Alfonzo, chief architect of Venezuelan oil policies, took the first steps to establish direct contacts with the Middle Eastern oil producing states. These efforts were postponed during his long exile from 1948 to 1958 under the military dictatorship. But in 1959, the indefatigable Pérez Alfonzo, jointly with Saudi Arabian oil minister Abdullah Tariki, became the driving force behind the creation of OPEC.

Beginning with John D. Rockefeller, powerful personalities have always played a major role in the oil business, and Pérez Alfonzo is a perfect illustration. Now in his early seventies and still very active, the OPEC architect has been the most innovative and resourceful of the oil-exporting nations' petroleum policy-makers. Although he was critically instrumental in uniting the producers, Pérez Alfonzo overestimated the capacity of the less advanced Middle Eastern states to comprehend, and act on, his plans to wrest control of world oil from the major oil companies by establishing a producer-consumer compact. Iran, with its relatively advanced culture and longer oil history than Venezuela, was psychologically damaged by its failure to achieve nationalization in the early 1950s under Premier Mossadegh. The lesson had been only somewhat less traumatic for Iran's Middle East oil producing neighbors.[3]

As one of the few men in the exporting countries with a broad grasp of international oil economics, Pérez Alfonzo had studied the historical process of oil development in the United States: from the establishment of the Rockefeller monopoly and its dissolution to the experiment with the free play of supply and demand which led to overproduction, the disastrous decline in prices, and subsequent government intervention through the Texas Railroad Commission's prorating program.[4] When the glut in global oil supplies in the middle and late 1950s eroded prices and producer income, Pérez Alfonzo reasoned that the producers should control, and prorate, the flow of oil entering world markets.

Venezuela's intensely exploited, but limited, oil reserves reinforced Pérez Alfonzo's awareness of the non-renewable characteristic of oil. He comprehended that even the Middle East's vast reserves would be insufficient to satisfy the huge growth in oil demand that began in the 1950s and has continued to the present.

The immediate problem facing Pérez Alfonzo upon his return to the Venezuelan Mines Ministry in 1959 was the steady decline in oil prices due to the glut in production. With the reopening of the Suez Canal, pressure to lower the prices of crude led to a series of sharp cutbacks in early 1959 by the international oil companies, making evident the breakdown in the international crude oil pricing structure. Venezuela's first move was to establish a government agency to watch over prices, production and exports as an instrument to carry out oil policy.

In April 1959, at the First Arab Petroleum Congress, Pérez Alfonzo headed the Venezuelan delegation of observers and took advantage of the meeting to show the Middle Eastern producers the steps that Venezuela had taken to control prices in Venezuela. In tandem with Tariki, Pérez Alfonzo pushed for the creation of an international producers' organization. The Middle Eastern producers, however, were hesitant. Iran, still traumatized by its experience with nationalization, was reluctant to come to the fore. In fact, Iran's observer at the Cairo Congress, Manucher Farman Farmaian, now Iranian ambassador to Venezuela, recalls that "Pérez Alfonzo almost twisted my arm to get me to sign" the "gentlemen's agreement" which was the best that the Venezuelan minister and Tariki were able to achieve.[5]

The document, which was the forerunner of the formal

[125]

creation of OPEC, called for the delegates to hand their governments three recommendations: 1) that each producing nation should consider the creation of a formal organization to coordinate policies; 2) that no one producer should take advantage of another's problems with the oil companies to improve its own relative position; and 3) that agreement to changes in prices should be granted only after previous consultation with other producers.

Following the Cairo congress, both Pérez Alfonzo and Tariki lobbied for an international prorating commission which would estimate worldwide oil demand and distribute the indicated production quotas among the exporting countries. Such a commission, in Pérez Alfonzo's view, would have included the participation of consumers.[6] Moreover, Pérez was insistent that OPEC take into account the interests not only of producers, but also of consumers and the oil companies—a commitment, written into the opening resolution of the organization, which calls for "securing a steady income to the producing countries, an efficient economic and regular supply of this source of energy to consuming nations, and a fair return on their capital to those investing in the petroleum industry." Nowadays, following the Arab oil embargo and the quadrupling of oil prices, it is ironic that one of the prime promoters of OPEC originally had sought the participation of the consumer in establishing oil supply and price.

Finally, following another series of price cutbacks by international oil companies in August 1960, the Middle Eastern producers were galvanized into action by the loss of millions of dollars in tax money. On September 10, 1960, Iraq, Iran, Kuwait, Saudi Arabia and Venezuela, accounting for over 80 percent of world oil trade, established the Organization of Petroleum Exporting Countries (OPEC) in Baghdad. In its initial statement, OPEC said that it would include regulation of production as one of the possible means for restoring crude oil prices to their previous levels, but output control was given increasingly less attention in subsequent OPEC meetings. This central goal, which Venezuela had promoted as fundamental for achieving stabilization of oil prices, proved to be impossible to achieve in the short and medium term, and only informally in the longer term. Neither Pérez Alfonzo nor any of the Venezuelan Mines Ministers who followed him were able to convince their OPEC partners of the wisdom of their views. In fact, Middle Eastern and African producers were suspicious of Venezuela's motives. Many thought that the South American producer, whose share of world markets was being seriously challenged by the new suppliers, was simply maneuvering to maintain its position.

However, if Venezuela failed in its central goal during the years before the oil price and producer control revolution in the 1970s, the country's influence in the organization remained strong as it continued to make important political and technical contributions to OPEC. It was this sharing of experience that aided the Middle Eastern producers in gaining the greater tax benefits that Venezuela already enjoyed in their negotiations with the companies.

Throughout the formative years of OPEC, when direct immediate benefits for Venezuela were few, the Acción Democrática administrations of Presidents Rómulo Betancourt and the late Raúl Leoni were often the targets of attacks in Venezuela by opposition parties that also opposed OPEC. The criticism was not entirely without foundation. The Middle Eastern nations, mainly Iran and Saudi Arabia, and later the new African producers, not only ignored Venezuela's call for programmed production growth, but took the opposite approach. They reasoned that they enjoyed relatively unlimited oil resources and needed large volumes of revenue to achieve accelerated national economic development. This meant that their emphasis was less on the Venezuelan objective of better prices, and greater per barrel income, than on sheer income growth through increased production. In the 1960s, Venezuela found itself competing with lower-priced Middle Eastern oil in its own backyard, the large South American markets of Argentina, Brazil and Uruguay.[7]

The story of Venezuela's OPEC participation is largely the story of a small but effective group. It has been Venezuela's great fortune that despite a small population base, growing from 7.5 million at the beginning of the 1960s to its present 12 million, it has had a number of capable and dedicated men to handle its OPEC affairs.

Pérez Alfonzo, the imaginative and impatient OPEC co-founder, was perfectly suited to the early pioneer efforts. However, it soon became evident that he would not be able to achieve his visionary goals in the short term through OPEC. In 1962, he saw his greatest ally, Tariki, deposed and replaced by Yamani, and he became deeply disillusioned with his brainchild. Toward the end of his period as Mines Minister in 1963, Pérez Alfonzo openly criticized the short-sightedness of his Middle Eastern and African associates.

At this critical point, another Venezuelan, Manuel Pérez Guerrero, took Pérez Alfonzo's place. He brought to the Mines Minstry and OPEC vast international experience dating back to his participation in the League of Nations in 1937, and intimate knowledge of the Middle East, acquired as a United Nations official, based in Cairo and in charge of technical aid for Egypt, Saudi Arabia, the Sudan, and Yemen. Between 1963 and 1967, Pérez Guerrero carefully nursed a fractious OPEC, advised the Middle Eastern producers in the prolonged and arduous tax negotiations with the international oil companies, continued trying to convince Venezuela's

OPEC partners of the wisdom of voluntarily limiting production and other policies.

In July 1965, at the Ninth OPEC Conference held in Tripoli, the organization resolved to adopt a transitory production program "calling for rational increases in production from the OPEC area to meet estimated increases in world demand." Pérez Guerrero termed the resolution a "victory for Venezuela" and explained that the individual historic development of each country was one principal factor in determining each country's "quota." He said that the measure would allow OPEC to "see that for every new barrel of demand there will be only one barrel of supply instead of the one-and-a-fraction being offered now." [8]

The proposed plan provided for a 10 percent rise in overall production in the 12 months ended June 30, 1966. The allotments for the eight OPEC countries were Iran (17.5 percent), Iraq (10.0), Kuwait (6.5), Saudi Arabia (12.0), Qatar (32.0), Libya (20.0), Indonesia (10.0) and Venezuela (3.3). Under the program, each nation would increase its production levels by the percentage allotted, taking into account population, revenue requirements, and the stage of development of the individual industries. Despite the announced goals, Libya immediately said that it did not feel constrained to limit its growth, and Saudi Arabia's Yamani said that the program was a "mere test" and gave it only "conditional acceptance."

In April 1966, when it became evident that the program would not achieve its goals, the eleventh OPEC Conference in Vienna announced a radical change in its outlook on production. Accusing the international oil companies of "manipulating" production, OPEC called for improvement in output growth; virtually a 180 degree move away from the starting point.

TABLE 1

How Formal Production Programming Failed in 1965
(thousand barrels daily)

	July '64 to June '65	July '65 to June '66	Actual % Increase	OPEC % Quotas
Saudi Arabia	2,091	2,406	15.1	12.0
Kuwait	2,355	2,351	−0.2	6.5
Iran	1,754	2,044	16.5	17.5
Iraq	1,294	1,350	4.3	10.0
Libya	1,062	1,344	26.6	20.0
Indonesia	474	496	4.6	10.0
Venezuela	3,445	3,453	0.2	3.3
Total	12,696	13,705	7.9	10.0

(Source: Petroleum Intelligence Weekly)

The production program was continued for another year, but finally became virtually meaningless as the major Middle Eastern producers as well as the new African sources failed to comply with quotas which paralleled those of the first year. In 1969, Venezuela once again tried to revive production programming, proposing that members with stable output could begin the program, and with the gradual incorporation of others with output or reserves problems. This initiative, however, also failed.

If Venezuela was unable to achieve the implementation of a formal prorating program in the first 14 years of OPEC's existence, in 1975 it took the lead in drying up the glut in supply that resulted from the sharp decline in demand. Although a number of other factors contributed to the cutbacks in production by OPEC members, the key producers initiated informal and voluntary controls, following the Venezuelan example. This action, however, reflected more the fact that the producers' enlarged incomes gave them an ample cushion of reserves, than the unconditional acceptance of Venezuela's traditional insistence on prorating.

TABLE 2

How Informal Production Programming Succeeded in 1975
(thousand barrels daily)

	1974	1975	Absolute Decrease	Percentage
Venezuela	2,976	2,346	− 635	−20.1
Ecuador	177	172	− 5	− 0.3
Saudi Arabia	8,480	7,077	−1,403	−16.5
U.A.E.	1,679	1,403	− 276	−16.4
Iraq	1,975	2,248	273	13.8
Iran	6,022	5,350	− 672	−11.2
Kuwait	2,547	2,054	− 493	−19.3
Qatar	519	439	− 80	−15.4
Algeria	1,009	933	− 76	− 7.5
Libya	1,521	1,510	− 11	− 0.7
Gabon	202	209	7	3.4
Nigeria	2,255	1,781	− 474	−21.0
Indonesia	1,375	1,313	− 62	− 4.5

(Source: Venezuelan Ministry of Mines and Hydrocarbons)

It was the frustrating lot of Pérez Guerrero and later of his successor, José Antonio Mayobre, an experienced international economist with the United Nations, to bide their time awaiting the moment when circumstances would allow Venezuela to implement its goals in OPEC. It is to the credit of the Betancourt and Leoni administrations, as well as the Acción Democrática party, that they fully understood that even though Venezuela's OPEC partners were unready for the South American producer's more advanced ideas, Venezuela could only achieve these goals through membership in OPEC. The political pressure was great and even Pérez Alfonzo, who

[131]

continued to advised the government and AD on oil matters, proposed that the countries unable or unwilling to comply with OPEC goals should be ousted from the organization.[9]

Ironically, it was not an Acción Democrática administration that saw OPEC's power expand explosively in the 1970s but its traditional political rival, the (Social Christian) Copei party whose founder, Rafael Caldera, became Venezuelan President in 1969 following a narrow electoral victory. Once again, personalities played a key part in Venezuela's position in OPEC. Caldera's Mines Minister, Hugo Pérez La Salvia, a civil engineer with no practical background in oil, encountered an OPEC cool to the new Venezuelan administration. This was understandable since Venezuela's OPEC partners had, with few exceptions, known only Acción Democrática party representatives since the outset, and viewed the Copei Mines Minister with suspicion. Moreover, peaceful change in government was an alien concept for most of Venezuela's OPEC partners, whose governments were authoritarian, and there is no indication that AD made any special efforts to smooth the transition.

Encountering an OPEC cool to the new Venezuelan administration, Pérez La Salvia angrily contemplated withdrawing from the organization following his return from his first OPEC Ministers Conference in Vienna in July 1969. The situation was ironic since in the past it had been the Arab members, most notably Iraq, who had threatened to quit OPEC while Venezuela had been the champion of conciliation and cohesion in the organization.

However, high-level political agreements between AD and Copei virtually guaranteed that the nation's basic oil policies, including OPEC membership, would not be radically altered despite changes in government. But at the beginning of his five-year term as Mines Minister, Pérez La Salvia's relations with other OPEC leaders, particularly Yamani, were often stormy. When Pérez La Salvia, impatient with other OPEC members, attempted to revive production programming in 1969 as well as other Venezuelan ideas, his efforts ran into strong opposition. His frustrations led to arguments with the Saudi Arabia oil minister, to the point where Venezuela (heretofore the mediator par excellence in OPEC) had to rely on the Persian Gulf sheikdoms to mediate its relations with Saudi Arabia.

This awkward situation, however, never broke out into a full-fledged conflict, thanks to growing OPEC power over the international oil companies in the 1970s. Additionally, the quiet behind-the-scenes efforts of Valentín Hernández served to smooth ruffled Saudi feelings.

VENEZUELA'S ROLE IN OPEC

The end to Venezuela's long wait for the right moment to assert OPEC power came in 1970. The first hint of what was to develop into the famous "energy crisis" became evident in Libya, which was to play a decisive role in the forthcoming revolution, backed by Venezuelan expertise.

Long a pioneer among OPEC countries in conservation, Venezuela established the first rudimentary principles in its 1918 mining code, and subsequently imposed progressively stricter norms. The basis for the modern concept of conservation emerged from policies adopted in the late 1940s, and when Pérez Alfonzo returned from his 10-year exile in 1959, one of his first acts was to invite Texas Railroad Commission experts to instruct Mines Ministry inspectors on conservation methods. The experience allowed Venezuela to draft basic rules for preventing waste in petroleum operations, which gained the virtual rubber-stamp approval in 1968 of less knowledgeable OPEC states.

In 1969, Libya requested, and Venezuela sent, a group of top-level technicians to investigate whether the major oil company concessionaires were violating Libyan conservation norms. The mission was headed by Arevalo Guzmán Reyes, a veteran technician who, beginning as a lowly inspector in back country oilfields, has become deputy Mines Minister today. Guzmán Reyes discovered a number of gross conservation irregularities which definitely precipitated Libya's decision to cut back production after years of explosive growth. Using the training acquired from the Texas Railroad Commission experts, the mission found that some companies were forcing production beyond the maximum rate of efficient flow, and threatening to damage the real potential of deposits. African output (including Libya's) had risen from 200,000 in 1960 to nearly 5 million barrels per day (b/d) in 1970. The cutbacks prompted by conservation-minded Libyan rulers were later increased as a means of pressuring foreign oil companies to accept new, higher taxes as well as enlarged Libyan control over their operations. The combined pressure on production produced a sharp reduction in the flow of Libyan oil to world markets from a high of 3.3 million b/d in 1970 to 2.7 million b/d in 1971, and to 1.5 million b/d by 1974.

The Libyan cutbacks, plus the shutdown of the Trans-Arabian Pipline, led to a production shortfall that caused prices to rise. This increase in prices, however, was not immediately reflected in additional revenue for all of the OPEC states. Throughout the 1960s world oil prices had declined steadily. Venezuela's realized prices had peaked in 1957 at $2.65 per barrel and by 1969 fell to a low of $1.81; government revenue per barrel had grown only erratically and was $0.89 in 1969. The posted price of Arabian light crude, later adopted by

OPEC as the marker crude for pricing purposes, had fallen from a high of $2.08 in June 1957, to a low of $1.80 by 1970. Continued tax action by the Middle Eastern nations had increased the states' per barrel income by between $0.05 for Iran and $0.13 for Saudi Arabia by 1970, up from the average income per barrel of $0.75 that these Middle Eastern exporters had in 1961.

In December 1970, Venezuela galvanized OPEC by moving decisively to reverse a decade of decline in prices. Pérez Alfonzo, having become aware of favorable circumstances, urged his Acción Democrática party to reassert Venezuela's leadership in international oil affairs. Using its Congressional majority, AD steamrolled through a radical reform of Venezuelan income tax laws, pushing oil company tax rates up from a graduated range of 20-52 percent to a flat 60 percent and empowering the executive to establish per barrel export reference prices for tax purposes, instead of negotiating these prices with the foreign companies holding concessions as in the past. Thus, regardless of what the oil sold for on international markets, taxes would be based on the tax reference prices.

The move stunned the oil companies and provided a vivid model for other OPEC nations who were meeting in Caracas at the time. OPEC followed suit by demanding sweeping new tax and price increases that later were recognized as the first step in the explosive series of oil price hikes which have continued to the present.

This dramatic action raised Venezuela's sagging influence in OPEC enormously. It was not so much that OPEC members had forgotten Venezuela's past leadership, but rather an attitude of "So what have you done lately" that had caused its influence to erode.

Venezuelan prestige rose again with the careful, step-by-step nationalization of its oil industry. The five-year process culminated January 1, 1976, with the state takeover of two score U.S. and other foreign oil companies. With the nationalization coming at a difficult time for all OPEC states, and with world oil demand depressed, Venezuela's successful takeover left a strongly favorable impression on its OPEC partners. Moreover, Venezuela's detailed reports to other OPEC members on the nationalization process enabled it to continue its traditional experience-sharing role among the oil-exporting countries.

In the midst of the headlong rush toward higher prices and taxes and along with greater control over oil by the producing states, a new Venezuelan personality began quietly to emerge in OPEC. Valentín Hernández, the first petroleum engineer to graduate from a Venezuelan university in 1948, had moved in the 1960s from successful private business to diplomacy. He first served as petroleum advisor to the Venezuelan Embassy in London, and later as envoy to various North African countries, including Libya, then Rumania and finally Vienna, site of OPEC's main office. It was Hernández who did the fence-mending for Venezuela in OPEC, using the easy-going nature of his Venezuelan plainsman origins to build close personal friendships with Yamani, Jamshid Amouzegar of Iran and other key OPEC ministers, much in the way that both Pérez Guerrero and Mayobre had earlier established close ties with pivotal OPEC personalities.

In March 1974, at the insistence of former Venezuelan President and AD party founder, Rómulo Betancourt, who had chosen Pérez Alfonzo to guide Venezuelan oil policies in the 1940s, Hernández was named Mines Minister in the new Acción Democrática administration of President Carlos Andrés Pérez. Since then, he has been instrumental in molding Venezuela's present OPEC stance.

Moderation, Hernández's leitmotif, means for Venezuela avoiding extreme positions within OPEC, such as the often politically-motivated actions of a Libya or Iraq, or the very conservative posture of Saudi Arabia. In this respect, Venezuela plays a balancing role: in the case of prices, for example, it neither insists on maximum or minimum increases, but rather tries to steer a middle road. While OPEC rarely follows a set decision-making pattern, Venezuela has continually sought consensus which, once achieved, it articulates from a respected position.[10]

In this role, Venezuela has a number of distinct advantages over the other 12 OPEC members. It is not directly involved in the Arab-Israeli confrontation (having avoided taking sides) and has finally achieved Arab OPEC members' respect for its studied objectivity. Additionally, unlike OPEC's other major non-Arab member, Iran, Venezuela is not involved in Persian Gulf regional probelms. This means that the South American producer can, and does, act as a standard-bearer in advancing new ideas and in mediating conflicts since Venezuela is not suspected of ulterior motives, as the Arabs frequently are.

Acceptance of Venezuela's OPEC role clearly indicates that the Arabs at last understand Venezuela is not seeking special benefits but rather a greater good for the group. This is of utmost importance in assuring Venezuela's effectiveness in OPEC, according to Hernández.[11] He feels that the Venezuelan character, as expressed in OPEC, appeals not only to the more radical members who recognize the South American producer's early efforts to redress foreign oil company injustices, but to moderates as well who admire Venezuela's levelheaded administration of policy goals.

Moreover, many of the thorn brackets of the past have become hedgerows. The Middle Eastern and African producers no longer see Venezuela as a rival producer and exporter they have to dethrone. There is a vast difference between the Libya of the mid-1960s—when ambitious government oil officials boasted to Hernández that they would soon surpass Venezuelan production—and Libya today, where such goals have been abandoned.[12]

As a matter of fact, Venezuela has seen its views on the need to husband oil reserves gain increasing acceptance among other OPEC nations. Even Saudi Arabia, earlier gearing up to 20 million b/d output at the insistence of U.S. officials, is now becoming aware both of the dangers of rapid depletion of its only major source of wealth, and of the inability of most OPEC countries to make effective use of the enormous revenues produced by a non-renewable resource.[13]

Hernández has also attempted to influence OPEC through extramural efforts such as close friendships with Yamani and other key personalities. What Venezuela seeks, in the case of Saudi Arabia, is to convince it to talk price and other policies outside of the somewhat ritualized and rigid forum of the OPEC conference. Venezuela's message for the Saudis is that it is not possible to maintain an intransigent position on prices, for example, in the long term. This is a delicate and crucial task since Saudi Arabia is by nature rather isolationist in outlook, and the pressure of OPEC's leftist radicals on the Saudis tends to harden their anti-communist stance. Another key concern, of course, is that Saudi Arabia not succumb completely to U.S. seduction. Venezuela feels that this not only would be perilous for OPEC, but also detrimental to Saudi Arabia's political stability, in a part of the world where there is little love for the United States and much territorial ambition. Moreover, Venezuela feels that excessive reliance by the United States on Saudi oil may resolve its short-term energy problems, but could boomerang by inducing the United States to slow its efforts to seek other non-oil energy sources. While it may appear contradictory to say that Venezuela would like to see the United States develop non-oil energy sources rather than depend overwhelmingly on OPEC oil, the South American producer is convinced that petroleum should be used decreasingly as a source of energy. Most Venezuelan oil experts feel that petroleum and natural gas should be dedicated to petrochemicals rather than burned.

In addition to its conciliatory, cohesive role in OPEC, Venezuela's influence also depends on a continuing flow of technical contributions, such as designing of a system of reference price differentials for different grades and qualities of oil, as well as in production technology. Although the Venezuelan Mines Ministry ranks as one of the world's best-informed and, since the creation of OPEC, has been responsible for a large number of technical advances, in recent years a manpower shortage as well as the growth in expertise among the other OPEC members has diminished its traditional pre-eminence. This decline, however, should be reversed with the nationalization of the Venezuelan oil industry. Now, instead of relying on a small group of experts in the Mines Ministry alone, Venezuela can draw on its 23,000-man industry work force to handle many studies for OPEC that it obviously could not have asked the foreign-owned companies to undertake. The industry, which has the highest concentration of skilled native talent of any OPEC country, can be expected to make important contributions in the future.

Hernández has not been alone in his efforts to increase Venezuela's influence among the key OPEC nations. Pérez Guerrero, now Venezuela's Minister of State for International Economic Affairs, has added another facet to the country's prestige as a key negotiator in efforts to use petroleum as a lever in different forums, including the North-South dialogue in Paris.

OPEC can easily be charged with "enlightened self-interest" for taking up the banner of the oil-poor less-developed countries. However, it must be noted that Venezuela was quick to warn of the danger of OPEC becoming isolated between equally hostile rich and poor nations, both groups suffering to a different degree from the impact of higher oil prices. Moreover, Venezuela has given more than lip service to the plight of its neighbors, helping Latin American and Caribbean nations finance the purchase of Venezuelan oil through special credits.

VENEZUELAN PETROLEUM AND THE INTERNATIONAL ENERGY PICTURE

The continuing bull market for Venezuelan influence in OPEC can be reasonably foreseen. The outlook for Venezuela's more tangible but nonrenewable asset is a great deal more complex.

In 1929, Venezuela became the world's largest net exporter of oil, producing over 9 percent—almost 375,000 barrels a day—of total world output. World depression caused output to drop in the early 1930s, but by 1935 growth was resumed, to rise to 1 million b/d in 1946, 2 million in 1955, 3 million in 1962, and peaking at 3.7 million b/d, the average for 1970.

To supply world demand between 1929 and 1970, Venezuela's oilfields underwent the most intensive exploitation of all the OPEC nations. Some 33 billion barrels of oil, not including wasted natural gas, have been drained from proven reserves since 1917, leaving Venezuela with around 18.5 billion barrels of proven reserves in 1976.

Venezuela's proportionally dominant role in world oil trade began to be challenged in the 1950s when the postwar surge in demand led to explosive growth first in the Middle East and, in the 1960s, in Africa. By 1970, Venezuela was overtaken by Iran, and later by Saudi Arabia, as world export leaders. Since 1970, Venezuelan output has declined steadily. The causes have been both political and technical. In 1959, when Acción Democrática returned to power, Venezuela reinstated its 1940s policy of granting no further concessions to foreign oil companies, causing a decline in major exploration efforts. The imminence of nationalization in the 1970s led to a decline in investments needed to maintain the potential in aging oil deposits. The huge jump in oil prices after 1973 made production increases unnecessary to produce additional government revenue, and in 1975 the administration of President Pérez announced that from 1976 through 1980 output levels would be held to an average 2.2 million b/d to reduce wastage of natural gas and to conserve reserves.

The growth of Middle Eastern and African production has also reduced Venezuela's participation in European markets, making the South American producer increasingly dependent on the United States, the single largest consumer of Venezuelan oil since 1928. Venezuela now sends about 66 percent of its 2 million b/d exports to U.S. and Canadian markets, with the remainder going to Caribbean, South American and European clients. In its role as the Western Hemisphere's largest oil exporter, Venezuela plays an important part in determining the pricing policies of other OPEC nations.

Venezuela has a number of factors in its favor as a world oil exporter, despite its proportionally diminished role in supplying accelerating demand. The characteristics that assure Venezuela an important place among world oil exporters are its traditional stability, security of supply and the unusually wide operational flexibility of the industry, the most sophisticated among all the OPEC countries. In contrast with the relatively narrow range of crudes offered by most Middle Eastern producers, Venezuela produces crudes ranging from the heaviest through the mediums, lights, wax crudes and condensates. Venezuela's 1.5 million b/d refining capacity is the largest among the OPEC countries. The Amuay refinery, one of Venezuela's fourteen, is the world's largest with a 630,000 b/d capacity. Venezuela's nationalized oil industry handles over 60 crudes or segregations of crudes and some 80-100 specifications of refined products. Additionally, few countries can boast of Venezuela's 120 million barrel storage capacity, which enhances the strategic importance of the South American nation's oil industry and its ability to meet short- and long-run commitments.[14]

Mines Minister Hernández is optimistic about Venezuela's future as an important contributor to world oil supply. The magnitude of this contribution, however, will depend on replenishment of depleted reserves, the immediate challenge facing the nationalized oil industry.

Petróleos de Venezuela, the state oil monopoly, plans to reverse the steady decline in major exploration efforts in Venezuela. It has earmarked over $3.6 billion of its total planned $5.5 billion investments through 1980 for activities directly linked to finding and producing more oil. The short-term goal is to at least replace the approximately 800 million barrels depleted annually from proven reserves at current production levels. For the medium and longer term, the focus will be on building up the country's potential.

The traditional basins are believed to hold an additional 20 billion barrels of probable reserves, which may be coaxed out through more efficient exploration methods, deeper drilling and secondary and tertiary recovery systems. Additionally, the country has one million square kilometers of largely untapped continental platform in the Caribbean and the Atlantic which has great promise, as initial exploration has shown.[15]

In the long run, however, Venezuela's future as a major oil exporter is linked to development of the Orinoco Oil Belt, one of the world's largest accumulations of non-conventional oil. The conservatively estimated 700 billion barrels of oil in the Belt, which extends some 375 miles along the northern bank of the Orinoco River, cannot be incorporated into national reserves until it has been proved that the oil can be produced, stripped of sulfur and metals and converted into a commercially marketable product at a profit. The government plans to invest over $800 million for the integral development of the Belt over the next five years, covering geophysical exploration, the drilling of test wells to evaluate the yield of existing production techniques and the development of better means to utilize the Belt's heavy crudes.

Due to the magnitude of the task, Hernández feels that Venezuela must undertake Belt pilot projects as soon as possible. Ideally, he notes, Venezuela should be able to produce around 200,000 barrels per day of Belt oil by the end of the decade. This would have great political significance, according to Hernández. "Based on total Belt reserves, we could produce at the rate of 200,000 barrels per day for centuries. This would show that Venezuela is still a source of oil to be reckoned with," Hernández believes.[16]

Hernández' concern over showing that Venezuela will continue to be a reliable source of imports is understandable. Its main clients, the United States and Canada, have expressed apprehension over the South American producer's ability to sustain even its present reduced flow over an extended period of time, let alone increase it in times of emergency, such as it did during the abortive 1967 Arab oil embargo and, to a lesser degree, in the more successful 1973-74 stoppage. Venezuela now ranks fourth among the OPEC states in terms of petroleum potential, with about 500,000 b/d of unused capacity. By way of comparison, in June 1976, Saudi Arabia had almost 3 million barrels of its 11.5 million b/d capacity shut in.

Once Venezuela has resolved the problem of replenishing its depleting reserves and is able to enlarge its potential substantially, the country will be in a position to consider increasing production levels. The pressure already exists. United States clients have been pressing Venezuela for more oil in efforts to offset partially growing dependence on the politically volatile Middle East and African producers. Venezuelan government planners have based expected income from oil over the rest of the decade on increases in prices averaging around 8 percent annually. As this growth, however, has failed to materialize totally, there is a strong temptation to compensate for the price shortfall by increasing output. In fact, industry insiders say that Venezuela will violate its 2.2 million b/d ceiling in 1976 by at least 100,000 b/d and it could rise to 2.4 million in 1977. When production rose to over 2.4 million barrels daily in September 1976, the Mines Ministry issued orders for a cutback to meet programmed production levels. Another element of pressure is growing domestic demand which is now equivalent to over 10 percent of total output, and is rising at 6-7 percent annually.

While there may be moderate short-term increases in Venezuelan production over the rest of the decade, depending on success in finding new reserves as well as on fiscal pressures, it is obvious that Venezuela will never again vie with major producers for a proportionally larger share of world exports. The very magnitude of present world demand excludes this possibility. In 1974, the 13 OPEC nations jointly

[144]

produced over 30 billion barrels in a single year, the same amount it took Venezuela 66 years to pump out.

"We have paid our quota," observes Hernández, adding that it is now up to Saudi Arabia and other producers with vastly larger proven reserves of conventional oil to take on the responsibility of satisfying the demands of consumers on a large scale. Hernández's views are generally accepted by Venezuelans of all walks of life.[17]

There are few indications there will be a substantial decline in oil demand, in prices, or in OPEC's power in the foreseeable future. Demand for oil is expected to grow from 49 million b/d in 1974, to 59 million in 1980 and 79 million in 1990. This means that world oil consumption will increase by 60% between 1974 and 1990. Growth in demand for oil between 1965 and 1973, when the energy crisis occurred, was 7.5% annually. Between 1973 and 1975, growth fell to an annual rate of 2.4% and between 1975 and 1977, is expected to grow at 5.2%. Even with a sloping off in demand for oil to 3.3% between 1977 and 1990, as alternate sources such as coal and nuclear energy make larger contributions, oil is expected to still supply 50% of world energy in 1990, with OPEC providing 60% of world output.

The cost of alternative sources of potential energy during the next 10 or 15 years, such as oil from shale or tar sands, or coal gasification and liquefaction, is such that a price between $16 and $20 per barrel (in 1974 constant prices) will be needed to achieve a satisfactory return on investment. This level is substantially higher than the 1975 price of oil delivered to the United States, which was about $12 per barrel in 1975 dollars.

Oil prices are coming under a number of pressures that indicate increases. For one, oil is becoming harder to find and produce. Up to 1970, the annual volume of new reserves discovered worldwide was greater than production levels. In 1970 they were equal, at 15 billion barrels. Since then, new reserves have been steadily outstripped by growing production. The volumes of new reserves are directly linked to the volume of investments made. Between 1965 and 1975, the world oil industry invested $121 billion to find and develop new reserves. If the industry invested the same amount over the next ten years, the new reserves would be substantially below market requirements for the period. In this case, requirements could only be satisfied by accelerating the depletion of present proven reserves, hardly a likelihood in view of growing concern over conservation among the producing countries.

The price of oil in the future will be affected by the fact that a vast amount of new reserves must be found, and most of the "easy" oil has already been discovered. New areas will be difficult and costly to find and exploit, while inflation will continue to push costs upward. Taking into account these factors, the world oil industry faces investments over the next decade of at least $480 billion to find and develop new reserves, plus an additional $475 billion for expanding the transport, processing and marketing facilities. This $955 billion outlay is four times greater than investments made between 1965 and 1975. Obviously, the only way to finance such an investment is by making it profitable, thus strengthening oil prices.[18]

The demise of OPEC appears unlikely in the short term. Even the organization's fiercest critics, such as Professor M. A. Adelman, state that OPEC appears to have more strengths than weaknesses.[19] Exxon Chairman Clifford C. Gavin predicted in mid-1976 that the United States would continue to rely on OPEC supplies until at least 1990.[20]

In assessing prospects for OPEC, Dankwart A. Rustow and John F. Mugno find that the organization is stronger and more durable than many competent observers have allowed and reject most of the proposals made for curtailing its power as rash and naive. They note that over the next five to ten years there is little likelihood of a sharp decline in oil prices and link a ceiling for price increases to alternate energy source costs.[21]

What role will Venezuela play? As we have already seen, there is the traditional demand for Venezuelan oil in its chief market, the United States. Despite the decline following the energy crisis, demand has increased in 1976. By mid-year, U.S. oil imports were at their highest point over the previous 18 months. The American Petroleum Institute reported during its annual convention in November that U.S. oil imports had risen by close to 16 percent in the first 10 months of 1976 and came to 7.4 million b/d in October alone. As the United States had not fully recovered from economic recession, this growth would appear to indicate that there will be steadily increasing demand for imported oil in the United States. As a traditional supplier, with its industry geared to U.S. requirements, Venezuela appears to have an assured outlet for present and increased exports.

Lest this appraisal appear overly optimistic, it should be noted that Venezuela is not seeking enlargement of its export volumes in the short or medium term but, rather, stable exports up to 1980 of around 2 million b/d. While Venezuela's "security of supply" has been repeatedly cited by Mines Ministers from Pérez Alfonzo to Hernández, it is an asset that is hard to measure in dollars and cents under normal circumstances. However, with world oil supplies subject to political pressures, traditional consumer concern with diversification of sources certainly favors Venezuela. In the past, some supply contracts have specifically called for back-up sources such as Venezuela in the event of shut-downs in less stable Arab sources.

Conclusion

In the past three decades, Venezuela has shown itself to have been an innovator among the oil-exporting nations, and over the 16 years of OPEC's existence a cornerstone of that organization. What is the outlook for the future, and will Venezuela be able to maintain its influential role among its oil-exporting partners?

In promoting its grand objective of cooperation among the world's major oil exporters, Venezuela has run an historical gamut. Its early pressures on oil companies to win greater income and control served as examples to Middle Eastern and African producers; its leadership was crucial for the creation of OPEC; and its moderate, ameliorating stance through the difficult 1960s helped to consolidate the organization as well as neutralize conflicts in the first half of this decade.

With its traditional role virtually assured, Venezuela now faces a number of challenges. One such challenge is whether Venezuela will be able to sustain its image of impartial support for OPEC as radicals intensify their challenge to conservative Saudi Arabia and its allies. In this respect, future OPEC unity may hinge to a large degree on the South American nation's ability to defend its grand objective of producer cooperation from divisive political infighting.

While present circumstances have allied Venezuela more closely to the Saudis, the moderation that has characterized its recent attitudes in OPEC is by no means immutable. A shift in the relative balance of producer power away from Saudi Arabia's pivotal position, changes in the Arab governments bringing more radical administrations to power among the key producers, or failure of largely Venezuelan-promoted efforts to use oil as a negotiating instrument with the industrialized world could lead to a radicalization of Venezuelan attitudes. Certainly if Venezuela is to retain its role as a catalyst of views prevailing in OPEC, it would have to reflect changes in the stances of its partners. None of these pressures can be ignored. Iraq has now undertaken intense efforts to explore fully its huge oil potential in order to build up output and reserve levels with the objective of joining Saudi Arabia and Iran as the major OPEC producers before the end of this decade. The assassination of King Faisal of Saudi Arabia was a telling example of the violent changes in leadership that characterize the Arab world, where instability has been the rule rather than the exception.

With a characteristic flair for conceptual ideas, Venezuela has been in the forefront of OPEC members in expressing its willingness to use oil as a negotiating instrument. More than any other OPEC nation, Venezuela has committed itself to achieving a new economic order. In addition to President Pérez's rhetoric and Pérez Guerrero's expertise in international negotiations, Venezuela has locked itself into fairly long-term oil and oil-dollar-aid agreements with its neighbors and international institutions despite the sacrifice that this represents for a country with limited oil production. The success or failure of this initiative will have a crucial impact on Venezuelan attitudes. Lack of results will certainly harden Venezuela's attitude toward the industrialized nations.

Venezuela's technical contributions to OPEC are likely to increase rather than decline in the future as a direct result of nationalization and its many challenges. Upon nationalization it became clear to Venezuelans of all walks that while the country had the largest concentration of native talent in the most complex of all the OPEC nations' industries, it was heavily dependent on international oil companies for marketing and technology. For the medium term, this dependence is likely to continue. The country, however, has undertaken efforts to shed this dependence by experimenting in marketing as well as in the establishment of a large-scale research and development center for the oil and petrochemical industries.

The chief asset that Venezuela enjoys is a wealth of experienced native oilmen of high caliber. It appears certain that the present generation of oil technicians and the incorporation of new personnel will guarantee a steady flow of technical expertise that Venezuela will share with its OPEC partners in the future.

TABLE 3

Venezuela's Prices and Profits

Year	Price $/bbl	Fiscal Share $/bbl
1958	2.50	0.93
1959	2.23	0.82
1960	2.12	0.77
1961	2.13	0.80
1962	2.08	0.83
1963	2.04	0.83
1964	1.96	0.87
1965	1.89	0.85
1966	1.87	0.83
1967	1.90	0.89
1968	1.92	0.91
1969	1.92	0.89
1970	1.93	0.98
1971	2.52	1.30
1972	2.99	1.63
1973	3.17	2.52
1974	10.45	8.48

(Source: Venezuelan Ministry of Mines and Hydrocarbons)

TABLE 4

Venezuela and OPEC: Output and Reserves
(000 bbls)

Country	Accumulated Output 1974	Percent	Output Began	Reserves End–1974	Percent
Saudi Arabia	23,095,664	17.7	1938	108,533,366	26.9
Algeria	4,013,534	3.0	1958	9,034,871	2.2
Ecuador	272,716	0.2	1918	1,424,000	0.3
United Arab Emirates	3,159,466	2.4	1962	25,746,842	6.3
Gabon	128,359	0.1	1957	652,050	0.1
Indonesia	5,928,778	4.5	1893	12,000,000	2.9
Iraq	10,088,331	7.7	1928	35,123,750	8.7
Iran	20,190,380	15.5	1913	68,050,000	16.8
Qatar	2,159,696	1.6	1949	5,437,850	1.3
Kuwait	17,428,902	13.3	1946	75,943,366	18.8
Libya	8,652,865	6.6	1961	23,000,000	5.7
Nigeria	3,935,215	3.0	1958	19,577,942	4.8
Venezuela	31,090,977	23.8	1917	18,568,000	4.6
Total	130,144,783	100.0	–	403,092,037	100.0

(Sources: OPEC, *Annual Statistical Bulletin, 1974;* Venezuelan Ministry of Mines and Hydrocarbons; *World Oil.)*

NOTES

1. A mathematical model for determining differences in crude oil prices based on diverse factors such as refinery yields and impurities was developed by Algeria and Venezuela. One fundamental aim was to establish uniform pricing systems to avoid conflicts among OPEC members. At the Bali conference, Saudi Arabia agreed to adopt this formula, although it said that acceptance was unofficial, provisional and flexible. Venezuela gained direct benefits due to the large volume of refined products it exports. (Mariano Gurfinkel, Venezue-

[151]

lan oil expert with the World Bank, United Press International dispatch from Washington, July 12, 1976).

2. Another view on this incident has been given by Juan Pablo Pérez Alfonzo upon his return from a 10 day trip to Iraq in November 1976. He reports that the Iraq delegation felt that if Venezuela had not left the conference room, OPEC would have moved to increase prices despite Saudi Arabia's withdrawal. The Venezuelan move, according to Iraq, tilted the balance in favor of moderation and postponement of a decision on prices. (Conversations with Pérez Alfonzo, December 1976.)

3. In 1951, Iran nationalized the Anglo-Persian Oil Company under the government of Premier Mohammed Mossadegh. Iranian oil was effectively boycotted throughout world markets and Mossadegh overthrown by a coup in 1953. Pérez Alfonzo, in conversations with the author, has said that if an Acción Democrática administration had been in power during this period, Venezuela would have moved to support Mossadegh. As this, however, was not the case, Mossadegh received no support from any of the oil-exporting nations.

4. The Texas Railroad Commission, set up in the 1890s to regulate railway operations, gradually evolved into the agency supervising oil and gas conservation in the state. The commission weighs demand and oversees distribution of supply from the state's 90,000 wells, based on the maximum efficient flow rate under conservation norms.

5. Venezuela and Iran attended as observers and, as such, would not normally have been authorized to sign any agreements with Arab producers. Pérez Alfonzo insisted that Farmaian sign the Gentlemen's Agreement and thus partially committed Iran, despite Farmaian's protests. (Conversations with Farman Farmaian and Pérez Alfonzo).

6. Franklin Tugwell, *The Politics of Oil in Venezuela* (Stanford: Stanford University Press, 1975).

7. As a logical result of the development of Middle Eastern and African sources, European consumers reduced Venezuelan exports to specific crudes required to produce special refined products, in favor of lower cost and closer sources. Venezuela was forced to accept this change in export patterns, but was less happy over the intrusion of extra-continental supplies on the east coast of South America. The memory of violated supply contracts certainly played a role in Venezuelan reluctance to extend special credits to Argentina, Brazil and Uruguay such as those given to other Latin American countries. (Venezuelan Mines Ministry sources).

8. See OPEC Resolution IX.61 and *Petroleum Intelligence Weekly*.

9. Although reliable Venezuelan sources have insisted that Pérez Alfonzo on more than one occasion called for Venezuelan withdrawal from OPEC, the former Mines Minister has told the author that he had limited his proposal to the ouster of members not complying with OPEC policies.

10. "OPEC decisions never follow exactly the same pattern. Sometimes they are taken secretly and announced later (the 1965 production program), sometimes they come out of the Economic Commission, and sometimes it is only at the level of the Conference itself that proposals are made and accepted," according to one former OPEC governor. More recently, price increase decisions have hinged on Saudi Arabia's acceptance. In the September 1975 Conference in Vienna, Yamani had orders from his government to accept no more than a 10 percent increase and in the May 1976 Conference in Bali, Yamani would accept no increase. In both cases, Venezuela was aware of Saudi Arabia's position well in advance of the conferences but was unable to modify it despite extra-mural efforts. (Venezuelan Mines Ministry sources).

11. and 12. Conversations with Valentín Hernández.

13. Since the initial boom in revenues in OPEC member states, there has been a steady reappraisal of the capacity of these largely

undeveloped nations to gain long-lasting benefits from major capital investments. In Venezuela, between 1959 and 1974, Bs. 164 billion (more than three times what the United States invested in the Marshall Plan) have been invested in the country, but there has been little to show, either in social or economic development, in proportion to the expenditure. Venezuela's present 1976-1980 national economic plan calls for close to Bs. 100 billion in investments over the five-year period and has been seriously challenged as misuse of revenue produced by depletion of a non-renewable resource. Pérez Alfonzo has written extensively on this problem, which he calls the "Venezuelan Effect."

14. Alirio Parra, Director of International Marketing, Petróleos de Venezuela, in the *Financial Times,* November 17, 1975.

15. Although Venezuela pioneered offshore drilling techniques in Lake Maracaibo starting in 1923, it was only in 1972 that the state oil firm, Corporación Venezolana del Petróleo, undertook offshore drilling in the Caribbean. Wildcat wells in the Ensenada de la Vela, on the western coast, have found a potential 300 million barrels of recoverable light crude, according to CVP. Further wildcat drilling in the Caribbean and Atlantic has been suspended until the areas are more fully evaluated, but a likely new area will be at the mouth of the Orinoco River. Trinidad, which shares the waters of the Gulf of Paria, has already made substantial discoveries in structures which overlap into Venezuelan territorial waters, attracting Venezuelan interest. (Venezuelan Mines Ministry sources).

16. and 17. Conversations with Valentín Hernández.

18. These figures and estimates have been drawn from a study made by former Venezuelan Deputy Mines Minister Hernán Anzola in 1976.

19. United Press International dispatch from Washington, August 10, 1976.

20. United Press International dispatch from Washington, July 24, 1976.

21. Dankwart Rustow and John Mugno, *OPEC: Success and Prospects* (New York: New York University Press, 1975).

[FIVE]

Venezuelan Foreign Policy Toward Latin America

John D. Martz

I. INTRODUCTION

The history of all our countries confirms and reaffirms
the conclusion that we cannot develop or progress
without uniting. The fortune of each and every one of us
cannot be a matter of indifference to the others. The
doctrine and action of the Government over which I
preside is adjusted to these sincere convictions of solidarity, of integration. ... In the past year I have
dedicated all my efforts toward Latin American unity and
integration, strengthening the ties and links of the Latin
American community.[1]

With these words to a continental meeting of intellectuals
on May 3, 1976, Carlos Andrés Pérez delineated the basic
thrust of Venezuelan foreign policy toward Latin America,

reiterating a message which the peripatetic President had carried to La Paz, Lima, Santa Marta, Mexico City and beyond. The resolution of internal problems throughout the hemisphere, he argued, was dependent upon continental nationalism, political unity, and economic liberation from restrictions imposed by the industrialized states. A similarly characteristic expression had been delivered at the commemoration of the 150th anniversary of the Battle of Ayacucho in December 1974. There the themes of regional independence and economic integration were writ large in Pérez's oratory. The struggle against poverty and under-development, he contended, required a concerted and united effort to which Venezuela was fully dedicated. As past victims of economic exploitation, the nations of Latin America were seeking to remedy the magnitude of injustices.

We aspire to a system of economic security without preferences, with justice, not privileges but reciprocal respect. This new international economic order for which we struggle cannot be built while artificial and unjust divisions remain in economic relations. . . .

We have to be active in the realization of those great plans which will permit us to fight poverty. Misery will enslave us as has been true to the present, if we do not combat and overcome all obstacles; Venezuela is ready with its program, and wishes an interchange of opinions and criteria on practical modes of action.[2]

If these and countless other public declarations were rich in rhetoric, there was also substance to Venezuelan foreign policy. From his inauguration in March 1974, Pérez had

[157]

moved self-confidently in the assertion of continental leadership. Within a few months Venezuela had committed $500 million apiece to the World Bank and to the Inter-American Development Bank; $500 million to the International Monetary Fund; $60 million to the Andean Development Corporation; $25 million to the Caribbean Development Bank; and some $80 million in support of a Central American coffee marketing company. Political unity was enhanced by initiatives favoring Cuban re-incorporation into the Latin American family of nations, while economic integration was pursued through collaborations with Mexico in creating the Sistema Económico Latinoamericano (SELA). And ranging even further, the government became an increasingly visible spokesman of Third World views in its criticisms of the industrialized world.

Despite the welter of activity on several different planes, however, Venezuelan foreign policy toward Latin America was by no means without its internal inconsistencies. Based more on pragmatic responses to many individual issues than on a clearly articulated ideological posture, it failed to develop an overall framework for policy-making. Thus internal coherence being sometimes absent, there were few bases upon which the prediction of future actions might reliably be made. National interests were well-defined in some areas, but in others did not emerge from hasty *ad hoc* decisions. The policy-making process itself often responded more to idiosyncratic factors of a given problem than to a "world-view" of hemispheric relations.

At the broadest level, to be sure, overriding national interests could be identified: a fundamental commitment to independence, self-determination, and a reduction of economic dependence. Moreover, these were extended from the national arena to embrace all of Latin America. Beyond this highly general posture, however, Venezuela took stances on particular issues which reflected an absence of internal consensus. And although the formulation of foreign policy was less directly susceptible to political pressures than domestic decisions, it was by no means immune to particularistic forces. Geopolitical and security interests were influenced by the military; economic policy toward such bodies as the SELA and the Andean Group was pressured by domestic business and commercial interests; and the use of petrodollars abroad elicited demands from opposition political parties to place greater emphasis on internal development.

At least five major theses emerge in the discussion to follow: (1) foreign policy demonstrates an idealism derived from the Bolivarian vision; (2) in less grandiose terms, foreign policy has suffered from the lack of clearly articulated guiding principles; (3) domestic as well as international pressures have helped to shape many specific decisions; (4) given the *ad hoc* nature of certain decisions, the sum of the parts of foreign policy does not constitute a coherent whole; and (5) as a result of the preceding, the possible failures of specific measures will mitigate against the effective reformulation of foreign policy toward Latin America in the near future. As a corollary of the latter, it will be noted in the concluding section that many of the Pérez initiatives appear to be on the verge of dissolution.

With the first of these arguments, it seems that the attempt of Carlos Andrés Pérez to resuscitate Bolivarian unity suggests a lack of realism by flying in the face of 150 years of Latin American fragmentation and nationalistic rivalry. Too often the government has offered cosmetic adulation of the President and his public role, at the expense of concrete and viable policy. Thus the necessity of canceling the June 1976 sesquicentennial celebration of the Congress of Panama, at which all chiefs of state were to have attended, signified a public failure which could have been avoided. The second thesis stresses the piecemeal nature of foreign policy formulation, and the absence of a meaningful philosophy out of which fully coherent decisions might be shaped. For better or worse, this stands in contrast to the experience of the Caldera government immediately preceding that of Pérez.

Third, the impact of such internal interest groups as cited above at times distorts the intended thrust of foreign policy. As a consequence, shifts of ground and alterations of policy sometimes occur, further weakening the cohesion which is being sought. This leads to our fourth point, encouraging policy-making which responds to specific problems at the expense of attention to inter-related issues. Finally, the formulation of future policy can be expected to reflect these same characteristics, thereby complicating Venezuela's actions in the next few years.

If this seems unduly critical, it should be noted that such problems are frequently encountered in the shaping of foreign policy, whether in Venezuela or elsewhere; for immediate reactions to pressing problems and a pragmatic view of the world are all too common. Indeed, the pragmatism of foreign policy under Carlos Andrés Pérez is characteristic both of his personal style and of his party, Acción Democrática. However, the rapidity with which Venezuela has moved toward hemispheric leadership and a deep-seated sense of urgency further contribute to bursts of impetuosity which produce impractical or ill-considered decisions. Several important Venezuelan initiatives are therefore nearing a dead end and, as described in the conclusions, will leave major problems for the future.

Evolution of Democratic Foreign Policy. As the Venezuelan role in hemispheric affairs became more pronounced under the Pérez administration, it was sometimes forgotten that the post-

1958 era had produced substantial continuity. The drive for leadership had begun following the ouster of the dictator Marcos Pérez Jiménez. It was the circumstantial confluence of several events, most importantly the massive rise of petroleum earnings, which provided the opportunity that the new government seized. The dictatorship had given way to the emergence of Latin America's most vigorously competitive political system. Despite a multiplicity of electoral organizations, a new "establishment" grew up around two parties, Acción Democrática (AD) and the Social Christian COPEI. From Presidents Rómulo Betancourt (1959-64) and Raúl Leoni (1964-69) of the AD, through Rafael Caldera (1969-74) of COPEI to the present *adeco* incumbent, Venezuela's voice was heard with growing attention.

Ideological conflict had been paramount during the Betancourt years; competition between Cuban socialism and Venezuelan democratic reformism as developmental models was acute. Betancourt adopted an equally uncompromising posture toward dictatorships of the Left and the Right. Thus the hallmark of his foreign policy was the so-called Betancourt Doctrine, which demanded the withholding of diplomatic recognition from illegitimate regimes. Leoni subsequently honored this cornerstone of AD thought, explaining: "We maintain our principles, often alone, [opposing] such [developments] as the repudiation of government by force and the usurpation of governments by violence." [3] Both AD administrations subordinated sub-regional to hemispheric-wide policy. Movement toward participation in the Andean Pact was halting, and Venezuela stood aloof from the Latin American Free Trade Area (LAFTA) until 1966.

Not until 1969, with the electoral victory of COPEI, did orientations toward international affairs alter perceptibly. Rafael Caldera, whose writings had extended the Social

[161]

Christian concept of social justice to the international sphere, adopted "ideological pluralism" as the cornerstone of Venezuelan policy.[4] His inaugural address in March 1969 was explicit. "It seems to me that public opinion favors the establishment of relations with countries of political organization and ideology different from ours, for their presence in the world and their influence on economic relations cannot be ignored."[5] Diplomatic ties were gradually renewed with a number of countries, including the Soviet Union in March 1970. Venezuela joined the Andean Pact, and discourse with Colombia was broadened over the territorial dispute concerning the border on the Gulf of Venezuela. Foreign Minister Aristides Calvani, a leading Social Christian theoretician, skillfully managed foreign relations. Moreover, the administration cast its shadow across national boundaries through the personal stature and statesmanship of Rafael Caldera. This was in part a reflection of the Caldera style of leadership, nourished by a career replete with international experience.

Of more direct importance, however, was growing concern over perceptions of Brazilian expansionism. The reverberations of Brazil's vaunted "economic miracle" were being heard through the Spanish-speaking republics, while Brazilian public and private investment in neighboring countries grew apace. Venezuela was also troubled by the surge of Brazilian penetration toward its borders, where villages were being colonized and airfields constructed. It was within this context that Caldera dramatically extended Venezuela's role with a continental tour in February 1973. Visiting six Spanish-speaking capitals of South America, he personalized ideological pluralism through an exchange of *abrazos* with such diverse chiefs of state as Rodríguez Lara, Velasco Alvarado, Allende, and Banzer.

Nothwithstanding the cosmetic quality to some of these

activities, the outline of an anti-Brazilian alliance was evident, and Itamarati (the Brazilian foreign ministry) expressed its wounded sensitivities to Caracas. A subsequent meeting of Presidents Caldera and Garrastazu Médici at the border town of Santa Elena de Uairén outwardly soothed relations, yet it was disappointing for Venezuela. Instead of moving toward collaboration with Brazil in guiding a united continent in defense of its interests against the industrialized nations, the government opted for a concert of Spanish-speaking nations. Brazil would necessarily be placed in a separate category. Such a judgment stood as a significant milestone of the Caldera government.

Hemispheric pressures favoring readmission of Cuba into Latin American councils had meantime been growing, and Caldera encouraged informal contacts with Havana. It was expected that the President would cap his stewardship of foreign policy by a climactic address before the United Nations during the course of a trip that would include an official stopover in Cuba. These plans were set aside in the wake of the September 1973 *golpe de estado* in Chile, the repercussions of which were substantial within COPEI as well as upon the Venezuelan electoral campaign. Thus it remained for the next administration to pick up the initiative on the Cuba question, as well as to restructure international relationships amid the torrent of petrodollars following the quadrupling of prices from 1973 to 1974.

The 1973 campaign had been fought almost purely on domestic issues, with foreign policy relegated to a secondary position.[6] In the economic sphere, there was a general consensus that nationalization of oil would occur during the next presidential term, but the candidates agreed, as Pérez put it, not to *"petrolizar las elecciones."* Foreign policy questions occupied but four pages of Acción Democrática's 78 page

[163]

platform, wherein a continuation of support for international and regional organizations was promised. One paragraph considered the emergence of changing relationships between the developing nations and the industrialized world, but went no further than decrying the evils of scientific and technological dependency.[7] And while both COPEI and the leftist parties favored recognition of Cuba in their electoral campaigns, Pérez's own platform simply promised to "maintain the principle of diplomatic and commercial relations with all the countries of the world."

The *adeco* candidate had been somewhat more specific in interviews. Noting that the Betancourt Doctrine had been devised to meet conditions prevalent a decade earlier, he viewed it as no longer useful. Thus accepting by implication Caldera's recognition policy, he also expressed a willingness to reopen relations with Cuba, although insisting that the initiative lay with Havana. There was little question that the movement toward Cuba would continue under the new administration, then; moreover it was apparent that both Acción Democrática and Rómulo Betancourt himself viewed the nonrecognition of unconstitutional or undemocratic regimes as an artifact no longer desirable in the world of the 1970s.

As the new administration soon proved itself rich in foreign policy initiatives, its championing of Latin American unity and solidarity provided an overarching umbrella under which less sweeping objectives were defined. The configurations of Venezuelan policy grouped themselves under three distinctive if overlapping rubrics: (a) initiatives at the full hemispheric level; (b) sub-regional actions, most notably an expansion of influence into the Caribbean and Central America; and (c) responsiveness to bilateral military/security problems, especially those with Brazil, Guyana, and Colombia. In the process, several important questions swiftly surfaced. What was the ordering of priorities? Would the pursuit of Venezuelan objectives stimulate cooperation or conflict in the hemisphere? Could its goals be sufficiently realized to maintain policy directions, or might possible failure require a redefinition of priorities? These questions are assessed in the concluding section. But first, attention is directed sequentially to the three preceding policy categories. Perhaps the most striking involves the use of economic muscle and diplomatic persuasion on behalf of broadly Latin American concerns.

II. Petroleum and Hemispheric Foreign Policy

Petroleum and Economic Influence. Pérez's inaugural address in March 1974 concentrated heavily on domestic issues, barely hinting at the possible configuration of foreign policy. There were flourishes characterizing Latin America as "our Motherland," and concomitant pledges to consult with hemispheric nations in advance of a conference on primary products, through which priorities and policies might be identified and communicated to the industrialized states. The new chief of state pledged that Venezuelan oil would support "the elaboration of our international Latin American policy and . . . the economy of our sister states, [along with] the common interests for the progress and well-being of our peoples." To this effect, oil income would provide for contributions to the Inter-American Development Bank, "with the single condition that it be used to develop those economic activities which today do not find institutional financing because of the sphere of interest of multinational corporations which, with their influence, can paralyze lines of credit to Latin America." [8]

[165]

Similar views were presented later in the year when Pérez sent a lengthy telegram to Gerald Ford following the latter's address to the United Nations.

IN LATIN AMERICAN AS IN THE OTHER DEVELOPING COUN-
TRIES WE AFFIRM THAT THE DEVELOPED COUNTRIES HAVE
BEEN ABUSING THE FUNDAMENTAL NEEDS OF THE LATIN
AMERICANS, ASIANS, AND AFRICANS. THE PRICES OF OIL, TO
CITE THE PARTICULAR CASE OF VENEZUELA, WERE FOR
MANY YEARS IN A FRANK PROCESS OF DETERIORATION
WHILE OUR COUNTRY WAS OBLIGED TO RECEIVE MANUFAC-
TURES PROVIDED BY THE UNITED STATES AT PRICES WHICH
GREW DAILY HIGHER, THUS LIMITING EVEN MORE THE
POSSIBILITIES OF DEVELOPMENT AND WELL-BEING FOR
VENEZUELANS. . . .

VENEZUELA CAN ONLY VIEW WITH SYMPATHY ANY EFFORT
TO RESOLVE THE GREAT QUESTIONS OF OUR TIMES IN
GLOBAL TERMS, BUT WITHOUT A WORLD PERSPECTIVE, IT
MEANS THE DOMINATION OF THE GREAT COUNTRIES OVER
THE SMALL. IT WOULD BE DANGEROUS, INEFFICIENT AND
DAMAGING IF GLOBAL AND UNIVERSAL SOLUTIONS FORGOT
THAT THE WORLD IS ALSO COMPOSED OF SMALL NATIONS.[9]

The obvious generality of such declarations reflected the action-oriented pragmatism of Acción Democrática, personified by Pérez himself. The inclinations of the new administration, unlike its Social Christian predecessor, were less consciously shaped by philosophical considerations. As foreign policy initiatives were undertaken, they sometimes appeared to be formulated on a piecemeal basis.

[166]

Perhaps the first major pillar to be erected was a willingness to employ petroleum earnings in the conduct of international relations. This was articulated at the April 1974 meetings of the Inter-American Development Bank (IDB) in Santiago. Delegates met amid growing criticism of United States influence, as demonstrated by the earlier denial of loans to the Allende government in Chile.

Manifesting Venezuela's drive toward hemispheric leadership, Treasury Minister Héctor Hurtado proposed a special fiduciary fund, to which his government would contribute $100 million annually for five years. The fund would be available to both private and public-sector projects, especially for industry, mining, and agriculture. The financing of exports of manufactured and semi-manufactured goods to markets outside Latin America was suggested, as well as the providing of capital to buy shares in nascent trans-Latin American corporations. Significantly, bonds emitted by the fund to internationa' financial markets would be guaranteed by the Latin American states rather than by the United States, as in the past. Hurtado proposed the application of three basic criteria. First, the region's less developed countries would receive preference; second, there would be insistence upon projects other than those for infrastructural development; and lastly, regional companies would be encouraged.

The underlying assumptions constituted an assertion of Latin American independence and an implicit challenge to North American domination. This was consistent with the initiative by Antonio Ortiz Mena, Mexican President of the Bank, to secure European capital as a means of reducing US influence. It was in the same vein that Hurtado suggested reorganization of the IDB into a "Latin American Bank," one in which the Latin American role in policy-making would be at least equal to that of the United States and Canada. While no immediate action on this point was forthcoming, it accurately mirrored Venezuelan thinking.

The use of petrodollars to finance a host of sub-regional enterprises grew rapidly during the first months of the new administration (see section III below), which was fully cognizant of the problem of increased oil prices for Latin American consumers. Although Venezuela well understood that the income supporting its economic foreign policy measures came at the expense of many of its neighbors, not solely the United States and Canada, it flatly rejected the notion of two-tier pricing, whereby Latin American oil importers might pay less than the prevailing international price. However, three separate mechanisms were devised to lighten the burden. Nor was it coincidental that each of them further enhanced the nation's growing hemispheric role. One approach took the form of a cash-loan; the second involved reimbursment to a third party; and the last comprised aid to development banks plus miscellaneous forms of aid.

The cash-loan plan was announced to the Central American presidents at their December 1974 meeting with Pérez in Puerto Ordaz. As outlined in the Declaration of Guayana, economic aid was pledged in the form of deferred payments. In essence, Central American importers would pay $6 per barrel—roughly 50 percent of the market price. The remainder, in local currency, would be placed as a virtual loan into the respective countries' development banks for domestic reinvestment. Interest was set at 8 percent, somewhat lower than the rates from international development funds, while repayment could extend over twenty-five years, much longer than could have been negotiated elsewhere. Although the full price of the oil would eventually fall upon the importers, the burden would thus be extended over a lengthy period, during which time the available funds would be channeled into development programs.

The second method called for reimbursement of other oil exporters for fuel purchased by consumers. Such an agreement was announced with Ecuador and Peru in October 1974. Under its terms, Peru would pay Ecuador approximately half the cost of its daily 25,000 barrel imports. Ecuador would receive the remainder from Venezuela, which would eventually be repaid by Peru. As a consequence, Venezuela was spared the relatively uneconomical shipment of small quantities to Peru; the Ecuadorean petroleum industry would benefit; and Peru would have lower transportation costs. This deferred payment was estimated at some $100 million during its first year. A similar agreement involving Cuba and the Soviet Union, through which Venezuelan oil would be shipped to Cuba while the Russians in exchange would supply Western European customers, was signed in November of 1976. Both Venezuela and the Soviet Union were thus spared major transportation expense.

Thirdly, contributions to international agencies and banks extended a more indirect but nonetheless meaningful form of aid on a massive scale. As noted below, these were to include such regional entities as the Caribbean Development Bank and the Andean Development Corporation. In October 1975 Pérez also proposed to the Organization of Petroleum Exporting Countries the creation of a $1.5 billion to $2 billion fund on behalf of Third World oil consumers. The availability of such nonrecoverable financing would soften the impact of increased prices, while serving to strengthen the unity of developing nations, whether producers or consumers. In 1976 OPEC agreed to a fund of $800 million, and Venezuela promptly pledged a contribution of $100 million.

In these actions, as with sub-regional economic measures

[169]

detailed later, Venezuela was by no means motivated purely by generosity. Indeed, although rejecting occasional charges of expansionism, it did not deny the intention of extending its diplomatic and political influence. As time passed, however, increasing domestic demands for internal development threatened to absorb an enlarged proportion of oil revenues. By late 1976, as the administration reached its halfway point, Caracas was making it clear that the financial investments and blanket loans of the early period would not be emulated during the remainder of the Pérez term. This shift did not mean, of course, that the broader goal of hemispheric unity and the effort to assert hemispheric leadership were to be abandoned. Certainly activities of a predominantly political nature constituted an important element of foreign policy.

Reordering Political Relationships. Concerns over the fate of the developing nations suggested a clear reorientation of attitudes toward the outside world. This was manifest in a growing advocacy of the Third World's cause, as well as in a restructuring of hemispheric relationships. With the former, the Pérez administration was insistently articulate. At the United Nations General Assembly in October 1974, for example, Foreign Minister Efraín Schacht Aristeguieta spoke of an international community characterized by a more equitable socio-economic order, buttressed by the unimpeded right of self-determination. Venezuela saw herself as explicitly aligned with the Third World in a struggle destined "for the benefit of all men, putting an end to odious distinctions between the large and small states, between weak and powerful nations, between rich and poor countries." The great powers bore a responsibility to share in the quest for formulas of understanding, so that a reordering of international relationships might be realized.[10]

In an interview one year later, President Pérez reiterated

[170]

these views over the sharing of responsible decision-making between the industrialized nations and the Third World. What was necessary, he argued, was "interdependence among equals rather than interdependence in which there are subordinates." Especially in the case of petroleum and energy problems, Venezuela was determined to avoid situations of confrontation, preferring broader dialogue and understanding. As a part of the Third World, his country spoke an increasingly common language. "We countries of the Third World aid one another; we cannot accept the fact that prices of our raw materials are manipulated in the great financial centers of the world. We also believe that an agreement has to be made that will establish an equilibrium in the terms of trade." [11]

Beyond such public pronouncements, concrete policy was developed on two important enterprises: the creation of a regional economic entity closed to United States participation, and the reincorporation of Cuba into the hemispheric fold. The former, despite evident political implications, was avowedly intended to foster the integrated economic development of the Latin American bloc. The initiative for its creation was shared with Mexico, whose president Luis Echeverría had championed the cause prior to Pérez's assumption of power. Conversations during Echeverría's four-day visit to Caracas in July 1974 included mutual commitments to proceed with the formation of the Sistema Ecónomico Latinoamericano (SELA), and both men dispatched official representatives elsewhere to stimulate discussion and enthusiasm. After Pérez travelled to Mexico City in March 1975, he and Echeverría issued a formal invitation to all Latin American countries for a conference to inaugurate the organization.

Nine objectives were set forth for the SELA. These included integrated economic development; creation of multinational Latin American corporations; the channelling of resources into both regional and sub-regional projects; defense of prices and markets for raw materials and also manufactured products; improvement of food supplies, including a multinational system of fertilizer production; stimulation of scientific and technical cooperation; and the directing of technical aid through appropriate sub-regional organizations toward the less developed members. Both Pérez and Echeverría insisted that the SELA would avoid strictly political activities, which should remain within the purview of the Organization of American States. Rather, it would enhance Latin American solidarity in its dealings with the industrialized world, as an identity of interests could be defined through a dialogue grounded on full equality.

Delegates from twenty-five states subsequently met in Panama from July 31 to August 2, 1975, unanimously resolving to promote intra-regional cooperation and economic development. A working group was created to write a draft statute for the SELA that would encompass earlier Venezuelan and Mexican statements. These increasingly familiar proposals included the development of Latin American multinational ventures; maintenance of the prices of raw materials, and coordinated marketing; measures to defend regional interests against actions by transnational interests; the channelling of resources into programs to stimulate regional development; and promotion of the exchange of technology and scientific information.

Fully conscious of the importance of support from such unenthusiastic states as Brazil and Argentina, the SELA's sponsors were cautious in their approach. Thus it was agreed that further preparatory work should precede formal elaboration of the SELA's internal structures. Panama was entrusted to organize the working group, which was to meet within 45 days and present its recommendations to a ministerial conference no later than mid-October. These tasks were completed on schedule, with twenty-three nations signing the organizational document on October 18, 1975.[12] Caracas became the seat of the Permanent Secretariat, and Venezuela agreed to fund the SELA's interim budget.

Héctor Hurtado reiterated that the SELA was not a political organization, but rather that its functions centered on the identification and articulation of a common position *vis-à-vis* the outside world. Realistically, however, political implications could not be ignored. Notwithstanding denials, the SELA constituted a potential challenge to the United States. Moreover, the definition of common positions within the SELA was also sure to be a demanding task. Already at the October meeting there were differences of outlook between Venezuela and Cuba over multinational companies. The former preferred substantial reliance on private enterprise to provide necessary capital goods and industrial needs, while the Cubans advocated preponderant state participation. A Mexican compromise defused possible conflict at the time, but it was instructive that *Granma* was soon to predict that the SELA faced a difficult road ahead. Serious obstacles clearly face the SELA, and may ultimately prove insuperable. At the same time, its creation represents a major facet of Venezuela's basic commitment to regional collaboration, and to a meaningful expression of Latin American interests in international circles. Without Caracas' unflagging commitment and energetic diplomacy, it is unlikely that the SELA would have seen the light of day.

In contrast, Venezuela proved less skillful in seeking Cuban readmission into Latin American circles. Carlos Andrés Pérez had expressed views not unlike those of Rafael Caldera:

> . . . I believe there are some matters which are fundamental and which identify interests of all countries of Latin America. We must accept ideological differences if we

are to join together in the common quest for independent decision-making. And by helping to solve political problems in Latin America, we also create conditions in which democracy may become the system of government all over Latin America.[13]

Thus he undertook a diplomatic campaign on behalf of Cuba in which the presidents of Costa Rica and Colombia—both personal friends—shared.

It was the original intention to lift OAS sanctions against Cuba at the fifteenth consultative meeting of ministers of foreign affairs, convened in November 1974 at Quito. A two-thirds vote was required to end the sanctions originally adopted in 1964; Venezuela, Costa Rica, and Colombia confidently co-sponsored the major resolution at Quito. However, right-wing regimes effectively played upon residual fears of renewed Cuban intervention, and the proponents of Cuba's re-entry found themselves outmaneuvered. The decisive vote was 12 in favor, 3 opposed, and 6 abstaining (importantly, the United States and Brazil included).

In Venezuela, the unexpected setback provoked a wave of criticism against Foreign Minister Schacht, as newspapers headlined the "Venezuelan Failure" at Quito. Former *copeyano* Foreign Minister Calvani, for one, was outspoken in citing ineffective planning and an inept performance at the conference.[14] The government largely centered public blame on the United States for what it viewed as misrepresentation by the State Department both before and during the conference. However, dissatisfaction with the Quito performance was manifest in early 1975 when Schacht exchanged positions with the Secretary to the Presidency, Ramón Escovar Salom. The Cuban problem was eventually resolved late in July of 1975 as the foreign ministers voted by majority rule to leave

OAS members free to deal with Havana as they saw fit. By that time Venezuela had received official Cuban representatives in Caracas. Adolfo Raúl Taylhardat, in 1971 Venezuela's first ambassador to the Soviet Union following the opening of relations with Moscow, was named his government's envoy to the Castro government.

III. Sub-Regionalism and Spheres of Influence

Along with its hemispheric concerns, Venezuela devoted detailed attention to its relationships with several sub-regions. It projected its interests vigorously into the Caribbean and Central America, in particular, but also emphasized its historic bonds with Andean neighbors. While a number of specific actions and commitments were welcomed by the recipients, they also engendered suspicions concerning Venezuela's long-range national interests. The sharpest such statement came from Trinidad-Tobago's Prime Minister, Eric Williams, who charged Venezuela with undertaking a "recolonization of the Caribbean." [15] Indeed, it was in the Caribbean that the specter of neo-imperialist encroachment first was raised against the Pérez administration.

The Caribbean. Both sub-regional and bilateral approaches were employed. The former concentrated heavily on the Caribbean Development Bank (CDB), which had been created in 1971 as a lending agency for the Commonwealth Caribbean. Venezuela was the first non-English speaking member upon its entry in 1973, and soon became a major source of development investment capital. By 1974 the first half of its membership share allotment requirement of $3 million was paid; more importantly, a $10 million loan was extended to the Bank's Special Development Fund (SDF).

The SDF largely channeled its own loans into governmental financial institutions on the smaller islands,[16] especially for infrastructural development. Even greater significance lay in the August 1975 negotiations of the Fondo de Inversiones de Venezuela (FIV) with the CDB, which produced the creation of a $25 million trust fund. This was designed to support Caribbean integration, while also encouraging industrial, agricultural, and agro-industrial development.

Venezuelan representatives also played a central role in the activities of the newly created eighteen-nation Caribbean Tourism Association. At its first meeting, convened in Caracas in 1974, Pérez pledged his support and recommended that Spanish join English as the official language of the Caribbean. The same year Venezuela came to the rescue of the regional airline LIAT Ltd., which served the smaller members of the Caribbean Community and Common Market (CAR-ICOM).[17] With bankruptcy facing LIAT's owners (the Court Line of Britain), the Banco Industrial de Venezuela extended a loan of $5 million to the several island governments to purchase the airline. Twelve percent annual interest plus a 2 percent service fee were charged. There was some criticism of these terms, but Trinidad-Tobago had refused to bail out the airline competitive with its own British West Indian Airways (BWIA), thus the only option was acceptance of the Venezuelan offer.

Such Venezuelan activities typified its decision to enter the English-speaking Caribbean, where commercial ties had historically been weak. The private sector followed the public into the region; a construction firm secured a contract for port development on St. Lucia, for example, whil another company became a participant in a new cement plant in Jamaica.

The Caracas government also pursued several bilateral agreements, which helped fuel Caribbean fears of hegemonic ambitions from the mainland. The most striking instance followed upon the April 1975 visit to Caracas of Jamaican Prime Minister Michael Manley. Venezuela was invited to join with Mexico for capital participation in an aluminum smelter to be built in Jamaica.[18] In exchange, Jamaica would be offered an equity share in the new Venezuelan smelter in Guayana. Moreover, Jamaica agreed to sell 200,000 tons of aluminum and 400,000 bauxite annually (the latter to reach 500,000 tons in the fourth year); purchases would continue for ten years.

Venezuela also promised to sell Jamaica petroleum for its industrial program under cash-loan terms similar to those already extended to Central America. Thus payment would be set at 50 percent of the world price, with the remainder to be made in local currency for reinvestment in long term development projects. An extension of scientific, technical, and cultural exchanges was proposed by Manley and Pérez, with the former promising that the teaching of Spanish would be expanded in Jamaica. The joint presidential declaration was replete with calls for closer ties throughout the Caribbean. While the meeting's concrete accords were of economic advantages to both nations, they also symbolized continuing Venezuelan penetration of the Caribbean.

The most vocal critic of the Venezuelan-Jamaican negotiations was Eric Williams. The Prime Minister of Trinidad-Tobago feared the impact of the smelter project on previous plans for a CARICOM aluminum plant, which had been negotiated a year earlier in talks with Manley and with Forbes Burnham of Guyana. Trinidad-Tobago was to provide power from its offshore natural gas supplies, while aluminum would come in equal portions from Jamaica and Guyana. Faced with the Manley-Pérez declaration, Williams withdrew from the CARICOM project, adding that the oil agreement would also

[177]

damage Trinidad's traditional position as major supplier of the CARICOM nations. As an added fillip, he charged Caracas with an uncooperative attitude in talks concerning fishing rights in the Gulf of Paria, temporarily breaking off again more than a decade of intermittent discussions.

Michael Manley promptly denied that the new agreement would be inimical to Caribbean interests, countercharging that Trinidad had consistently dragged its feet in CARICOM affairs. Nor was Williams supported by other Caribbean leaders, many of whom were already indebted to the Pérez government. Eric Gairy of Grenada had been promised loans from Caracas, and the same was true of Antigua's George Walter and Robert Bradshaw of St. Kitts-Nevis. Barbados had secured a cash-loan accord for the purchase of oil, and conversations with Guyana presaged an understanding on bauxite and petroleum, with Venezuela exchanging refined oil for Guyanese ores. All of these measures deepened Venezuela's impact throughout the Caribbean, as did the 1976 one-year oil agreement with the Dominican Republic.

Central America. The Venezuelan presence was also being felt on the Central American isthmus. It was the December 1974 meeting at Puerto Ordaz which heralded Venezuelan entry into the sub-region. Carlos Andrés Pérez and his fellow chiefs of state negotiated the cash-loan plan described above. But the Declaration of Guayana went further, most notably in Venezuela's offer of $80 million in support of the Central American coffee market. A preliminary meeting in Caracas the preceding month had already outlined the establishment of La Compañía Café Suaves Centrales, a marketing agency to protect the prices of mild coffees. With the international price then experiencing a period of decline, the participants viewed the Company as a means of stabilizing prices through controlling their export levels. At Puerto Ordaz the Venezuelans agreed to provide some 70 percent of the requisite financing, and in January 1975 Café Suaves Centrales was officially inaugurated, with the Central American producers joined by Mexico, Ecuador, and Venezuela. Discussions at Puerto Ordaz also touched upon other problem areas. Venezuela contributed a $60 million loan to the Banco Centroamericano de Integración Económica (BCIE) for developmental programs, and gave informal assurance of assistance to Honduras' efforts to recover from the destruction of Hurricane Fifi.

Both before and after Puerto Ordaz, moreover, several additional bilateral agreements were negotiated. Early in 1975, for example, the Fondo de Inversiones de Venezuela (FIV) issued a loan to the Compañía Salvadoreña de Café to finance Salvador's coffee retention plan, while an oil refinery in Costa Rica and a pulp factory in Honduras were also to be aided. Construction of the refinery, with a daily capacity of 400,000 barrels, was conceived as meeting the domestic needs of the Central American market along with exports to non-regional customers. Venezuela would supply the crude oil while pledging 50 percent of the necessary capital—$100 million. By mid-1975 the FIV had also agreed to finance the local costs of six separate projects in Costa Rica. In Honduras, 50 percent of the estimated $300 million required for a pulp and paper factory would be paid by Venezuela, with the remaining capital to be provided by Argentina and Mexico.

With Venezuelan influence thus extending into Central America, Caracas also moved toward strengthening of ties between Spanish- and English-speaking countries, as reflected in the prospective Caribbean merchant fleet. By no means a new notion, the idea was encouraged by both Venezuela and Mexico, and in May 1975 representatives of seventeen nations met in San José, Costa Rica.[20] The projected Flota Mercante del Caribe was viewed as a means of stimulating regional trade and redressing the existing imbalance of shipping facilities with North American and European competitors. Advocates also contended that further regional collaboration might spin off from the Flota Mercante, such as shipbuilding and repair facilities, and processing plants for Caribbean foodstuffs.

In addition to its economic programs and projections, Venezuela also expressed its positions on two predominantly political sub-regional disputes—the Panama Canal, and the Belize controversy. With the former, warm approval was given in support of Panamanian claims against the United States. Pérez indicated a strong personal commitment and encouraged the attendance of Panama's leader, Omar Torrijos, at conferences with Central American leaders. There were also meetings of Pérez and Torrijos with Presidents Alfonso López Michelsen of Colombia and Daniel Oduber of Costa Rica to discuss and review the situation. The evident depth of Venezuela's conviction was amply demonstrated at the July 1975 meeting near Santa Marta, Colombia, in celebration of that city's 450th anniversary. The presidents of Venezuela, Colombia, and Panama were in attendance, as was the new OAS Secretary General, Alejandro Orfila of Argentina. Among the major points of the resultant Declaration of Santa Marta was unqualified support for Panamanian sovereignty over the Canal. Pérez's speech linked Panama's winning of jurisdiction over the Canal to broader concerns.

When Panama regains sovereignty over the Canal—the irreversible will and decision of the Panamanians, uncon-ditionally supported by all Latin America—the traffic of Colombian and Costa Rican ships between the coasts of the Atlantic and the Pacific will be free, [serving] as the highway of one common country, an open door to understanding, solidarity, and concord.

[180]

I declare from Santa Marta that we observe and prepare that ephemeral Bolivarian ideal which ties all American to this 450 year old city. . . . The most precious goals which raise us toward Bolivar's glory are Latin American integration; [access to] the sea for Bolivia; and the Canal of the Panamanians.[21]

In a similar vein, Venezuela viewed Guatemalan claims over Belize as an obstacle to Latin American unity. In more concrete terms, Caracas perceived the sensitivities of her Caribbean friends over the plight of the English-speaking territory, leading to Pérez's announcement in November 1975 that Venezuela would not support Guatemala in the controversy.

The Andean States. Policy toward the sub-region closest to home was largely based on the Andean Pact. Venezuela initially had been cool toward Andean integration, and four years lapsed after the signing of the Cartagena Agreement before Rafael Caldera brought in his nation in February 1973. The Venezuelan private sector had been staunchly opposed to the Andean Pact, basing its opposition in large part upon the country's higher labor and production costs. Both political and economic factors—some of them highly technical—thus mitigated against the style and content of the foreign policy activism Venezuela demonstrated in the Caribbean and in Central America. To be sure, a $60 million contribution from the FIV was deposited in the Corporación Andina de Fomento (CAF), a separate entity established in 1970 which served as financial agent for the sub-region.[22] However, the complexities of its economy created special problems for Venezuela.

A case in point centered upon efforts by the Pact's administrative junta to devise a development plan for the automotive industry. In seeking to divide production facilities on an equitable and profitable basis, the administrative junta's

[181]

proposal meant for Venezuela a reduction of its share of the automotive manufacturing capacity from 54 percent in 1973 to one-third of the total, leading to a projected loss of $150 million by 1980. The Cámara de la Industria Venezolana Automotriz (CIVA), believing its activities the cornerstone of national industrialization, protested angrily. Long months of wrangling led to increased allocations for Venezuela, but as of mid-1977 final agreement was still pending. Similarly, efforts to outline a petrochemical program largely foundered on the disparate needs and demands of member states, notably Venezuela. In mid-1975 a petrochemical accord was accepted after four years of negotiations, but was so drafted as to leave its efficacy in serious doubt. A host of related problems also continued to complicate the process of integration. In October 1976 Chile effectively withdrew from the Pact, leaving a much weakened organization whose future was uncertain.

Obstacles to Venezuela's influence in the area were less evident in its bilateral dealings, although these responded primarily to idiosyncratic relationships with the individual countries. Venezuelan-Colombian ties continued to mirror the contradictions of warm official relationships confronted by substantive disagreements (see below).[23] Policy toward Ecuador was based primarily upon its emergence as an oil exporter and the second Latin American state to join OPEC.

Moving further southward, much of Venezuela's initiative revolved about ceremonial trips by Carlos Andrés Pérez. The most widely publicized manifestation came with the December 1974 celebration of the Battle of Ayacucho. The only non-military man among four attending chiefs of state, Pérez performed with his customary gusto. Private discussions were held with the Cuban foreign minister; with Torrijos of Panama; and with Hugo Banzer regarding Bolivia's renewed campaign for an outlet to the Pacific. For some, the occasion marked a passing of nationalistic leadership from Peru to Venezuela. Certainly the role of the latter was important in preparing the eight-nation Declaration of Ayacucho proclaimed on December 9, 1974.[24] Pérez's trip to La Paz in August 1975 for Bolivia's 150th anniversary ceremonies produced both an effusive public welcome and a clearly sympathetic if broadly phrased statement favoring the passageway to the sea. Pérez also volunteered his services as mediator between Bolivia and Chile.[25]

IV. Bilateral Rivalry and Conflict

With Venezuela's foreign policy toward Latin America relying so much upon its economic wealth, the sub-regional emphases were pronounced, and existing patterns of dominance in Caracas' relations with less developed countries were reinforced. An element of paternalism was inevitable as Venezuelan economic and diplomatic power aroused resentment on the part of several beneficiaries. At the same time, there were long-standing sources of bilateral conflict which remained unresolved, notably the Colombian and Guyanese frontier disputes. Moreover, the extension of Venezuelan influence complicated relations with larger states, particularly Brazil.

Colombia. Relations during the 1960s had been exacerbated by the massive illegal migration of Colombians across the border in search of better jobs and higher wages. Further, the estimated annual flow of 200,000-300,000 head of cattle smuggled into Venezuela complicated the situation. Of greatest potential economic significance, however, was the unresolved question of the Gulf of Venezuela boundary and contiguous offshore oil deposits. The Caldera government had engaged in bilateral talks held in Rome, but these were interrupted when Venezuela rejected Colombian demands that the issue be submitted to international arbitration.

Despite the friendship of López Michelsen and Pérez, solid bases for agreement remained difficult to identify following their respective inaugurations in 1974. While Colombia sought to explore compromise solutions—for instance the joint exploration and exploitation of subsea deposits—Venezuela made lengthy reference to earlier treaties and to international law in rejecting these proposals. Public opinion was strongly opposed to any understanding which might be interpreted as surrender of territorial sovereignty, and the Venezuelan armed forces were particularly firm on the question. Thus domestic pressures left the Pérez administration limited room for maneuver and it consequently sought to downgrade the issue. Communications have continued to flow between the two foreign ministries, with both parties repeating cordial expressions of mutual respect, but to the present moment Venezuela has dragged its feet on defusing the potentially explosive controversy.

Guyana. If anything, this border controversy is even more complex. Historically, its origins emerged in the 1895 conflict with Great Britain over some two-thirds of what was then British Guiana. In 1899, an arbitral tribunal awarded the British most of the contested area, a decision which still rankles. Rómulo Betancourt reopened the issue in 1962, and four years later Raúl Leoni's government secured the Geneva Accord, which created a mixed commission to explore the matter at greater length. Guyanese independence in 1966 did not interrupt diplomatic efforts. After four more years of difficult negotiation, the Caldera administration in 1970 signed the Protocol of Puerto España, which called for a twelve-year suspension of talks. The Guyana legislature duly ratified the agreement, but the Venezuelan congress was unwilling to do so. While the *modus vivendi* froze the dispute in place, it left a residue of mutual mistrust for the incoming Pérez government. Tensions which had flared in 1970 gradually relaxed, permitting a temporary shelving of the problem while other matters received priority. Discussions with Georgetown over exchanges of oil for bauxite moderated more bellicose attitudes for a time. However, the routing of Angola-bound Cuban troops through Guyana in 1975 inflamed Venezuelan attitudes once again.[26]

Brazil. Policy toward the continent's most powerful nation has been outwardly quiescent, but the potential for rivalry is unavoidable as both nations drive toward progressively greater hemispheric and extra-continental prominence. Burgeoning Brazilian activity along portions of the 1300-mile border has fanned Venezuelan preoccupations. In 1966 Brazil created the Superintendencia do Desenvolvimento da Amazonia (SUDAM), an autonomous entity committed to development of the region and to its effective integration into national life. A multifaceted program receiving high priority in Brasilia envisaged colonization of the area, the opening of military bases, and the construction of a network of airfields capable of handling jet aircraft (45 were operable by 1973, with 126 projected by 1980).

During the Caldera years the Venezuelan response was two-pronged. First, the government created its own Comisión para el Desarrollo del Sur de Venezuela (CODESUR), heralded in its public relations campaign as initiating *"la conquista del Sur."* In addition, Rafael Caldera's diplomatic energies were directed toward strengthing the ties among the Spanish-speaking nations, as previously noted. Underlying Venezuelan attitudes toward Brazil possess an element of ambiguity. The dominant theme, however, was reflected in

[185]

both public and private resentment over Richard Nixon's statement in 1973 that Brazil was the "natural leader" of Latin America, presenting a developmental model consistent with North American policy preferences. The generally unsatisfactory and diplomatically innocuous meeting of Caldera with Garrastazu Médici in 1973 helped to sharpen Venezuelan concern, and from that point forward, the disjuncture in the policy objectives of the two nations has become dominant in Venezuelan attitudes.

The continuing thrust of Brazilian frontier colonization has not gone unnoticed in Caracas.[27] The town of Boa Vista—the major pole of Brazilian Amazonian development—has increased in population from a few hundred to some 80,000 in less than two decades. The construction of airfields has led to growing dismay on the part of Venezuelan military leaders. Yet the *adeco* government of Carlos Andrés Pérez, decidedly unenthusiastic about promoting CODESUR because of its identification with COPEI, has been relatively inactive in regard to the "sleeping frontier." And for all the Pérez initiatives in other areas, there has been limited public evidence of a clearly defined posture toward Brazil. With the exception of a visit by Foreign Minister Escovar Salom to Brazil in late 1975, relations have been conducted with an aura of formality at less elevated echelons of the hierarchy.

Venezuela is quite conscious of the Brazilian presence on the border, and of its economic and political influence throughout the hemisphere. Yet there has been an apparent reluctance by the Pérez government to articulate a clear position. Earlier, Caldera had implicitly reached the decision to pursue national and international interests apart from Brazil. On January 2, 1976 the current president told foreign newsmen and guests that he anticipated a significant growth in exports of petroleum to Brazil as a consequence of Venezuelan nationalization.[28]

For Venezuela, despite the public imprecision of its policy toward Brazil and the absence of a clearly enunciated policy, there is a less strong sense of alarm under Pérez than was the case with Caldera. Restiveness over the border situation is perhaps exaggerated, although the armed forces are by no means the only ones to be preoccupied. The psychological element remains central to Venezuelan attitudes, as suggested by the ferocity with which the press and non-governmental political elites responded to Henry Kissinger's gratuitous public recognition of Brazil as having great-power status in February 1976.

That the two nations may ultimately seek more cordial and collaborative ties is by no means inconceivable. Brazil might well continue to be confronted by serious balance of payments problems, alleviation of which could come through an accord with Venezuela on petroleum products. Moreover, conflict with the United States and other industrialized countries over export markets could enhance Brazil's sense of solidarity with Venezuela and Mexico toward a new international economic order. Thus there need be no sense of inevitability about future disagreement between Venezuela and Brazil. At the same time, it remains to be seen how long the pragmatism of the Pérez government will permit the short-term luxury of imprecision in the articulation of policy toward Brazil.

V. Conclusions: Toward the Future

While the overarching commitment to Latin American unity and integration has been evident, a delineation of specific

[187]

Venezuelan policy priorities is elusive. In at least one sense, the category of bilateral relations bearing the potential for conflict may be the most fundamental. Whatever the outcome of both hemispheric and sub-regional policies, territorial integrity and national security necessarily lie at the core of foreign policy interests. Latent political conflict with Brazil, Colombia, and Guyana also incorporates important economic concerns as well. While bilateral diplomatic negotiations are not being uniformly emphasized at this writing, in the long run Venezuelan policy toward Latin America must focus clearly and directly on these military/security problems.

Of greater immediacy—if ultimately less basic to national survival—are the other two categories. Sub-regional policies in particular will continue to provide a fertile field for the extension of Venezuelan power and influence. Penetration of the Caribbean and Central America can be expected to continue. Although increasing domestic economic pressures will diminish the flow of public funds into the area, the basic thrust will continue. Venezuelan private investment will also increase the nation's presence, notwithstanding the inevitable sensitivity of recipient countries. Thus both the Caribbean and Central American elements of Venezuelan foreign policy, notably the former, will remain important. Prospects for the Andean region are far less promising in the light of the Pact's rapid deterioration, the latter being an inevitability with Chile's withdrawal. This in turn augurs poorly for the SELA; while the efficacy with which it was conceived and born remains impressive, the eventual success of the organization is by no means assured.

The implementation of foreign policy at all three levels— hemispheric, sub-regional, and bilateral—also carries seeds of conflict. Competition with Brazil will continue; the departure of Luis Echeverría from the Mexican presidency may affect the present spirit of cordiality; and resentment from such nations as Argentina and Peru is more likely to increase than diminish. Among the sub-regions, Caribbean and Central American worries have already been suggested. Eric Williams' charges are but the most widely publicized. In May 1975, for one, the Guatemalan magazine *Competencia* editorialized that the Mexican-Venezuelan partnership reflected "obvious expansionist designs on Central America and the Caribbean, whose principal instrument of persuasion will be oil." Dominican President Joaquín Balaguer complained at an IDB meeting that Venezuela was in the process of beggaring its neighbors. Thus, given the magnitude of Venezuelan activities beyond its borders, further underlined by the *élan* with which the nation has been operating, tensions will periodically be experienced. The realities of oil are obviously central to the problem. But the consequences are mixed for both Venezuela and the Third World consumers. With the latter, the effective victory and continued domination of OPEC is highly satisfying. This has moderated any serious inclination to challenge either OPEC in general or Venezuela in particular; the avowed movement toward a "new international economic order" is psychologically and economically uppermost. Yet the fact remains that the Latin American oil consumers have suffered from high prices more heavily than have the industrialized nations. Even the three-pronged Venezuelan policy designed to soften the immediate blow is in a sense a stopgap measure. In the end, the money is to be repaid, along with accumulated interest.

The Venezuelan response, in citing its arrangements in Central America and elsewhere, customarily argues against the thesis that oil producers are the source of the problem. Rather, the historical responsibility lies with the great industrial centers, and their complaints are designed to destroy

[189]

Third World solidarity. Carlos Andrés Pérez has noted that criticizing the oil producers is tantamount to blaming the thermometer for a high fever. The ultimate and decisive resolution of existing inequities will only come through a restructuring of basic global relationships, whereby an equilibrium might emerge between producers of raw materials, on the one hand, and those of manufactured and capital goods on the other.

Such debate is profound in its complexities, and lies well beyond the scope of this discussion. Suffice it to say that Venezuela's relationships with Latin American consumers of petroleum will be increasingly responsive to such pressures as time passes. Will the pursuit of Venezuela's foreign policy objectives produce more harmonious relationships, or will they provoke escalating levels of intra-regional conflict? At this juncture, the indicators appear mixed. Hemispheric affairs are likely to be at least indirectly enhanced by the continued Venezuelan exercise of leadership among Third World nations, whereby the voice of Latin America will be increasingly respected. Moreover, promotion of the SELA as well as the accrual of short-term benefits from Venezuelan economic policy in Central America and the Caribbean also suggest a possible strengthening of hemispheric solidarity.

The adoption of a foreign policy designed to maximize broad objectives nevertheless remains susceptible to the pressures of domestic factors. To begin with, highest priority in the final analysis continues to be given to Venezuela's internal development, and this is unlikely to change. Consequently, national resources will be channelled primarily into a growing array of massive economic reforms and enlarged social programs; foreign policy will receive comparatively less energy and attention. Moreover, national interest groups will also constrict the government's freedom of action. The armed

[190]

forces have adopted a posture which limits options toward Colombia and Guyana. It is also possible that preoccupation with Brazil's Amazonian development will necessitate compromise on Pérez's part. Similarly, the business community remains deeply troubled over the potential impact of full Venezuelan collaboration in the Andean Pact. Links between the private sector and public elites are powerful, and no government in Caracas can be indifferent to such interests. In contrast the enthusiasm of the private sector over Caribbean penetration is evident.

Returning once again to the fundamental objective of hemispheric unity, prospects by the close of 1976 had dimmed perceptibly in comparison with the situation when the administration took office. The two greatest sources of difficulty remained Cuba and Brazil. The Pérez administration has never enjoyed a clear national consensus in support of its warming toward Cuba. A controversial clash with Cuban authorities at Venezuela's Havana embassy, centering on the status of would-be political refugees, produced editorial criticism in Caracas. The large size of the Cuban mission to Venezuela also provoked suspicion. When Fidel Castro embarked upon his Angolan intervention, the climate of official sentiment also cooled markedly. One result was Pérez's joining with other chiefs of state in calling off the projected sesquicentennial celebration in Panama, to which Castro had been invited.

The relationship between Caracas and Havana has remained in a state of flux. Following the October 1976 sabotage of a Cuban airliner in which Cuban exiles carrying Venezuelan passports were implicated, Pérez sent a strongly sympathetic message to Castro expressing profound indignation and regret. At the same time, powerful opposition from the large Caracas colony of Cuban exiles—most of whom had become naturalized Venezuelan citizens—was manifested anew by the machine-gunning of the Cuban embassy from a passing car. The initiative in the relationship is clearly on the side of Castro, at least for the immediate future. Barring new Cuban adventures in Africa or, more damagingly, in Latin America, the Pérez administration will probably maintain its stance of cordiality. Both official and private economic and commercial exchanges will grow, with Venezuela remaining an advocate of normalization of hemispheric ties with Cuba. Should Castro's priorities dictate foreign interventionism, however, Venezuela will then be subjected to virtually overwhelming domestic pressures to freeze or to reduce the Caracas-Havana connection.

With Brazil, pressures for the articulation of a clearer policy have been gradually increasing. In 1976 the drumfire of alarmist reports in Venezuelan papers and newsweeklies built toward a crescendo. Both civilian and military sources spoke to the issue of greater Brazilian activity along its nothern border area. In June a Senate commission quizzed members of the foreign ministry on the situation, and the President himself linked criticism of Henry Kissinger's posture toward Brazil with the latter's move to develop a nuclear capability. In the long run, two options appear possible. Following the inclinations of Rafael Caldera and Arístides Calvani, Venezuela can focus on its ties with both Spanish- and English-speaking countries as a means of providing a counterbalance to Brazilian power. This, of course, would constitute in part a denial of the vision of a united, fully collaborative Latin America in its dealings with the rest of the world. Alternatively, efforts might be undertaken, as during the creation of the SELA, to remain responsive to the sensitivities and objectives of Itamarati. It could attempt a closing of the breach through both symbolic gestures between the two presidents and concrete economic and trade agreements. By mid-1977 there were as yet few indications that Venezuela had made a choice. If one were to engage in reasoned speculation, however, it would appear most probable that as visions of Bolivarian unity continue to suffer setbacks elsewhere in the hemisphere, Venezuela will find itself drawn into a closer and mutually supportive relationship with Brazil. This is clearly the preference of the latter, and its goal is likely in time to elicit a sympathetic response from Caracas.

At the broadest level, in sum, Venezulean initiatives momentarily enhanced the prospects for greater hemispheric solidarity and unity. Yet the equation is far from neat, especially given the unresolved policy stance toward Cuba and Brazil. The Andean Pact has been seemingly shattered by Chile, and the SELA will perhaps be damaged in the process. Moreover, the years immediately ahead will not see the quantitative wealth and diversity of overseas economic and financial commitments which marked the first two years of the Pérez government. As Kuczynski notes, growing domestic demands upon existing resources are multiplying as the republic has nationalized its petroleum industry. A shift in emphasis over the utilization of oil revenues has already taken place. Thus, while both the present administration and its successor can be expected to continue Venezuela's activist foreign policy, potential sources for conflict remain.

Finally, there are a pair of psychological factors which provide important if somewhat intangible inputs into the Venezuelan milieu. Historically, the nation was relegated to a minor role in hemispheric affairs. The experience since 1958 has been insufficient to create a tradition out of which the capacity to enunciate and carry forward foreign policy flows easily and naturally. The quality of the diplomatic corps itself is decidedly uneven, although with time greater professional-

[193]

ization should produce a higher overall level of performance. Moreover, there is a diffusion of policy-making responsibilities among a number of individuals and groups: the ministers of mines, finance, planning, and international economic affairs; the president of PETROVEN; the presidential advisory commission on foreign affairs; and respective congressional commissions all play a part. Even without an activist president such as Pérez, many decisions necessarily must be resolved only at his desk.

Perhaps even more fundamental is Venezuela's singular position as a democratic island in a sea of authoritarian regimes. As a bastion of pluralistic politics in Latin America, Venezuela is highly conscious of its image. The projection of responsible democratic leadership permits a moral legitimacy which few countries in the hemisphere now possess. A striking illustration came after the assassination in Washington of the Chilean, Orlando Letelier. His body was returned to Venezuela for burial, where President Pérez participated in the various ceremonies. This represented a further assertion of Venezuela's democratic vocation, at the same time seriously affecting already cool relations with the government of Chile. It thereby underlined a fundamental weakness in Venezuela's effort to provide hemispheric leadership, although embodying Caracas' legitimate claims to moral authority in international affairs.

We noted at the outset our theses concerning contemporary Venezuelan foreign policy toward Latin America, and have elaborated upon them. Taken in conjunction with the "neo-imperialist" seeds of conflict in Central America and the Caribbean, added to the impending collapse of the Andean Group and the adolescent growing pains of the SELA, and compounded by the crucial relationships with Cuba and Brazil, in both of which the initiative lies in their hands rather than

Venezuela's, there are valid grounds to question Venezuelan capacity to realize its most ambitious objectives in the hemisphere. Carlos Andrés Pérez remains an activist in foreign policy, stubbornly committed to the ideals of regional unity, and determined himself to personify Venezuelan leadership in Latin America. His vision and ambition will not lightly or easily be discarded. Yet the obstacles are profound, and many forces continue to lie beyond the influence of Venezuelan economic power and moral suasion. Thus it will not be surprising if the next few years see some diminution of foreign policy activism and a less sweeping definition of goals and objectives. Venezuela may well employ its yet powerful economic resources in a more subtle and less grandiose fashion, emphasizing instead its commitment to democracy. This latter stance may prove felicitous if, as some have speculated, United States policy toward Latin America undergoes change with the Carter Administration. At the least, Venezuela will remain an important and influential actor in the international affairs of Latin America and, barring a collapse of its present political system, will increasingly speak out on behalf of the historic ideals of freedom and human rights.

NOTES

1. For the text, see *Resumen* (Caracas), 16 de mayo de 1976, p. 14.

2. *Resumen,* 22 de diciembre de 1974, p. 16.

3. For an English version of Leoni's full statement, see *Venezuela Up-to-date,* 12 (Winter 1968-69), p. 8.

4. Among his many statements and discussions of the subject, see

Rafael Caldera, *El bloque latinoamericano,* 2d ed. (Mérida: Universidad de los Andes, 1966); *Especificidad de la democracia cristiana* (Barcelona: Editorial Nova Terra, 1973); and *Justicia social internacional y nacionalismo latinoamericano* (Madrid: Seminarios y Ediciones, S.A., 1973).

5. Rafael Caldera, *Discurso a la nación* (Caracas: Imprenta Nacional, 1969).

6. For extended treatment of electoral issues, see John D. Martz and Enrique A. Baloyra, *Political Participation and Mobilization: The Venezuelan Campaign of 1973* (Chapel Hill: University of North Carolina Press, December 1976).

7. Carlos Andrés Pérez, *Acción de gobierno* (Caracas: n.p., 1973), p. 78.

8. Carlos Andrés Pérez, *Discurso a la nación* (Caracas: Imprenta Nacional, 1974).

9. For official translations which were placed as full-page advertisements in leading North American dailies, see issues from September 22-24, 1974.

10. The text appears as "Discurso del Canciller de Venezuela ante la Asamblea de las Naciones Unidas," *Resumen,* 20 de octubre de 1974, pp. 4-7.

11. "Interview with President Pérez: What the Third World Wants." *Business Week,* October 13, 1975, as reproduced in *Venezuela Now,* I, no. 6 (October 15, 1975), pp. 22-23.

12. Constitutional complications prevented immediate signing by Grenada and Barbados, but in due course they too adhered to the SELA accord.

[196]

13. "Interview with President Pérez," reproduced in *Venezuela Now*, 23.

14. For a thorough discussion and dialogue, see *Resumen*, 24 de noviembre de 1974, which includes lengthy interviews with both Calvani and Schacht.

15. From a speech to Williams' Peoples National Movement; the text was reported throughout Venezuela in its press the week following.

16. The Caribbean Development Bank identifies as "less-developed territories" the islands of Antigua, Cayman, Dominica, Grenada, Montserrat, St. Kitts-Nevis, St. Lucia, St. Vincent, the Turks and Caicos, and the non-U.S. Virgin Islands.

17. These included Antigua, Dominica, Grenada, Montserrat, St. Kitts-Nevis-Anguilla, St. Lucia, and St. Vincent.

18. Venezuela received 10 percent ownership in the plant; other shareholders were Jamaica 51 percent, Mexico 29 percent, and Kaiser Aluminum, 10 percent.

19. The agency was slow to become operable, for shortly thereafter a disastrous frost destroyed much of the Brazilian harvest, thereby assuring high prices for the Central American coffee producers.

20. Mexico and Venezuela were joined by all the Central American countries; Caribbean states to send delegations included Barbados, Cuba, the Dominican Republic, Guyana, Grenada, Haiti, Jamaica, and Trinidad-Tobago.

21. The text appears in *Resumen*, 10 de agosto de 1975, p. 13.

22. Authorized to finance up to 25 percent of the cost of integration

programs, it only began to exercise a meaningful role in 1974, after devoting initial years largely to a host of feasibility studies.

23. An anecdotal illustration of the Pérez-López Michelsen friendship was the fact that following completion of Pérez's successful electoral campaign, he sent a key adviser, Diego Arria (later Governor of the Federal District) to Colombia with audio technicians who advised López's campaign team.

24. Among its major provisions were commitments to collaboration in winning economic independence; controlling natural resources; protecting the prices of raw materials; regulating foreign investment; and controlling multinational activities. A definition of Latin American nationalism was also articulated: *"El nacionalismo latinoamericano constituye la toma de conciencia de nuestros pueblos sobre su realidad profunda y su verdadera personalidad, fruto del mestizaje de sangre, fusión de culturas y comunes vivencias históricas, sociales y económicas."*

25. Diplomacy with Chile and Argentina has been less active. With the former, coolness toward the repressive military regime has been noticeable from the outset. In the Argentine case, Venezuelan overtures toward Buenos Aires have produced little response. Already outstripped by its Brazilian rival, Argentina has been less than pleased with Venezuela's growing prominence.

26. The Caracas media have also disseminated a host of reports alleging the presence of Cuban "advisers" at Guyanan military training camps.

27. For example, see the two-part series by Nikita Harwich Vallenilla, "La frontera dormida," *Resumen*, 20 y 27 de julio de 1975, pp. 28-36 and pp. 6-10.

28. Conference at Miraflores Palace, January 2, 1976, from notes by author, who attended.

[SIX]

The United States and Venezuela: Prospects for Accommodation

Franklin Tugwell

INTRODUCTION[1]

During the last decade and a half, and especially since 1970, Venezuela has emerged as an independent and assertive actor in international politics. In Latin America it must now be counted among the handful of countries—others include Brazil, Peru, Mexico and Cuba—able to exert significant influence beyond their borders; at the global level it has won a recognized place as a leader of the developing nations in the ongoing dialogue about the future of the international economic order.

For the United States, Venezuela's active diplomacy is significant for several reasons. It presents a clear test of America's ability to adapt constructively to a rapidly changing geopolitical configuration in the Western Hemisphere. At stake also is a system of long-standing economic and political bonds between the two countries. In comparison to most other Latin American countries, Venezuela is more thoroughly tied to, and generally oriented toward, the United States. As I have pointed out elsewhere in this book, it is a vitally important source of imported oil, sending over a million barrels of crude and petroleum products to American shores every day. It is also a valuable customer: in 1975 Venezuelan purchases of American goods and services totaled more than $2.3 billion.

It is the object of this essay to analyze the challenges Venezuela's new role poses for American statecraft, and to consider the possibilities for future U.S. policies that may more successfully promote the welfare of both countries. With respect to these matters, I advance three main theses. The first is that, while the United States has on several occasions granted Venezuela special treatment in pursuit of hemispheric Cold War objectives, it has nevertheless often been short-sighted in failing to recognize, in day-to-day policy decisions, the long-term security value of Venezuelan petroleum. The second is that because of the distinctively conciliatory and constructive character of Venezuela's diplomatic style, there are opportunities, not just sources of irritation, to be found in Venezuela's role as an advocate of Latin American economic independence and as a spokesman of the developing nations. The third is that the most difficult, but most important, future task of American statecraft as it concerns Venezuela is to see beyond the frictions between the two nations (frictions which will surely persist in many lesser policy areas) to the long-term significance of Venezuela's effort to build a stable and legitimate democracy, an effort which will very likely come under serious strain in the near future.

To clarify and support these conclusions, I briefly review

[200]

recent Venezuelan-American relations and then turn, first, to those issues arising out of Venezuela's status as a principal supplier of oil to the United States, and second, to the broader problems and tensions stemming from Venezuela's new diplomatic activism in behalf of causes opposed by the United States. In the final section I attempt to assess some of the implications of a very mixed policy legacy and consider future problems and possibilities.

BACKGROUND

To place current Venezuelan-American relations in perspective, it is helpful to begin by recalling the remarkable convergence of policy objectives that brought the two countries together during the early 1960s in support of an ambitious development program and in the conduct of an energetic diplomatic offensive within the Hemisphere. It was the combination of Kennedy's Alliance for Progress and Betancourt's determination to protect his vulnerable government with an assertive foreign policy that created the conditions for this period of unusually close cooperation and friendship.[2] The developmental aspirations and democratic character of the Venezuelan regime fit neatly the strategic objectives of the Alliance, and Kennedy, many of whose advisers had close personal ties to Betancourt, chose Venezuela to be the "showcase" for his Latin American policy. Accordingly, the American president went out of his way to demonstrate his support for the government in Caracas. Foreign aid; a presidential visit; the appointment of Puerto Rican Teodoro Moscoso (a friend of Betancourt) as the U.S. Ambassador to Venezuela; the extradition of Pérez Jiménez to face trial in Venezuela—all served to reinforce the conclusion

CONTEMPORARY VENEZUELA

that both countries shared a deep commitment to human rights and democratic development.

Although the United States soon grew uncomfortable with the Betancourt Doctrine, which asserted the obligation of Hemispheric governments to use diplomatic sanctions to protect democratic regimes against their authoritarian enemies (domestic and foreign), Venezuela's break with Cuba in late 1961 and Castro's decision to make Venezuela the principal target in his effort to promote new revolutionary movements in Latin America, assured a continuing "fit" between the central policy objectives of the two countries. Caracas subsequently supported the US decision to force the withdrawal of Soviet missiles from Cuba—Venezuelan naval vessels actually participated in the OAS-approved quarantine of Cuba—and in 1963, following the discovery of a cache of arms traceable to Cuba, brought formal charges of aggression against Castro in the OAS.

Overall, Venezuelan leadership in the effort to isolate Castro in the Hemisphere was an important contribution to American Cold War strategy in the region, and in return policymakers in Washington for a period downplayed such irritants as the growing tension between American oil companies and the Venezuelan government, and Caracas' trenchant opposition to military dictatorships, some of which (e.g., Brazil) Washington actively supported.

The close ties of the early Cold War years, however, eroded steadily after the mid-1960s as the guerrilla challenge in Venezuela and Latin America subsided and as Venezuelan governments began to take a more independent stance on many policy issues. Raúl Leoni strongly criticized U.S. intervention in the Dominican Republic in 1965, and he and his successors frequently expressed their discomfort with American policy in Vietnam. Venezuela also became increasingly committed to the promotion of "Third World" causes, both in the United Nations and its agencies, where representatives from Caracas supported the "Group of Seventy-Seven," and within Hemispheric forums, where Latin American solidarity, often in opposition to the United States, emerged as an important policy concern.

These changes, combined with frictions arising over OPEC and oil trade matters, contributed to a gradual cooling of Venezuelan-American relations in the late 1960s and into the 1970s. In order to better assess the prospects for accommodations in the future, it is helpful first to examine the most important sources of conflict in greater detail.

OIL, OPEC AND THE UNITED STATES MARKET

Oil is, of course, Venezuela's lifeline, and conflicts over the status of the oil industry and over oil trade have been irritants in U.S.-Venezuelan relations for many years. At the heart of Venezuela's oil policy since 1958 has been the conviction that control of the production and commerce of petroleum by private foreign companies is fundamentally incompatible with the nation's interests. Successive governments sought to restrict the freedom of action of these companies, extract more income from them, and prepare for their eventual domestication. As I noted in my chapter on nationalization, the result was a drawn-out, often bitter, process of conflict and bargaining. The existence of a smouldering hostility between branches of some of the largest U.S. private corporations and the government of Venezuela created an ever-present source of tension between the two countries. No American administration was able to ignore this circumstance when dealing with Venezuela. Thus, although close Venezuelan-American

[203]

ties during the Alliance heyday for a period led policymakers in Washington to downplay oil company petitions for assistance, in the absence of an overriding concern for national security a confusion of private and public goals and obligations has tended to obscure opportunities to promote other, often more important, long-range American interests. Among the specific sources of tension and disagreement between Venezuela and the United States, two prominent ones, related to oil prices and supply, need to be discussed in greater detail.

Consider prices first. Since the production lifetime of Venezuela's regular oil reserves is relatively limited, the government is strongly committed to maintaining high prices. In the past this has been true even if it meant some sacrifice in terms of production quantities. Indeed, hoping to conserve oil for the future and at the same time help OPEC handle the recent market surplus without price erosion, Venezuela has made significant reductions in production on a voluntary basis. Another reason for Venezuela's commitment to high prices, probably more important in the long run, is that the utilization of the Orinoco heavy oil deposits, upon which Venezuela hopes to rely increasingly after the next decade, will require very high prices. Production of marketable petroleum from this region may cost from $7 to $10, perhaps even more, per barrel. This means, in contrast to oil currently being produced, that government income per barrel is likely to be very low. Assuming costs in the range indicated, and little real increase in prices, Venezuela would have to produce enormous quantities to realize the same fiscal dividend—up to sixteen million barrels per day.[3]

At preparatory and full OPEC meetings Venezuela has consistently sought to persuade its fellow members to raise both prices and tax levels by substantial amounts, the latter to increase producer income but also to place an effective floor

[204]

under prices. At Quito in 1974 Venezuela proposed a very substantial increase in taxes but its proposal was dropped, in favor of a very small increase in royalties along with stable prices, after the Saudis indicated they favored a 20 percent reduction in prices.

More recently, again to protect high prices, Venezuela has increasingly assumed the role of mediator in OPEC. As the world oil surplus of the mid-1970s increased tensions within the price "camps" in the organization, Venezuela has often been the initiator and promoter of compromise. In the critical Vienna meeting of September 1975, for example, the final decision to raise prices by 10 percent was the result of careful Venezuelan diplomacy. As one source reported it, Venezuela "emerged in a central role as a responsible conciliator with President Carlos Andrés Pérez personally telephoning the Shah of Iran and the Crown Prince of Saudia Arabia in pursuit of a compromise." [4] Venezuela has also sought to negotiate a compromise to the current stalemate within OPEC over pricing policy (the "two-tier" controversy).

Clearly therefore, one of the most significant areas of conflict of interest between the United States and Venezuela is over oil prices. American energy policy, as enunciated, has as a central goal the denial to OPEC of the power to set international oil prices, plus the reduction of oil prices if possible, though not below the Minimum Safeguard Price (MSP) of $7 per barrel chosen by the members of the International Energy Agency (IEA). Even partial success on the part of the United States and the IEA in these areas would have very serious consequences for Venezuela.

This conflict of interest is real and, as posed by stated U.S. policy, is not susceptible to compromise—it is zero-sum, in the classic sense. However, it would appear that the American commitment to this objective is weakening quickly. The reasons for the change are beyond the scope of this essay, but its effect may be to blunt the edge of actual conflict on this issue. Indeed, the most widely accepted forecasts of international price trends suggest that prices are not likely to decrease in a way that will be threatening to Venezuela.[5]

The question of petroleum supply is also important to both countries. Venezuela needs stable, secure markets. And American policies with respect to Venezuelan imports may affect significantly the degree of U.S. dependence upon insecure sources of oil. The forecasts of the Federal Energy Administration (FEA) and others now indicate that the United States is not going to achieve energy independence in the foreseeable future—Project Independence notwithstanding. This is not surprising. What it does mean, however, is that the United States, for security reasons, must begin paying much more careful attention to its overall pattern of oil supply, acknowledging the importance of those supply sources that create the least vulnerability to manipulation or embargo. Unfortunately, U.S. energy policy administrators have not yet accepted the full implications of this conclusion. A key problem in this respect seems to be their current inability and unwillingness to consider the imposition upon the private companies (those currently controlling import levels and origins) of a government-determined preferred "profile" of import sources.[6]

The most serious disagreement between the two countries concerning oil supply has been over the treatment of Venezuelan petroleum in the overall U.S. oil import system. Put in the simplest, most direct way, the Venezuelan government feels, and has argued for years, that it should be granted a special status in its trade relationship with the United States because of its role as a major supplier of oil and oil products.

Venezuela gives several reasons for this claim: (1) It has for years been one of the most important sources of petroleum imports to the United States. (2) Though a member and founder of OPEC, it has never embargoed the United States or used its oil as a means of political blackmail; indeed, its trade pattern as it currently stands is one of such interdependence that such an action would be virtually impossible. (3) During times of crisis—World War II, Korea, Vietnam, the various Middle East wars—it remained a reliable provider of petroleum. (4) Although it has nationalized the industry, it has paid adequate compensation, which all the important companies have accepted (although the companies have accepted, many do not feel that the amounts paid were adequate), and, perhaps more important, it has established a good working relationship with the large American multinationals, thus assuring the continuation of supply to its established American market. (5) Finally, it is a fellow democracy.

For a number of different reasons, including the complicated interest group struggle affecting U.S. decisions on oil imports, the influence of the major oil companies with a stake in Venezuela, the general lack of central coordination in energy policy matters in the United Stats, and the lack of congressional expertise in these matters, Venezuela has been repeatedly denied the special status it has requested. When mandatory oil import control was established in the United States in 1958-59, Venezuela suggested an intergovernmental agreement among the hemispheric countries supplying oil to the United States (Canada, Venezuela, and to a lesser degree, Mexico) in order to prorate supply according to U.S. requirements. Such an agreement would grant hemispheric producers a "preference," recognizing their status as more secure sources of oil. The United States decided instead to exempt Canada and Mexico from the mandatory system, but to leave Venezuelan status untouched.[7]

The mandatory import program was a source of continual strain and friction between the United States and Venezuela until its termination in 1973. Drifting along without a real energy policy, and seeking to protect the interests of American corporations operating in Venezuela, the United States government repeatedly turned down Venezuela's petitions for preferential status in the U.S. market—this, despite the recommendation of a high-level task force that a hemisphere preference be adopted in order to avoid increasing reliance on less secure Arab oil.[8] The only exception to this was with respect to imports of heavy fuel oil, and in this case the exception was made for the wrong reasons from Venezuela's standpoint: American refineries preferred to produce as little residual fuel oil as possible, preferring instead to turn their crude into more profitable commodities such as gasoline and use imported fuel oil to supply the U.S. demand. With this exception, however, Venezuela could accomplish little. The large international companies had firmly decided upon a "non-hemispheric preference" with respect to imports since costs were lower in the Middle East and North Africa and since they strongly resented Venezuela's tougher controls, tax laws, and impending takeover.

In 1972 and early 1973 American representatives initiated discussions with Venezuela concerning the development of the heavy oil deposits in the Orinoco basin in eastern Venezuela. These discussions were held before the large price increases in the fall of 1973, and President Caldera was looking eagerly for capital in order to assure a healthy future rate of production. The United States suggested the possibility of guaranteed market access for Orinoco oil, but in return asked for long-term guarantees of security and profits for the American companies that would provide the necessary investment capital. As might be expected, however, the negotiations were stillborn. Indeed they proved a political liability to Caldera when it became public that they had taken place. Although security in marketing was desirable, Venezuela was in the midst of an election campaign in which both major candidates had acknowledged the need to "accelerate" reversion. Under these circumstances, the government was unlikely to agree to new guarantees to American oil companies.

After the energy "crisis" and the embargo by the Organization of Arab Petroleum Exporting Countries (OAPEC) in 1973-74, a few Venezuelans hoped that they would finally receive the special status they desired. This, however, did not come about. On the contrary, when the old import control program was finally abandoned, subsequent regulatory changes tended to place Venezuelan imports, especially fuel oil, at a price disadvantage in Venezuela's traditional East Coast U.S. market. The severity of this disadvantage was reduced in the spring of 1976 administrative adjustment in what is known as the Entitlements Program (designed to equalize the benefits among refiners accruing from the price difference between domestic and imported oil), and Venezuelans are hoping that Congress will acquiesce to the Administration's request that fuel oil prices be decontrolled, thereby improving its competitive standing in the American market. But the basic attitudes toward Venezuela remain clear.

And then, adding insult to injury, the U.S. Congress included in the important 1974 Trade Act, signed by President Ford in January 1975, a provision excluding by definition all OPEC members from the benefits conferred by the new Generalized System of Preferences (GSP) authorized by the Act. This was apparently done partially because of the misconception (quite common) that it was OPEC, rather than OAPEC, that embargoed the United States. Both President Ford and Secretary Kissinger subsequently urged a reconsideration of this provision, introducing legislation in both houses of Congress which would modify the "OPEC" clause in such a way as to permit Venezuela (and Ecuador, also affected) to benefit from GSP adjustments. However, despite considerable urging, including a personal appeal by the Secretary, Congress at the time of writing does not appear willing to act on the request.

Carlos Andrés Pérez reacted vigorously to the special discrimination in the Trade Act. He sent an urgent message to all member states of the Organization of American States (OAS) requesting a special meeting of the OAS Council to consider the action, and a meeting of that group two weeks later produced a resolution (twenty votes in favor) condemning the act and expressing "profound preoccupation with the deterioration of inter-American solidarity provoked by certain clauses of the law." [9] There was a great deal of sympathy among the other Latin American countries for the Venezuelan position on this issue. The precise effect of the exclusion is not yet known although one estimate is that about $35 million worth of annual Venezuelan exports to the United States of manufactured goods will be affected. Oil is not affected directly.

The real damage of the Trade Act, of course, is symbolic. It confirms the worst fears and frustrations of the Venezuelans with respect to their hope for recognition of the special role Venezuelan oil has played in supplying American needs. For practical purposes, there can be no doubt: Venezuelan oil is the same as Arab oil in U.S. eyes.

If its heavy reliance on the U.S. market is one source of insecurity for Venezuela, another is its dependence on large U.S. corporations for the marketing of its product. After taking over the industry, Venezuela was not able to place its oil at the levels desired—approximately 2-2.2 million barrels a day (mbd) in exports—without some very tough bargaining with the former concessionaires. These companies sought to use their new position as "off-shore buyers" to force the government to bring its prices down below the levels government negotiators had set as conforming with OPEC's standards. Venezuelan negotiators held out, and finally placed the amount they intended, but only after some very frightening moments. Since the original negotiations, the market has improved and it seems clear that Venezuela will succeed in its marketing effort. But the lesson was not lost; Venezuelans were made to feel very insecure indeed. PETROVEN will now have to handle marketing, and this is the area of the petroleum industry which Venezuelans are least prepared to handle. To make matters worse, Venezuela's marketing job is very difficult compared to that of the other OPEC countries. As one observer has noted, "there is not much doubt that the nationalization operation is a very much more ticklish one than any attempted in other areas such as the Middle East. Venezuela exports a much larger proportion of finished products than any Middle East country." [10] Actually, just under half of Venezuela's exports are in the form of refined products. All of this adds up to a different but very pronounced form of dependence on the international companies, and a new and direct vulnerability to the world oil market.

Given these circumstances, it is not surprising that the Venezuelan Government and PETROVEN management have already made it clear that they hope to reorient the country's market in two ways:

1) To circumvent the international companies wherever possible without sacrificing price realizations. There are

several ways of doing this and Venezuela is actively exploring all of them. First there is the possibility of state-to-state arrangements. These have proven difficult since most governments have tried to bargain for price reductions, which Venezuela has not been willing to entertain. (Actually, most experts feel that the much discussed state-to-state alternative is not going to materialize in the immediate future, except for small amounts, but may grow with time.) Second, there is the option of direct agreements with individual refineries and individual public utilities. Here the possibilities are better and it is very likely that Venezuela will be moving in this direction in the near future. This will allow long-term, secure agreements that need not damage prices, but will displace the companies as intermediaries.

2) To diversify markets, so that a company decision to supply from other sources a critical, large volume Venezuelan market, such as the U.S. East Coast heating fuel market, would not damage Venezuela as severely. In this respect there is considerable concern in Venezuela about the encroachment of Mexican oil in this traditional Venezuelan market area. Caracas is also strongly interested in providing an increasing proportion of the import requirements of other Latin American countries. Brazil, one of the largest importers among the developing nations, is the object of special attention. Venezuela now has less than 2 percent of the Brazilian market, and Carlos Andrés Pérez has stated several times that he hopes to increase that percentage considerably. As economies grow in Latin America generally, Venezuela expects demand to increase and hopes to become a more important source of supply to the countries of the region. Whether or not it will be able to do so, or to what extent, is now unclear. Changing marketing and refining patterns will take time and may exact a

price in lost income. The commitment, however, remains and has important implications for the United States.

THE "OPEN" HEMISPHERE AND THE NEW INTERNATIONAL ECONOMIC ORDER

In the last half decade Latin America has, so to speak, "opened up" as far as international relationships are concerned. There is more heterogeneity, and a new fluidity in bilateral and multilateral ties. Visible too is a kind of groping for a regional understanding about legitimate collective objectives and appropriate policy means. Most of the larger and more prosperous Latin American countries have grown more experienced, more self-confident, and more self-assertive, accepting the responsibility for shaping their own future. This is true especially of those countries that have begun to consolidate strong central governments. Related to this trend is the new inclination on the part of a number of states to dismantle, or at least modify, the U.S.-designed hemispheric institutions created originally to handle Cold War problems, and to replace these with ones that (1) address the more immediate issues of development and facilitate the cooperative action needed to boost that development, and (2) tolerate diversity and ideological experimentation.

For a number of countries this has led also to a hesitant, but growing, advocacy of a more openly adversarial relationship with the United States. The new relationship would keep Washington at arm's length, available for bargaining on problems of clear concern to most or all Latin American countries, but distant enough to open up Latin America as a region to a more active pattern of subregional international interactions—this to be increasingly shaped by the Latin American "middle powers" themselves—and to allow Latin America to engage more actively in the ongoing dialogue and bargaining over global economic arrangements.[11]

As mentioned earlier, Venezuela has in recent years been an eager supporter of these changes in the international relations of the Western Hemisphere and has worked diligently, in surprisingly diverse ways, to build a reputation as a leader of the process of transformation. In doing so it has experienced some success, but in the process has found itself increasingly a source of irritation and concern to the United States.

In addition to organizing a series of consultative meetings of Latin American heads of state, Venezuela was a prime mover, with Mexico, in the creation of the Sistema Económico Latino-americano (SELA), an institution Venezuela hoped would facilitate communication among Latin Americans and provide a constructive framework for an adversarial dialogue with the United States on key development issues. And in the Organization of American States, Venezuela supported the effort to reassimilate Cuba as well as the reform of the Rio Treaty codifying the acceptance of "ideological pluralism" in the Hemisphere. It also joined Mexico and others in asking the abolition of the special Inter-American Defense Commission Against Communism. These measures in support of ideological pluralism deserve special mention because they reflect an important change in the doctrinal orientation of Venezuelan foreign policy that has taken place since the middle 1960s. As noted earlier, in the first years after the ouster of Pérez Jiménez, Betancourt viewed foreign policy as an instrument in his effort to prevent a resurgence of authoritarianism—of the left or right—in Venezuelan politics. The United States supported the Betancourt Doctrine in principle during the early days of the Alliance for Progress, but Cold War anxieties soon made Washington uncomfortable with Venezuela's stress on the primacy of human rights and the defense of democracy. The United States, of course, continued to encourage Venezuela's efforts to isolate and weaken Cuba. By the mid-1960s, however, Venezuelan presidents too had begun gradually to mute their adherence to the Doctrine. The polity had grown more secure against conspiracies assisted from abroad and Betancourt's successors found the Doctrine an impediment in their efforts to promote regional economic cooperation and to establish Venezuela as a leader in the search for Latin American solidarity. Rafael Caldera formally abandoned the policy after assuming office in 1969.

At the global level, Venezuela has cultivated a leadership role in the bargaining between developed and underdeveloped countries as a member of the Group of Seventy-Seven in the United Nations and UNCTAD. Because of its activities as a member of OPEC, and as an oil producer generally, Venezuela has acquired considerable experience in the conduct of economic diplomacy. Few Latin American countries have been so extensively involved in this way at the global level, although many have greater experience within the Hemisphere. In these forums Venezuelan representatives have done their best to legitimize the role of non-market arrangements designed to improve the position of developing nations. Thus, Caracas has promoted and supported other cartelization efforts, including those in bauxite, copper, sugar, iron ore, bananas and coffee, and has backed the idea that prices for raw materials from underdeveloped countries and prices from manufactured goods from developed countries should be considered together at the international economic bargaining table.

The attitude of the United States toward Venezuela's new diplomatic activism may be characterized as one of "passive

[215]

disapproval." This is not surprising; indeed, the list of specific sources of U.S. irritation with Venezuelan diplomacy is quite long:

1) OPEC
2) SELA
3) the oil nationalization
4) raw material and primary product cartels
5) the Andean Pact and (in general) restrictions on private capital
6) the sesquicentennial "summit" program
7) the initiative to legitimize pluralism in the Rio Treaty system
8) Venezuela's sponsorship of the move to re-assimilate Cuba into the OAS and the Inter-American System
9) Venezuelan backing of Panama in the canal negotiations
10) Venezuelan efforts to bring Latin America more fully into the rich/poor adversarial dialogue
11) Venezuela's hostility to the Chilean military regime
12) the special OAS condemnation of the 1974 Trade Act, engineered by Venezuela.

Economic independence and ideological pluralism, collective institutions excluding the United States, Latin American involvement in the North-South dialogue over the international economic order—all of these promised to complicate, if not derail, hopes for a new understanding, and acceptance, of the limits within which the United States was willing to see the new Latin American international relations operate.

Commendably, and reflecting the low salience of Latin American matters generally during the Nixon and Ford years, the United States does not appear to have gone to great lengths, or turned to "irregular" means, to force Venezuela to modify its positions on these issues. As mentioned, U.S. policymakers did deny Venezuela preferential status for its oil imports; but Venezuela's new wealth made many of the standard economic levers, such as denial of access to loans from regional or global lending institutions, unavailable. And the Venezuelan elections of 1973 probably provided few opportunities for covert intervention, since no major candidate took a position that was likely to please the United States on these issues. From available evidence, it appears as though the United States relied mainly on occasional notes of disapproval, such as the one sent by President Ford on the nationalization decision, plus other gestures, such as the tapping of Brazil for a special role, to signal its displeasure.[12] These were ineffective, if not counterproductive. The prospect of Brazilian-American co-hegemony in the region's geopolitical future, for example, was hardly likely to lead Venezuela to abandon its new diplomatic activism.

FUTURE

As they stand today, the relations of the United States with Venezuela are friendly but guarded, reflecting disagreement between the countries on a broad range of issues. Although Venezuela is not viewed as a major problem area by American policymakers, its control of significant oil resources and its role as a key advocate of self-assertiveness and solidarity on the part of developing nations do pose some difficult challenges to American diplomacy.

In analyzing possible U.S. responses to these challenges, it is important at the outset to stress the importance of maintaining boundaries between issues, of preventing conflicts and disagreements on some issues, especially those that may not be amenable to compromise, from obscuring opportunities for accommodation in other areas. Oil is a case in point. Despite

[217]

the residual anger of some oil company officials, the nationalization is an accomplished fact. Among import sources, Venezuela is one of the most desirable, and the United States has a strong interest in getting as much oil from there as possible in the future. Furthermore, the American companies with the largest holdings in Venezuela are likely to continue to receive substantial income from oil operations there due to very favorable post-nationalization "technological assistance" contracts.

Overall, therefore, it is evident that the United States has a substantial stake in the success of the nationalization venture. American recognition of PETROVEN's legitimacy, and even assistance to the Venezuelan government in assuring the technical efficiency and managerial success of the nationalized industry, would probably have several beneficial consequences: it would indicate U.S. acceptance of a nationalization process that has been one of the most orderly, democratic, and cautious; it might predispose those in charge of PE-TROVEN's marketing decisions to continue the longstanding supply arrangements with the United States once the company is on its feet; [13] and it might assist Venezuela in increasing proven reserves, perhaps even by bringing new offshore discoveries and, later on, Orinoco deposits, "on stream."

Unfortunately, the history of United States policy provides strong incentives to the Venezuelans to diversify their markets as much as possible, reducing their dependence upon the United States and upon American oil companies. The mandatory oil import program, the Entitlements program, the Trade Act discrimination, and the special recognition granted Brazil, all carry a very clear message: for a variety of reasons, including American policy incompetence and lack of coordination in energy matters, the United States cannot be relied upon to reward or even recognize the security value of Venezuelan oil.

Actually, the components of a more enlightened policy are rather easy to prescribe, although it is more difficult to imagine the circumstances under which they might be adopted. To begin with, the United States should dismantle existing ad hoc disincentives, such as the Trade Act exclusion, which has no pertinence to overall energy policy. Next, the United States should accept the need to devise a comprehensive oil import plan, a plan which would, on the one hand, take into account a "profile" of preferred import sources, and would, on the other, involve the exercise of authority over import decisions rather than leaving these largely to private companies. Such an import plan, of course, would make sense only within the framework of a larger, comprehensive, realistic—not another Project Independence—national energy plan. Finally, as part of the process of determining import needs and sources, it would seem advisable to form a regional system of consultation involving both consumers and producers—a kind of Western Hemisphere Energy Institute—to exchange information and try to coordinate regional supply decisions, especially between the United States and such countries as Canada, Mexico, Brazil and Venezuela.

With respect to U.S.-Venezuelan conflicts over Venezuela's new diplomatic activism, several points seem worth stressing. The first is that none of the sources of irritation mentioned, viewed as tangible threats to American interests, are likely to prove as serious as they may seem, at least not as far as Venezuela's role is concerned. Following its first flurry of diplomatic initiatives, Venezuela has become more cautious and less ambitious as it has become aware of the obstacles to collective action of any kind in Latin America. It has also

[219]

become increasingly aware that, despite its own willingness to overlook ideological differences in the pursuit of solidarity, others are not so willing. Diversity, independence, and self-assertiveness are often insuperable impediments to unity. In addition, as Kuczynski points out, it is unlikely that Venezuela will be able to continue to utilize its financial power to support its diplomatic initiatives in the way it has in the past; on the contrary, it will almost surely become increasingly preoccupied with domestic developmental goals, and will lose the financial leverage which was so important in the three or four years after 1973.

The second point is that, with respect to these issues of regional and international diplomacy, it may in fact be desirable for the United States to have Venezuela take a leadership role. Among those countries aspiring to an international status within the region, Venezuela is one of the most friendly to the United States. Further, Venezuelan foreign policy has in recent years been flexible, conciliatory and constructive. These terms refer not just to a willingness to work together with others to resolve problems but, more important, to a strong inclination wherever possible to build institutional and associational frameworks to handle problems on a more organized, long-term basis. They refer also to a willingness to disaggregate conflicts and prevent adversarial aspects of a relationship from overriding and obscuring opportunities for cooperation in other areas. Actually, a close review of Venezuelan conduct reveals that the tendency to respond in this fashion is extraordinarily pervasive, extending beyond the founding of compromisory institutions to its conduct as mediator and conciliator once these have been established. The list of new organizations and institutions that Venezuela has helped create is really quite long. OPEC, the Andean Pact, and SELA are among the best known. But it is important also to note the response to conflict situations that did not in the end lead to the founding of formal organizations. Venezuela's early suggestion for a world petroleum organization (in the late 1950s and early 1960s) to bring together consumers and producers is one example; another is its idea of a hemispheric energy policy and consultation system. (Both were patronizingly rejected out of hand by the United States, incidentally, and these rejections in part led Venezuela to promote OPEC as an alternative.)

The conciliatory, constructive character of Venezuela's foreign policy can be traced to many sources. First, and perhaps the most important, it parallels the process of institution-building and compromise, described so well by Levine, in which Venezuelan leaders have been engaged domestically. Second, it reflects the experience gained in the conduct of oil diplomacy, where important benefits, often after years of failure, accrued to the nation precisely because policymakers prevented other conflicts from overriding the compromises needed for success. The key point here is that these tendencies may prove highly beneficial to the United States. If allowed, Venezuela may actually prove a useful bridge-builder and mediator between the developed and underdeveloped countries, facilitating the design of new institutions to control and channel conflict.

Finally, there remains the broader question, alluded to earlier, of America's role as a long-term ally in the struggle to stabilize and institutionalize the democratic system in Venezuela. This requires emphasis for several reasons. First, U.S. policy in the Nixon-Ford years has provided grounds for serious doubt about American commitment to the growth of democracy, *per se,* in the world, especially where conflicts with other interests have been involved. The second reason is that an extrapolation of current political and economic trends suggests that Venezuela may be approaching a time of considerable economic and political difficulty, a major turning point in its overall development strategy. And a constructive, helpful U.S. attitude may be of critical importance.

Although most observers will agree that Venezuela has done quite well in responding to the short-term challenge posed by its income windfall since 1973, there remain very fundamental structural problems in the economy which must be overcome before self-sustaining growth, independent of oil production and its revenues, will be possible. These problems may be attributed in large measure to a system of accommodations and compromises that was necessary to insure the early survival of the democratic political system in earlier years.

Venezuela's current development plans, described by Kuczynski in his chapter, are somewhat awe-inspiring, but the products of the new state-created heavy industries will require complements in the rest of the economy if the country is to generate essential exports. As one observer has put it: "Now the country is plunging suddenly into a vast program of heavy industry, but these steel, aluminum, and petrochemical projects can only hope to grow if a medium-sized industrial sector emerges rapidly to provide the multiplier effect that it needs." [14] And the state, still deeply addicted to a constant growth in income stemming from oil, is under growing pressure to provide an expanded system of social welfare to compensate for persistent underemployment and unemployment.

In sum, an enormous amount needs to be done, and time may actually be much shorter than many realize. Barring large-scale price increases, Venezuela seems likely to enter a period of fiscal leveling-off after about 1979 and lasting into the 1980s, as oil income ceases to grow. As President Pérez has already announced, the government in the short term will

[222]

be forced to rely on a substantial program of borrowing in order to maintain the flow of capital investments required by the country's ambitious programs. At the same time, the government will be forced to come to grips with difficult administrative as well as political problems, the latter resulting from increased "sectoral" conflicts (between the state and the private sector, the state and labor) and over such issues as the performance of the public sector and the extent and form of its regulation of domestic and foreign economic activities. Venezuelan leaders are aware that these problems lie ahead and that oil-generated income bonanzas only postpone conflicts, they do not resolve them. Indeed, it is to this challenge that President Pérez referred when, during the presidential campaign, he stated several times that the next government (1974-79) would be the last chance for the survival of democracy in the country.

The United States has a stake here too, not merely because of shared values of political life, but because having a successful, friendly, open democracy located at the top of the South American continent is an asset of enormous long-range importance to American security, and perhaps even to the quality of political life in the Hemisphere as a whole. Therefore despite the impediments Venezuela has created to a "New Dialogue," and such things as its support of Panamanian claims in the canal conflict with the United States, American policymakers should be thinking hard about the critical period coming up for Venezuelan development in the early 1980s, and be prepared to respond in the most creative way possible. This will be especially difficult if the restructuring of the Venezuelan economy produces, as I feel it very likely will, serious clashes with Venezuelan and foreign economic interests. The real stakes involved require a constructive, long-range conception of the development process in

Venezuela, not short-term "damage-control" reactions that may do more harm than good.

Notes

1. In the preparation of this paper I have drawn freely upon material in my earlier essay on "Venezuelan Foreign Policy," prepared for the Office of External Research, U.S. Department of State, Spring, 1975.

2. Until the ouster of Pérez Jiménez, relations between the two countries were quite cordial. Venezuela during the early years of the Cold War remained staunchly anti-communist and cooperated with American oil companies in allowing a rapid expansion of the foreign controlled industry. But when the dictatorship was overthrown, tensions between the two nations increased. Vice President Nixon's official visit in March 1958 revealed an unexpected legacy of anti-Americanism among the Venezuelan people, and subsequent disputes between oil companies and the transitional junta caused further anxiety in Washington about the country's political evolution. However, a successful transition to constitutional government in Caracas plus a change of executive in the United States altered matters abruptly.

3. Actually, much of the public discussion in Venezuela that accompanied the nationalization process and the drafting of the controversial Article Five (allowing foreign participation with the state) was unrealistic in this respect, suggesting that in a short time the government should plan to save its "regular" oil for domestic future uses and instead use the "heavy" Orinoco oil for export. As indicated, heavy oil is unlikely to replace regular oil; as far as fiscal income is concerned, it just will not bring in enough after costs.

4. *Latin American Economic Report,* Oct. 3, 1975. For more on this role see the essay by Kim Fuad in this book.

5. See the *Report on Project Independence,* revised in 1976, published by the Federal Energy Administration. Informative also are: (1) "Energy Outlook: 1976-1990," Exxon (Dec. 1975); (2) Dankwart A. Rustow, "U.S.-Saudi Relations and the Oil Crisis of the 1980s," *Foreign Affairs* (April 1977); and "The International Energy Situation: Outlook to 1985," (Washington, D.C.: Central Intelligence Agency, April 1977).

6. There are many ways in which this could be done, but discussion of these is beyond the scope of this essay. Note: American dependence on Saudi Arabian oil has actually doubled in the years since that country engineered an oil squeeze and embargo against the United States.

7. See, for further details, F. Tugwell, *The Politics of Oil in Venezuela* (Stanford, Calif.: Standford University Press, 1975), pp. 67-106.

8. United States Cabinet Task Force on Oil Import Control, *The Oil Import Question: A Report on the Relationship of Oil Imports to the National Security* (Washington, D.C.: U.S. Government Printing Office, 1970).

9. *Latin America* (London), Jan. 31, 1975.

10. "Survey of Venezuela," *Financial Times* (London), byline Hugh O'Shaughnessy. In the same issue, PETROVEN Director Alirio Parra says that: "Petróleos is the only major state company that must face and resolve marketing problems convering over 60 crudes or segregations of crudes and some 80-100 specifications of refined products."

11. See, for further comments on key regional trends, among others: Riordan Roett, "The Changing Nature of Latin American International Relations: Geopolitical Realities," in Kalman Silvert, et al., *The Americas in a Changing World* (New York: Quadrangle,

1975), pp. 95-111; and Kalman H. Silvert, "The Kitsch in Hemispheric Realpolitik," Ch. 2 of R. Hellman and H. J. Rosenbaum, eds. *Latin America: The Search for a New International Role* (New York: Wiley, 1975). See also Abraham Lowenthal, "The United States and Latin America: Ending the Hegemonic Presumption," *Foreign Affairs* (Oct. 1976).

12. In view of the magnitude of the nationalization, the absence of a stronger U.S. protest is worth noting. The decision to stand back and allow the takeover to proceed with minimal protest and diplomatic row was a difficult one, taken only after a struggle within the American foreign policy bureaucracy. That those favoring a hardline response were defeated reflects, it would seem, both company desires to secure amicable post-nationalization ties to an important continuing source of oil supply plus growing recognition, within the Department of State, especially, of the future strategic importance of petroleum. See the forecast studies cited in footnote 4.

13. In the short run, of course, these patterns will be maintained out of necessity.

14. "Survey of Venezuela," *Financial Times* (London), p. 19.

[SEVEN]

Venezuela's Role
in International Affairs

Robert D. Bond

I. Introduction

In the fifteen years prior to the "energy crisis" of 1973-74, Venezuela was quietly and gradually emerging as an important actor in hemispheric and international affairs. Venezuela played a leading role in founding OPEC and in redefining the relationship among host governments and the international petroleum companies, Venezuela's Betancourt Doctrine influenced the course of Latin American politics, and Venezuela stressed Latin American solidarity as a counterpoise to U.S. influence in the region. But it was the Arab oil embargo of 1973-74 and the subsequent quadrupling of petroleum prices that provided Venezuela with a dramatic opportunity to chart its own course in international relations. The events of those two years not only demonstrated the strategic importance of Venezuela's petroleum in determining the degree of U.S.

dependence on Middle East oil, but also provided Venezuela with a financial windfall. In 1973 Venezuela earned $4.7 billion from its 3.4 million barrels daily (mbd) production; in 1974, with the quadrupling of oil prices in effect for the entire year, petroleum revenue rose to $10.5 billion despite a drop in production to 3.0 mbd.

President Carlos Andrés Pérez, inaugurated in March 1974, took full advantage of favorable international circumstances and the influx of petro-dollars to propel Venezuela decisively onto the international scene. At home, the Pérez administration selfconfidently nationalized the iron ore and petroleum industries, and initiated an ambitious industrialization program. In Latin America, Venezuela moved to assert its claim to continental leadership by championing the formation of the Sistema Económico Latinoamericano (SELA), by promoting the reintegration of Cuba into the Latin American community, and by disbursing most of its official development assistance (over 3 percent of GNP in 1974) to neighboring countries to offset the higher price of petroleum. On the wider international scene, Venezuela gained recognition for its prominent roles both in establishing OPEC policies and as spokesman for Third World demands for redistribution of international economic and political power. In 1975 Venezuela was elected co-chairman of the Paris Conference on International Economic Cooperation (CIEC), which subsequently became the principal North-South negotiating forum.

President Pérez capped nearly three years of activist Venezuelan foreign policy in November 1976 with a neatly balanced 15-day round of international state visits, stopping in Italy, the Vatican, Great Britain, the Soviet Union, Spain, Portugal, and the Dominican Republic. He launched his trip with an address to the United Nations, the first ever by a Venezuelan Chief of State. In his speech Pérez spoke as if

[228]

Venezuela were the voice of Latin America, OPEC, the Third World, and Western democratic nations. One Venezuelan commentator characterized the President's speech as a kaleidoscope of recent Venezuelan foreign policy positions, in all their clarity and ambiguity: Venezuela speaks at one and the same time as a country that is Latin American, developing, a member of the Third World, "Western," democratic, not non-aligned but critical of alignments, a supporter of just causes independently of the nature of the regime but critical of dictatorships, a defender of the right of OPEC to fix petroleum prices but mindful of the need for prudence so that price hikes do not excessively damage the economies of petroleum importing countries.[1]

President Pérez's energetic diplomacy has stimulated important questions about Venezuelan foreign policy, at home and abroad. How can democratic Venezuela purport to speak for the nations of Latin America, the Third World, and OPEC? What are the priorities of Venezuelan foreign policy, and how do these relate to the nation's development needs and to domestic political realities? How can Venezuela speak so stridently about the necessity of redistributing international political and economic power when there is a crying need to redress domestic inequities? Is Venezuela's emergence as an important "middle power" a temporary or lasting phenomenon?

It is not possible in this essay to discuss, let alone answer, all these questions: the reader will find illumination from each of the preceding chapters. By highlighting the major themes encountered in previous chapters, however, this essay attempts to offer an overall assessment of the origins, conduct, and probable future of Venezuelan foreign policy.

In the analysis which follows I develop four main themes. The first is that Venezuelan foreign policy is explainable

[229]

mainly in terms of the domestic political and economic development strategy followed by the political elite from 1958 to the present. Second, Venezuela's democratic experience has played an important role in shaping the style of its foreign policy behavior. Third, Venezuela will reevaluate its foreign policy priorities in the near future to take account of domestic development needs and the changing international political context. The fourth theme is that Venezuela will probably continue to play a significant role in hemispheric and international affairs, at least for the next decade.

II. THE POLITICAL AND ECONOMIC BASES OF VENEZUELAN FOREIGN POLICY

To understand contemporary Venezuela's international role, it is essential to begin by considering the linkage between domestic political and economic concerns and the conduct of the nation's foreign policy. Since 1958, Venezuelan foreign policy has been strongly influenced by domestic political and economic goals and by the distinctive development strategy adopted by Venezuela's leaders in pursuit of these objectives. Four development goals have been pursued: institutionalization of the democratic political system; control and eventual nationalization of the petroleum industry; economic growth that is less dependent on oil earnings; and greater equity in the distribution of the benefits of economic development.[2] The development strategy followed relied upon a constant flow of oil income to ease the transition to a democratic, industrialized Venezuela.

This special configuration of development goals and strategy has strongly influenced, and continues to shape, the style and substance of Venezuelan foreign policy. In addition, the

[230]

fact that the objectives of economic growth less dependent on oil and of greater equity in the distribution of the wealth growth creates have not yet been achieved has important implications for the future orientation of Venezuela's regional and international diplomacy.

POLITICAL DEMOCRACY

The primary, overriding goal of the Venezuelan leadership since 1958 has been to create a viable democratic polity. Venezuela's political leaders returned from exile convinced that the establishment of a democratic system capable of controlling and channeling conflict must take priority over all other development goals. Social and economic reforms were not to be abandoned, but their accomplishment was to be subordinated to the prior goal of reconciling potentially hostile elements in Venezuelan society to democratic rule. In essence, Venezuela's new leaders decided that a fundamental restructuring of Venezuelan society would have to be postponed until democracy was firmly established.

The task of forging the compromises necessary to the success of this strategy fell to the leaders of Acción Democrática (AD), particularly to President Rómulo Betancourt (1959-64). Betancourt had to seek accommodation with those powerful groups AD had alienated by its overzealous reform efforts during the *trienio* (1945-48): the major opposition political parties, the military, and the economic elite.

Before attempting to reconcile either the Armed Forces or the private sector to democratic rule, AD first had to reach agreement with the major opposition political parties on the limits to political competition. The arrogant electoral activities of AD during the *trienio* had convinced COPEI and the

Democratic Republican Union (URD) that there was no place for them in the political system; the result was that these parties failed to come to the defense of democracy when the military overthrew President Gallegos in 1948. To secure the support of these parties for democratic rule, AD signed a pact in 1958 in which the three agreed to form a coalition government of national unity regardless of the outcome of the December elections. Positions in the Cabinet were to be divided, and each party was to have a voice in the formulation of public policy and a share in patronage.

The agreement among the parties to share political power contributed importantly to the survival of democracy in the early 1960s. Without this arrangement, it is arguable whether President Betancourt could have overcome a series of events which made the transition from dictatorship to democracy extremely difficult. These included a recession in 1960, two damaging divisions within AD in which more radical elements split off to form independent political movements, Castro-inspired guerrilla activity, and military rebellion from the right and left. The URD left the coalition in late 1960, but COPEI stayed throughout Betancourt's presidency. The continued presence of COPEI in the government was especially important because of that party's support among elements in the middle class, the private sector, the Church, and the military.

President Leoni (1964-69) continued the practice of coalition government, but his successors, Rafael Caldera and Carlos Andrés Pérez, felt free to select their Cabinets without regard to coalition considerations. By the late 1960s, the increasing legitimacy of the democratic system had made mechanisms for restraining political competition unnecessary. Today, Venezuela's political leaders almost invariably embody compromise, conciliation, and negotiation as key political values.

Remarkably little is known in detail about how the

Venezuelan Armed Forces were reconciled to democratic rule, but it is possible to identify the general factors that contributed to the process.[3] Undoubtedly one important factor was the adroitness displayed by Venezuelan presidents in purging disloyal elements in the Armed Forces, in taking great care when making key military appointments, and in consulting regularly with military leaders on issues of concern to them (e.g., boundary disputes, questions of national security). A second factor was the emergence of guerrilla insurrection in Venezuela. This development provided the military with an important new role to play in national defense and united the military behind democratic government as an alternative to communism. A third reason for the acceptance of civilian rule by the military was the increasing support for the system being displayed by the private sector and the middle classes. Finally, all Venezuelan presidents have seen to it that the Armed Forces are well-equipped and well-paid.

Persuading the economic elite in Venezuela to accept reformist democratic rule was no doubt facilitated by the corruption and gross economic mismanagement characteristic of the final years of the Pérez Jiménez dictatorship. By 1958 many leaders in the private sector had come to the conclusion that some form of democratic rule was the only alternative to growing social and political unrest in Venezuela. The key to achieving accommodation with the private sector, however, was the government's adoption of an economic development strategy that did not directly challenge the prerogatives of the economic elite.

Every democratic government in Venezuela has walked a tightrope between the short-run necessity of avoiding conflict with the private sector and the long-run goal of restructuring the economy to promote more equitable and less dependent economic growth. To achieve these conflicting objectives,

[233]

Venezuela's leaders devised a two-track development strategy: Certain areas of the economy were left in the control of the private sector (commerce, manufactures), while basic sectors of the economy (steel, petrochemicals, electricity) were reserved primarily for state enterprises. By a judicious use of the state's petroleum income, Venezuela's leaders believed it would eventually be possible to reorient and restructure the economy; meanwhile, in the short term, they were prepared to compromise with the private elite and to live with a relatively inefficient manufacturing sector. In practice, this meant adopting high protective tariffs for domestic industries, maintaining low levels of individual and corporate income taxation, and consulting with business leaders on decisions that might adversely affect their interests (e.g., land reform, labor legislation, economic integration).

There are direct relationships between the pattern of Venezuelan political development and the conduct of the nation's foreign policy. The most obvious example of their interaction is the Betancourt Doctrine of the early- and mid-1960s, with its stress on the international defense of democracy as a corollary to the establishment of Venezuelan democracy. But of more lasting significance is the fact that the strategy of reconciling potential enemies to democracy gave the private sector as well as the military an important voice in determining Venezuelan foreign policy. The private sector, for example, was successful in delaying Venezuelan entry into both the Latin American Free Trade Association (LAFTA) and the Andean Common Market because of concerns that economic integration would damage private economic interests. Undoubtedly, the private sector will continue to influence the nation's prospects for achieving economic diversification and more equitable economic growth.[4] The extent of the influence of the Venezuelan Armed Forces over foreign policy is not so easily specified, but the military definitely is consulted on the formulation of policy toward Brazil and the Caribbean, and it reputedly has a veto over the negotiation of Venezuela's boundary disputes with Colombia and Guyana. President Pérez, for example, would like to resolve the dispute with Colombia over the Gulf of Venezuela, perhaps through an agreement jointly to develop petroleum resources in the area, but he has not done so despite several meetings with Colombia's President, López Michelsen.

Venezuela's democratic experience has also imparted a characteristic *style* to Venezuelan foreign policy. As Daniel Levine indicates on page 22, above, "the style of action characteristic of domestic politics in Venezuela, with its stress on building institutions *within which* differences can be resolved, spills over into foreign policy." Several examples of the Venezuelan preference for compromise and for creating international institutions and for using others to deal with conflict can be adduced, including its initiatives in founding SELA and its participation in CIEC, but the most striking illustration is its role in OPEC. Kim Fuad's chapter on Venezuela and OPEC provides two noteworthy examples of the compromise-oriented and institution-building style of Venezuelan foreign policy: (1) Juan Pablo Pérez Alfonso, the prime promoter of OPEC, originally sought to construct an organization which would take account of not only the interests of producers in establishing oil supply and prices, but also the interests of consumers and the oil companies; and (2) Venezuela has consistently been the champion of conciliation and cohesion in the organization.

CONTROLLING THE PETROLEUM INDUSTRY

The process of institutionalizing democracy in Venezuela was greatly facilitated by the constant flow of fiscal resources from the petroleum industry. Indeed, it is doubtful that Venezuela's leaders could have successfully implemented the political strategy of compromise and conciliation without the oil cushion. Oil income was the key to Venezuelan development in two respects. First, the relatively steady increase in the government's income from oil made it possible to satisfy at least some of the demands of competing Venezuelan groups without having to resort to a policy of redistributing existing wealth. Second, oil income enabled the government to follow the two-track economic development strategy that avoided direct conflict with the private sector.

The need for a constant flow of oil income largely determined the government's petroleum policy. The principal goals of this policy were: (1) in the near term, to maximize government revenues from oil by taxing international oil company profits at high levels and by building an international oil cartel to raise prices and control supply; (2) to limit the damage potential of the oil companies' activities; and (3) to prepare for the eventual nationalization of the industry.[5] The protracted conflict and the intricate process of bargaining which occurred between Venezuela and the foreign oil companies, culminating in the nationalization of the industry on January 1, 1976, have been comprehensively analyzed elsewhere.[6] Here, I will consider briefly three implications of the outcome for Venezuelan foreign policy.

First, the petroleum industry in Venezuela declined moderately as a result of the long period of conflict between successive Venezuelan governments and the foreign oil companies. Throughout the 1960s the oil companies, knowing that nationalization was approaching, were reluctant to explore for new reserves and unwilling to invest in new refining technology.[7] Consequently, Venezuela inherited a petroleum industry that, although in generally good shape, will require large

[236]

sums of capital for revitalization. How Venezuela responds to this challenge will have important effects on the future direction of Venezuelan foreign economic policy.

A second consequence of the long bargaining process was educational. In struggling to domesticate the industry, Venezuela's leaders gained an invaluable fund of information about the workings of the international oil industry. As Fuad notes in his chapter, the Venezuelan Mines Ministry ranks as one of the world's best-informed. Venezuela put this knowledge to good use domestically in exercising care in nationalizing the industry, and it will prove important in managing PETROVEN, the new state petroleum enterprise. The knowledge gained in negotiations was also employed internationally to solidify Venezuela's position in OPEC by making valuable technical contributions to other members of the producers' organization. Venezuela is undeniably the intellectual leader in OPEC.

Finally, the conflict with the multinationals over the control, price and supply of petroleum reinforced an ideological dimension in the convictions of Venezuela's leaders. Venezuela's experience with the international petroleum industry taught its current leaders about the inequities of the international economy and the need for solidarity in dealing with multinational companies. This learning experience is responsible in part for Venezuela's alignment with the Third World on the issues of commodity agreements, trade, indexation, and technology transfer.

Balanced Economic Growth and Greater Equity

To this point in the analysis, Venezuela's distinctive route to development could be labeled a success story, at least in the

[237]

terms set by the Venezuelan political elite. Today, the democratic political system is stable and vigorous, and the country has smoothly and successfully nationalized the petroleum industry. However, progress toward the other two development goals—balanced economic growth and a more equitable distribution of the benefits of development—has not been served well by the development strategy followed by Venezuela's leaders. In fact, it is apparent that the goals of democracy and nationalization of the oil industry were achieved at the expense of the goals of diversified and more equitably distributed economic growth.

Documenting that Venezuela has not been especially successful in diversifying its economy is not difficult, as Pedro-Pablo Kuczynski shows in Chapter 2. For the past half-century the contribution of petroleum to the Venezuelan economy has remained relatively constant: 90 percent of merchandise export earnings, 65 percent of government income, and 20 percent of the gross domestic product (GDP). In 1975, due to the increase in world petroleum prices, the petroleum industry accounted for 96 percent of export earnings, 77 percent of government income, and 29 percent of GDP. Private industry in Venezuela, still heavily dependent on protection from imports, is relatively inefficient and thus far has not been able to generate a significant export capacity in manufactured goods. In agriculture, over 50 percent of the farmers produce for their own consumption, basic infrastructure is lacking, and the country still has to import foodstuffs to feed its people.

The goal of distributing income more equitably is equally far from achievement. Income distribution in Venezuela is more skewed than in Latin America generally, with the lowest 20 percent of income groups receiving only 3 percent of total income; furthermore, this situation has remained unchanged for the past two decades. The statistics on unemployment are unreliable, but it is clear that significant problems of under-employment and poverty exist in Venezuela. Even a casual visitor to Caracas or to the Venezuelan countryside sees ample evidence of stark poverty alongside tremendous wealth.

Due to the quintupling of oil prices, Venezuela now has another opportunity to realize these objectives. The response of Carlos Andrés Pérez's administration has been to launch the nation on an ambitious five-year public and private investment program in basic industries, agriculture, and human resources. The public investment target for the 1976-80 period is an estimated $25 billion. This average annual target of $5 billion is a threefold increase over public investment expenditures of about $1.5 billion in 1974.

There are grounds for guarded optimism about Venezuela's prospects for realizing the aims outlined in the new five-year plan. Financing the development plan from oil earnings, domestic savings, a modest increase in taxes, past savings accrued in the Venezuelan Investment Fund, and external borrowing on very favorable terms should not prove difficult. The key to the financing, of course, is the balance between a continued high flow of oil income and the maintenance of expenditures within manageable limits. This will depend upon successful management of the newly nationalized industry, continued high international petroleum prices, and careful administration of public enterprises. Of the planned develop-ment projects, the investments in capital-intensive heavy industry (steel, aluminum), electricity, and perhaps human resources are likely to be successful; investments in agriculture and petrochemicals are more problematic.

If successfully realized, the public investment plan would lay the basis for a new pattern of self-sustaining, diversified economic development. But even if the state can administer the public investment program effectively—about which there is serious concern in Venezuela—areas of economic vulnerability will persist. One is that the Venezuelan economy will continue to depend on oil as its mainstay for a long time to come. In Pedro-Pablo Kuczynski's words, "Even ten years from now, non-oil exports would not amount to more than about one-fifth of total merchandise exports, and that would already be a major achievement" (page 81). A second concern is that, due to the highly capital-intensive nature of the five-year plan, little direct employment will result. The government will still be faced with the problems of unemployment, underemployment, and poverty, and it will have to devise a strategy to improve the lot of its citizens. A third worry is that the strategy of creating government-owned export industries does not deal directly with the problem of revitalizing and making more efficient the private industrial sector. And in moving toward diversified economic growth, the Venezuelan government will finally have to motivate the private economic elite to become more dynamic and efficient.

III. Venezuelan Foreign Policy

Venezuelan foreign policy is an intriguing blend of personal style, pragmatism, idealism, and moralist impulses. At its most fundamental level, however, Venezuelan foreign policy is directed toward the achievement of the country's development program. The priority foreign policy issues for Caracas are those that bear directly on the success of the nation's drive to transform itself into a modern, industrialized democracy. The realities of the Venezuelan development process result in the following cluster of Venezuelan foreign policy objectives: (1) the maintenance and maximization of government oil revenue;

(2) the achievement of Third World demands for a "new international economic order"; (3) the extension of Venezuelan influence in Latin America beyond strictly security measures; and (4) accommodation with the United States.

THE MAINTENANCE AND MAXIMIZATION OF GOVERNMENT OIL REVENUE

Maintaining, and if possible increasing, the flow of oil income to government coffers within practical and conservationist production levels is the highest priority of Venezuelan foreign policy. This objective is perhaps even more important today than in the past, given the massive public investment program recently embarked upon by Venezuela and the need for capital to develop the petroleum sector. Additionally, it is oil and OPEC that make possible the achievement of Venezuela's other foreign policy goals.

As Tugwell notes in the previous chapter, the key to maintaining the oil lifeline is OPEC. The nature of Venezuela's petroleum reserves firmly binds the nation to the goals of OPEC: price control, production control, and coordination of related policies. Venezuela's current proven reserves are estimated at 18.5 billion barrels. At present production rates of 2.2 million barrels per day the country could conceivably run out of oil by the year 2000. Venezuela also has a conservatively estimated 700 billion barrels of non-conventional oil, heavily laden with sulfur and metals, in the Orinoco Oil Belt. To develop this source, the price of oil must be maintained at current levels. Given this petroleum profile, it is hardly surprising that Venezuela is committed to high prices.

Venezuela has consistently sought to secure the cooperation of the world's oil producers in controlling prices and supply.

Over the years this has meant lending technical assistance to other oil producers, taking the first steps in winning greater income from and control over the oil companies as an example to Middle Eastern and African producers, and persuading the other OPEC members to raise taxes or prices. More recently, Venezuela has played a mediating role in OPEC. Although its petroleum profile and its development needs place it in the camp with those members favoring high prices (e.g., Iran and Indonesia), Venezuela has nevertheless pursued compromise with Saudi Arabia and its allies in the interest of organizational cohesion. To achieve the overall goal of OPEC unity, Venezuela is prepared at present to accept price increases pegged to the rate of world inflation.

Venezuela is well-suited for this "broker" role in OPEC for two reasons: (1) it is not involved in Persian Gulf regional affairs; and (2) it enjoys great prestige in the organization derived from its long experience in petroleum diplomacy, its technical expertise and its demonstrated willingness to make sacrifices for the benefit of OPEC unity. In OPEC, Venezuela's compromise-oriented style of diplomacy finds its major expression.

Venezuela will probably continue to play a mediating role in OPEC because of the importance of the producers organization for securing the oil lifeline, but there are several possible future challenges to this orientation. First, Venezuela will need large amounts of capital to finance its development plans in the early 1980s. If there is a leveling off of fiscal income in 1979 or 1980, as Franklin Tugwell predicts (page 222), Venezuela might become more adamant on the issue of price increases. The need for increasing oil income might force Venezuela to step-up production and/or join the camp of revenue maximizers in OPEC; either or both of these actions would put Venezuela in opposition to Saudi Arabia, the kingpin of the oil cartel. The MIT World Oil Project has calculated Saudi Arabia's optimum price pattern, and it shows a price rise less than the rate of inflation for the next 10 years, followed by a more rapid rise. This price pattern is clearly in conflict with Venezuela's development needs. Consequently, a dramatic change in Venezuela's OPEC role is a distinct possibility. A second challenge is the apparent determination of Saudi Arabia to link oil prices to the resolution of the Middle East conflict. Venezuela has thus far avoided taking sides in this dispute (although President Pérez did endorse a Palestinian homeland in April 1977) and it refused to participate in the 1973-74 oil embargo. Venezuela's position of neutrality apparently has not soured its relations with the Arab members of OPEC, but the potential for discord is obvious. Third, the Middle East is a politically volatile region, and changes in Arab governments could produce a new dynamic in OPEC. Venezuelan policy would have to adapt to reflect the new circumstances.

A new dimension to Venezuelan petroleum diplomacy has resulted from its nationalization of the oil industry. Venezuela is now in charge of marketing its own petroleum. Consequently, Venezuela has added two activities to the conduct of its petroleum policy at the international level: (1) it is attempting to make direct sales arrangements with governments, individual refineries, and public utilities to reduce its reliance on private oil companies; and (2) it is attempting to diversify Venezuela's dependence on specialized markets (e.g., the heavy fuel market of the Eastern Seaboard of the U.S.) to reduce the damage potential of a company decision to supply the market from alternative sources. By the end of 1976, Venezuela had already demonstrated some success in diversifying its markets, especially *vis-à-vis* the United States.

Championing the New International Economic Order

A major thrust of Venezuelan foreign policy under Carlos Andrés Pérez has been the advocacy of Third World demands for a fundamental restructuring of the present international economic order. Among OPEC countries, Venezuela has been the principal champion of using petroleum as an instrument for negotiations toward the construction of a new international economic order, and it has taken the lead in proposing that petrodollars be recycled in ways to benefit developing countries. In the past three years, Venezuela has participated actively and in solidarity with the Third World in all international forums where "new international economic order" (NIEO) issues have been discussed.

The extent of Venezuela's international lending, and the degree of its involvement in the North-South negotiations, make it clear that achieving a new international economic order is a priority item on Venezuela's foreign policy agenda. However, the rationale for championing Third World demands for a NIEO is at first glance not so obvious. Unlike the goal of securing the oil lifeline, it is not immediately apparent how the achievement of a NIEO contributes to Venezuela's economic development.

Much of the explanation for Venezuela's activist, pro-Third World policy lies in the linkage between petroleum diplomacy and NIEO demands. Venezuela's leaders see a clear connection between support for the NIEO and the continued political effectiveness of OPEC. Caracas is not immune to mounting criticisms that Venezuela and the other OPEC countries are benefiting at the expense of other Third World countries. President Pérez acknowledged as much in his speech to the United Nations:

An international intrigue, fostered by transnational interests and by certain developed countries, spreads the myth that we, the oil producing countries, are responsible for the inflationary process the world is suffering. We need not prove the fallacy of such a statement; it has already been done by world authorities here at the United Nations. The truth is that the position adopted by OPEC is contributing decisively to the opening up of a dialogue between developed and developing nations.[8]

By emphasizing how OPEC solidarity with the Third World will lead to a new economic order, Venezuela provides justification for its demands for higher oil prices.

The desire to deflect "beggar-thy-neighbor" criticism of Venezuelan petroleum policy was the motivation in part for Venezuela's international lending program. The disbursements to the World Bank, the regional development banks, and the IMF oil facility, and especially the oil financing agreement with the Central American countries and Panama, all reflect this orientation. In fairness to Venezuela, it should be stressed that its international financing effort has been a large one, particularly in comparison to that of other OPEC countries. Most of its loans, however, have been on relatively "hard" terms.

Venezuela's active participation in the NIEO negotiations is certainly not based on a cost/benefit analysis of what the program demanded by the Third World would mean for Venezuela's economic development. Rhetorical support for UNCTAD's integrated approach to raw materials and commodities makes excellent sense in terms of legitimizing non-market arrangements, but it is doubtful that the UNCTAD program would represent an economic gain for Venezuela. The nation would undoubtedly be called upon to make a sizable contribution to the Common Fund to finance buffer stocks, and Venezuela is a net importer of the commodities whose prices would be increased. It is equally difficult to see how Venezuela has much of an economic stake in the other NIEO issues, with the possible exception of technology transfer. At least in the mid-term, greater access to the markets of developed countries is not central to Venezuelan economic development, and debt-relief appears to be irrelevant.

In many respects, Venezuela's firm alignment with the Third World is the result of the moralist impulses and personal desires of its leaders. Venezuelan policy toward the NIEO is made by a few key individuals—President Pérez, Minister of State for International Economic Affairs Manuel Pérez Guerrero, Mines Minister Valentín Hernández, Finance Minister Héctor Hurtado, and Foreign Minister Ramón Escovar Salom—who view the achievement of the NIEO almost as a righteous crusade. In advocating the NIEO in international forums, for example, Venezuela characteristically presents its arguments in terms of the ethical duties and moral obligations of states. As noted above, this moralist strain in Venezuelan foreign policy derives from the country's experience with the oil companies: for seventeen years Venezuela's leaders struggled to obtain what they felt was a just price for Venezuelan petroleum, to have a greater voice in decisions affecting its oil lifeline, and to gain control of the foreign companies operating within its borders. One result of this learning experience has been to produce a highly emotional and strongly moral response among Venezuela's leaders to the aspirations of the Third World. It is important to note here that the moralist impulse in foreign policy is not limited to the current AD leaders: President Caldera, leader of COPEI, and his foreign minister, Aristides Calvani, initiated Venezuela's

Third World policy, and they too spoke and acted on the basis of moral conviction.

Personal factors are also important in shaping Venezuela's NIEO policy. Championing Third World demands clearly accords with President Pérez's desire to be viewed as a leader of international stature. Additionally, the personal reputation of Manuel Pérez Guerrero, the main proponent of Venezuela's NIEO policy, also contributes to Venezuela's alignment with the Third World. Pérez Guerrero is an experienced, highly skilled international diplomat who enjoys wide respect at home and abroad.

The personal and ideological dimension to Venezuela's Third World policy is significant in explaining the country's active involvement in the North-South negotiations, but its importance should not be interpreted to mean that Venezuela behaves like a twentieth century Joan of Arc in international forums. On the contrary, the pragmatic, compromise-oriented style characteristic of Venezuelan politics and of Venezuela's role in OPEC is also displayed in the North-South negotiations. For example, Manuel Pérez Guerrero and the Venezuelan delegation were instrumental in negotiating the compromise agreements that permitted the Seventh Special Session of the United Nations in 1975 to end on a successful note. Indeed, it is probably fortunate for the industrialized countries that Venezuela has assumed a leading role in the North-South dialogue.

Although Venezuela at present firmly supports Third World demands for a "new international economic order," it is debatable whether this position will be an enduring element of Venezuelan foreign policy. On the one hand, Venezuela's pro-Third World policy is a natural extension of Venezuelan petroleum diplomacy, it strikes an emotional, moral chord among Venezuelan leaders, and it corresponds to the personal

[247]

ambitions of the current Venezuelan leadership. On the other hand, Venezuela's pro-Third World policy does not contribute so obviously to Venezuela's economic development, it does not have a strong constituency among the informed Venezuelan public, and it is clearly subordinate to the foreign policy goal of maximizing government oil income. With regard to the latter points, three observations are pertinent. First, in the 1980s Venezuela's development needs will require the nation to push for international oil price increases at least equal to the pace of world inflation. This petroleum policy will undoubtedly produce tensions in Venezuela's relations with Third World countries hard hit by the petroleum price hikes, and criticism of Venezuela will mount. If Venezuela has to choose between maximizing government oil income and solidarity with the Third World, the latter is sure to be the loser because development at home is the overriding priority. Second, Venezuela's days as an international lender are about over; in the future, Venezuela will not be able to use petrodollar diplomacy to deflect Third World criticism. Finally, it should be noted that the personal nature of Venezuela's commitment to the Third World makes the current NIEO policy highly susceptible to a change in administrations. In this regard, it should be noted that Mexico's policy of strident "Third Worldism" ended when President López Portillo assumed office in December 1976.

VENEZUELA AND LATIN AMERICA: THE DRIVE FOR AN EXPANDED ROLE

Since 1974 the most active, yet least coherent, area of Venezuela's diplomacy has been its policy toward Latin America. In contrast to his democratic predecessors, Carlos

Andrés Pérez has not formulated a consistent Latin American policy to guide Venezuela's actions in the hemisphere. Rather, he has responded to specific issues on an *ad hoc* basis, the result of which is a Latin American policy that is internally inconsistent and often only marginally related to Venezuela's interests. This pattern of policy incoherence is evident at the hemispheric, sub-regional, and bilateral levels of Venezuela's Latin American diplomacy.

At the fully hemispheric level, the primary thrust of Venezuelan policy has been to champion Latin American independence and unity. Under Carlos Andrés Pérez, Venezuela has taken a number of initiatives in pursuit of the Bolivarian vision of a strong, united Latin America. One such endeavor was the convening of Latin American heads of state in a series of consultative meetings on the anniversaries of key events in the struggle for Latin American independence 150 years earlier. Two such meetings were held (at Buenos Aires in September 1974 and Lima in December 1974), but the sesquicentennial celebration of the Congress of Panama scheduled for June 1976, which was to be attended by all chiefs of state, had to be cancelled. A second effort to resuscitate Bolivarian unity was the creation of SELA, an organization Venezuela hoped would facilitate Latin American interaction and possibly provide a forum for confrontation with the United States on economic issues. A third initiative was Venezuela's attempts to have Cuba readmitted to the Latin American community. A fourth and fifth were Venezuela's staunch support of the Andean Common Market and of Bolivia's campaign for an outlet to the sea.

Venezuela's efforts on behalf of Latin American unity did not meet with extraordinary success. The Panama Congress was cancelled because some Latin American chiefs of state objected to Fidel Castro's attendance; SELA has been slow to get off the ground due to reservations on the part of Southern Cone countries; Cuba's intervention in Angola aroused new suspicions about its intentions with regard to neighboring countries; Bolivia still aspires to an outlet to the sea; and Chile withdrew from the Andean Pact. As John Martz suggests above, Venezuela's efforts to revive Bolivarian unity were probably doomed from the outset because they flew in the face of "150 years of Latin American fragmentation and nationalistic rivalry." However, Venezuela's initiatives had an important, if unintended, consequence: they accelerated a decade-long trend toward greater autonomy and fluidity in the international relations of Latin American states. For several reasons, it is no longer appropriate to speak of the international politics of Latin America as if they were a mere reflection of traditional United States-Latin American relations. These include: the movement from bipolarity to multipolarity; a growing economic interest in Latin America on the part of Europe and Japan; the willingness of Latin America to act collectively at the international level; and the emergence of increasingly self-confident, assertive governments in the region that have "given real meaning to the 'state' in the 'nation-state' concept." [9] Venezuela's attempts to diversify its external relations and thereby move out of the U.S. orbit, as well as its championing of Latin American independence and solidarity, contributed to an "opening up" of hemispheric interactions. The newly emerging system of inter-Latin American relations will be increasingly shaped by the prime candidates for regional leadership—Brazil, Mexico, and Venezuela. The challenge now facing Venezuelan diplomacy is to define a policy toward Latin America which takes account of this new reality, rather than attempting to breathe new life into a 150-year-old dream

While it was pursuing the idealistic goal of Latin American

unity at the hemispheric level, Venezuela's actions in several sub-regions aroused suspicions that it was trying to carve out spheres of influence. Charges of neo-imperialism were first voiced in the Caribbean, but Central American states soon followed suit. (Venezuela's highly publicized support for the Andean Pact has not provoked similar charges). In the Caribbean and Central America, Venezuela has indeed been very active diplomatically, taking strong stands on the Panama Canal and the Belize boundary dispute, arranging special loan agreements with countries in the area to offset the higher price of petroleum, offering to finance development projects, and joining in several sub-regional joint economic ventures. Although Venezuela will not have the funds to continue its petrodollar diplomacy at a high level in this sub-region in the future, there is no question that it has permanently extended its influence in the area. It should be noted, too, that Venezuela's expanded role in Central America and the Caribbean has not generated conflict with Mexico, the other "middle power" in the region. Relations between the two countries have been excellent throughout the Pérez presidency.

With regard to the Andean States, Venezuela's interest has waned as the Andean Pact encountered increasing difficulties in moving toward full integration. The Venezuelan private sector has a strong say in Andean integration, as evidenced by its continuing and successful opposition to a joint development plan for the automotive industry. The Venezuelan business community is still preoccupied with the consequences of full integration with the Andean States, and its concern will limit the President's discretion in making policy toward this sub-region.

Venezuela has been relatively less active at the bilateral level, notwithstanding the existence of several long-standing

[251]

sources of conflict with its neighbors. These include a Venezuelan claim to two-thirds of Guyana's territory, a dispute with Colombia over the delimitation of the boundary in the Gulf of Venezuela, a dispute with Trinidad-Tobago over fishing rights and maritime boundaries, and a Venezuelan preoccupation with the expansion of Brazilian influence along portions of the 1300-mile border they share. Despite its hemispheric-wide campaign for Latin American unity, Venezuela has not moved to resolve any of these disputes (with the possible exception of the delimitation of the waters of the Gulf of Venezuela). These latent conflicts involve economic and military/security concerns and therefore will not be susceptible to easy diplomatic negotiations.

Perhaps the clearest example that Venezuela lacks a well-defined policy toward Latin America is the reluctance of the Pérez government to articulate a position on Brazil. By any standard of national self-interest—economic, political, or military/security—Venezuela should have a well-conceived policy toward its southern neighbor. Brazil is the largest country in South America, equal in size and population to the rest of the continent combined, and its economic and military strength is impressive. Brazil's potential as the overwhelming power in the region, coupled with the talk by its leaders of "manifest destiny," makes Brazil a priority item on the foreign policy agenda of every neighboring South American state. Yet there is no public evidence that the Pérez government has decided on how to deal with the nation it may contend with for regional leadership. In marked contrast to this posture of indecisiveness was the policy of the Caldera government. President Caldera sought to limit Brazilian expansionism by initiating a campaign to develop and populate the Venezuelan border with Brazil and by trying to forge an informal alliance

[252]

among Spanish-speaking nations. President Pérez has done neither, nor has he moved toward closer ties with Brazil.

The reasons for the Pérez government's failure to define a coherent policy toward Latin America may be found in the way Venezuelan foreign policy is made. First, both tradition and the Venezuelan constitution grant the President wide discretion in the conduct of the nation's international relations. This makes the foreign policy-making process highly sensitive to presidential directives, especially in non-oil matters. President Pérez, who assumed office with virtually no experience in foreign affairs, has elected to exercise his prerogatives to the fullest extent in determining Venezuela's policy toward Latin America. In formulating Venezuela's hemispheric policy, Pérez seems to be guided more by a Bolivarian vision of a unified Latin America and by a desire for personal aggrandisement (which has important domestic political payoffs) than by a well-conceived notion of Venezuela's national interest.

A second reason for policy incoherence is that the Foreign Ministry, which is mainly responsible for Venezuela's Latin American policy, is the least professional of all the ministries dealing with foreign policy. For several reasons, including the relatively low level importance of diplomacy until recent years, frequent changes of governments, and the predominance of political and personal criteria in selecting personnel, Venezuela has never developed a professional foreign service.[10] Further, the Foreign Ministry has been content to define its role in traditional diplomatic terms, leaving the all important areas of international petroleum policy and foreign economic policy to the Ministries of International Economic Affairs, of Mines and Hydrocarbons, of Finance, and to CORDIPLAN, the state planning agency. In this regard it is instructive that the Institute for Foreign Trade (ICE), created

[253]

in 1970 to provide expertise for the Venezuelan government about the implications of government policies for foreign trade, quickly took control of the Foreign Ministry's powers in foreign economic policy by assembling a young, talented, and hardworking staff. The ICE is nominally under the direction of the Foreign Minister, but in practice it operates in a largely independent fashion; since 1974, it has functioned as a source of foreign economic policy initiatives for Manuel Pérez Guerrero, Minister of State for International Economic Affairs. The Foreign's Ministry's lack of professionalism makes it unable to design and implement a consistent policy toward Latin America; nor is it capable of curbing presidential excesses in this area.

A third reason why Venezuela has been unable to formulate a policy toward Latin America fully consistent with its national interest is the influence of domestic pressure groups. More than in other areas of foreign policy-making, domestic interest groups are very active on the Latin American front. As John Martz phrased it (p. 159, above):

> Geopolitical and security interests were influenced by the military; economic policy toward such bodies as the SELA and the Andean Group was pressured by domestic business and commercial interests; and the use of petrodollars abroad elicited demands from opposition political parties to place greater emphasis on internal development.

The importance of these groups to the viability of the democratic political system restricts the government's freedom in making Latin American policy.

Venezuelan policy toward Latin America is likely to change

[254]

significantly over the next few years. Prediction about its evolution is difficult because of the factors discussed above (high susceptibility to presidential initiatives, a non-professional foreign ministry, and the influence of domestic pressure groups), but it is possible to engage in reasoned speculation on the probable future orientation of Venezuelan policy toward Latin America. First, Venezuela will probably abandon its goal of a unified Latin America, in practice if not in rhetoric. Venezuela's efforts in pursuit of this objective have consistently met with frustration, primarily because of the nationalism prevailing in Latin America. One caveat should be mentioned, however: Venezuela will probably continue its active support of SELA because creating and nurturing organizations to deal with conflict situations is characteristic of Venezuelan foreign policy. Second, although Venezuela will soon cease its active petrodollar diplomacy, it will continue to expand its economic and political influence in the Caribbean and Central America. This subregion is a natural sphere of influence for Venezuela, and economic and military interests support a heightened Venezuelan presence. Third, the Venezuela-Cuba relationship will remain a sensitive one for Caracas. President Pérez has never enjoyed public support for rapprochement with the nation that assisted Venezuelan guerrillas in the 1960s, and criticism came to the fore when Cuba's involvement in Angola became known. Likewise, the Venezuela-Soviet Union-Cuba oil agreement signed by Pérez in Moscow in November 1976 was not well-received in Venezuela. A decision by Cuba to commit troops in Africa or in the hemisphere could easily lead to a chill in diplomatic relations. Finally, Venezuela will probably try to limit Brazil's increasing influence in the region, perhaps by building an alliance of Spanish-speaking countries capable of resisting

[255]

Brazilian pressure. President Pérez's recent public comments on human rights in the Americas and on the dangers of nuclear proliferation, widely interpreted as a thinly veiled criticism of Brazil, may be an indication that his government is preparing to abandon its fence-straddling position *vis-à-vis* its southern neighbor. Relations between the two countries have never been especially warm, and economic and political ties are minimal.

THE UNITED STATES AND VENEZUELA: ACCOMMODATION OR CONFLICT?

At present, relations between the United States and Venezuela are friendly but guarded, reflecting long and close ties at many levels but also a number of disagreements which arose between the two governments during the Nixon-Ford years. These included oil (Venezuela's leading role in pushing for OPEC price increases and its decision to nationalize the petroleum industry), the "OPEC Amendment" to the 1974 Trade Act (which excludes Venezuela from the benefits of the Generalized System of Preferences even though it did not participate in the Arab oil embargo), Venezuela's championing of the cause of developing countries in the North-South dialogue, and its initiatives to remove Latin America from the U.S. orbit. Venezuela's diplomatic activism encountered staunch U.S. disapproval, typified by strong notes from President Ford to President Pérez protesting Venezuela's OPEC policies and its nationalization decision.

There are compelling reasons for the United States to seek accommodation with Venezuela on oil policy and related matters. First, Venezuela is the United States' most secure source of imported oil. The United States currently imports 1 million barrels of Venezuelan petroleum per day (13 percent of total U.S. oil imports), down from 1.6 million barrels in 1973. Venezuelan imports therefore affect the degree of U.S. dependence on Middle East oil. The United States has an obvious strategic interest in seeing to it that Venezuela's newly nationalized petroleum industry runs efficiently and that Venezuela continues to export most of its oil to its traditional U.S. market. Second, Venezuela's compromise-oriented diplomatic style provides the United States with significant opportunities to ameliorate conflict in regional and international negotiations. Third, Venezuela is a fellow democracy, one of only two in South America.

Franklin Tugwell, in the preceding chapter, outlines a more enlightened U.S. policy toward Venezuela. It has four main points: (1) the United States should dismantle disincentives, such as the OPEC clause of the 1974 Trade Act; (2) the United States should not let disputes with Venezuela over its activist diplomacy spill over into oil policy; (3) the United States should devise an oil import plan which takes account of preferred import sources *and* has the power to control import decisions rather than leaving these largely to private companies; and (4) the United States should join with Venezuela to form a regional "energy institute" for the purpose of coordinating hemispheric supply decisions. However, it is very doubtful that the Carter administration will adopt the policy Tugwell prescribes. The Carter administration apparently recognizes Venezuela's importance to the United States, and it appears willing to tolerate frictions in the relationship in lesser policy areas, but it does not seem capable of taking the concrete steps in oil policy essential to improving U.S.-Venezuelan relations. For example, the Carter energy pro-

[257]

gram has run into serious opposition in Congress, particularly the provisions which entail a transfer of power from the private oil companies to the government. In addition, the Carter administration has yet to mount a serious campaign to replace the OPEC amendment to the 1974 Trade Act with one that allows the President to apply it to the real offenders.

On the surface, United States-Venezuelan relations are likely to improve over the next few years. Once again, there is a convergence of policy objectives between Washington and Caracas in certain areas. This was made clear during the Pérez state visit to Washington in June 1977, in which both Presidents publicly agreed on such issues as the importance of respect for human rights in the Americas, the need for the United States to negotiate a new and equitable treaty with Panama, and the desirability of the United States' initiatives toward Cuba. But agreement on these policy objectives does not significantly affect the bedrock issues in U.S.-Venezuelan relations—oil and Venezuela's drive to make its economy less dependent on oil earnings. In these two crucial areas little agreement was reported, and prospects are far from promising. Oil will remain a source of tension in the relationship. Venezuela is committed to the maintenance of high prices and of OPEC unity, while the United States has as a primary goal of its energy policy the denial to OPEC of the power to set international oil prices. And even though the United States is interested in exploring ways in which it can assist Venezuela in increasing proven reserves and in exploring for new sources of petroleum, these discussions will pose a delicate political problem for any Venezuelan administration. For example, before departing Caracas for Washington, President Pérez felt it necessary to reassure Venezuelans that no foreigners would be allowed to participate in the development of the Orinoco Oil Belt. Consequently, it seems unlikely that little more than a cosmetic improvement in U.S.-Venezuelan relations will transpire in the near term.

IV. Conclusion

The prospects are good for Venezuela to continue playing an important role in hemispheric and international affairs over the next ten years. Oil is the key to this future, and fortunately for Venezuela the international and domestic petroleum outlooks are encouraging. Internationally, there are few indications that there will be a significant decline in oil prices or in the power of OPEC through 1990. Domestically, Venezuela's state oil company is running efficiently, and it quite possibly may be able to achieve its short-term goal of replenishing the approximately 800 million barrels depleted annually from proven reserves. This would guarantee a continued production rate of 2.2 mbd for some time to come. In the longer term, Venezuela's future as an oil producer depends on the successful exploitation of the Orinoco Oil Belt.

Paradoxically, Venezuela's greatest asset—petroleum wealth—is also a liability. Although it has provided the government with sufficient funds to undertake many ambitious social and economic projects, and thereby facilitated the institutionalization of the democratic political system, the oil bonanza has also had a negative effect by postponing urgently needed solutions to some of the country's basic problems. Foremost among these is the necessity of developing a diversified economy less dependent on oil earnings, one capable of meeting the basic needs of the Venezuelan people. For all its oil riches, Venezuela remains a country with huge disparities in the standards of living of its population. Accordingly, social tensions are widespread in Venezuela. The

[259]

population is increasing by about 3.2 percent annually—one of the fastest rates in the world—and this results in rising demands for education, housing, jobs, and other basic social services.

Venezuelan leaders are well aware that significant progess must be made toward the postponed development goals of balanced economic growth and of a more equitable distribution of its benefits within the next decade. To delay actually "sowing the oil" would jeopardize Venezuelan democracy and would sharply limit the influence Venezuela could exert at the international level. The response of the Pérez government to this challenge has been to initiate a drive to transform Venezuela into a modern, industrialized democracy. Over the next five years, Venezuela will invest about $25 billion in development projects, much of it in capital-intensive heavy industries. If successful (and there are grounds for guarded optimism), this public investment program would lay the basis for a new pattern of diversified economic growth. In the short-term, however, this capital-intensive industrialization strategy will do little to alleviate unemployment and poverty in Venezuela's *barrios*. The government is gambling that the proven strengths of the political system (effective leadership and strong party organization) and a continued flow of oil revenues will enable Venezuela to make the transition to an industrialized economy capable of redressing domestic inequities. This is probably a good gamble. Oil earnings and foreign borrowing should provide sufficient revenues to fund the industrialization program; social discontent among Venezuela's poor is likely to remain latent; political parties of the extreme left have never been strong in Venezuela; and the military is unlikely to intervene in the governmental process short of a dramatic political breakdown.

In summary, Venezuela's prospects are good, especially in

comparison to those of other developing countries. Nevertheless, the nation is clearly entering one of the most difficult and challenging periods in its history. By the mid- to late-1980s it should be evident whether Venezuela will be able to diversify its economy, on the basis of its industrialization program, or whether it will sink into economic stagnation and begin a process of social, political, and economic decay. At that time, the question of whether Venezuela's emergence as an important international actor is a lasting or temporary phenomenon will be answered.

NOTES

1. Carlos Gueron, "Evaluación preliminar de un viaje preliminar," *Resumen,* 12 de diciembre de 1976, p. 26.

2. Franklin Tugwell, "Venezuelan Foreign Policy," Research Paper prepared for the Office of External Research, United States Department of State, Spring, 1976.

3. See Gene Bigler, "Armed Forces Professionalization and Patterns of Civil-Military Relations in Venezuela," in John Martz and David Myers (eds.) *The Democratic Experience in Venezuela* (New York: Praeger, 1977).

4. See my "Business Associations and Interest Politics in Venezuela: The FEDECAMARAS and the Determination of National Economic Policies." Ph.D. Thesis, Vanderbilt University, May 1975.

5. Franklin Tugwell, *The Politics of Oil in Venezuela* (Stanford: Stanford University Press, 1975).

6. *Ibid.*

7. *Ibid.*

8. The text of the address by Carlos Andrés Pérez is in *Venezuela Now,* Vol. 2, No. 9, November 30, 1976. The quote is from p. 42.

9. Riordan Roett, "The Changing Nature of Latin American International Relations: Geopolitical Realities," in *The Americas in a Changing World* (New York: Quadrangle Books, 1975).

10. Eva Josko de Gueron, "La Politica Burocrática y la Formulación de la Politica Exterior en Venezuela," unpublished paper, Instituto de Estudios Politicos, Universidad Central de Venezuela, Caracas, Venezuela, 1975.

Index

122-32; production programming, 129-31; prospects, 146-49, 259; Venezuela's role in, 38, 133-40, 241-43

Orinoco Oil Belt, 47, 70, 72, 101, 143, 204, 208-09, 224n, 241, 259

Panama, 63-64, 77, 180-81

Paz Galarraga, Jesus Angel, 17

Pérez, Carlos Andrés, 7-8, 9, 38-39, 91, 101, 105, 107, 114-16, 136, 141, 149, 156-60, 165-66, 169-70, 173-74, 178, 182, 212, 228-29, 246-47, 253, 258

Pérez Alfonso, Juan Pablo, 51, 100, 121, 123-28, 131, 135-36, 152n, 235

Pérez Guerrero, Manuel, 128-29, 131, 136, 139, 149, 246-47, 254

Pérez Jiménez, Marcos, 11, 19, 39n, 51, 106, 161, 201, 224n, 233

Pérez La Salvia, Hugo, 132-33

Persian Gulf, 121, 133, 137, 242-43

Peru, 35-37, 94, 169

Petróleos de Venezuelo (PE-TROVEN), 71, 101-17, 142-43, 211-12, 218, 237

Political system, Venezuela: challenges, 23-32, 233-34, 260; guerrilla insurrection, 18-19; management of conflict, 12-13, 22, 40-41n, 42n, 233-34; leadership, 14, 18, 27, 43n; 1973 election campaign, 16, 24-25, 163-64; origins, 10-12, 231, 233; party organization, 14-18, 25-26, 28; style of action, 13, 235; *trienio* period, 11-12, 231

Prieto, Luis B., 17

Private sector, 31, 233-34, 261n

Public enterprises, 92-99, 117n

Ravard, Rafael Alfonso, 104, 115

Rockefeller, John D., 124

Sadli, Mohammed, 120

Saudi Arabia, 121, 127, 138, 141, 148-49, 243

Schacht, Efraín, 170, 174

SELA, *see* Latin American Economic System

Soviet Union, 162, 169, 251

Tariki, Abdullah, 100, 124-26, 128

Texas Railroad Commission, 124, 133-34, 152n

Torrijos, Omar, 180, 182

Trade Act of 1974, 112, 209-10, 219, 256-57

Trinidad-Tobago, 175-77

Trujillo, Rafael, 19-20

United States-Venezuelan relations: under Betancourt, 201-203, 214-15; during Nixon-Ford years, 216-17, 221, 256; under Pérez, 257-58; oil policy, 111-14, 141, 144, 203-12, 243, 257-58; and the Trade Act of 1974, 112, 209-10, 219, 256-57

Uruguay, 128, 153n

Uslar Pietri, Arturo, 52